South Asian Children and Adolescents in Britain

Ethno-cultural issues

Edited by

ANNIE LAU, MD, MRCPsych, FRCP (Can)
*Clinical Director of Child and Adolescent Mental Health Services,
Redbridge Health Care Trust*

W

WHURR PUBLISHERS

LONDON AND PHILADELPHIA

© 2000 Whurr Publishers Ltd
First published 2000
by Whurr Publishers Ltd
19b Compton Terrace
London N1 2UN England and
325 Chestnut Street, Philadelphia PA 19106 USA

British Library Cataloguing in Publication Data

A catalogue record for this book
is available from the British Library.

ISBN 1 86156 127 X

Printed and bound in the UK by Athenaeum Press
Ltd, Gateshead, Tyne & Wear.

Contents

Foreword

There is an extensive literature on the problems facing first, second and later generations of immigrants to the United Kingdom. Some of it is scientific, a lot is political and in more recent years relates to being black. However being black, Muslim or African covers a wide range of very different people and unfortunately such people are seen as strangers or are grouped by 'the majority' as similar or at least as part of a racial minority. None of the problems is really new and indeed this is reflected in accepted and traditional English literature.

Race, ethnicity and culture are terms used often without thought as to precise meaning. Race implies genetic difference at the level of species, and racial difference strictly does not apply to man, for whom there are no true genetic incompatibilities; something of which the ethnologists of the last century were aware[1]. There is only one human race. 'Ethnicity' helps little more, the Thesaurus equating this to race and common practice using the word for a variety of meanings. To which ethnic groups do a 'black' Protestant and a Caucasian Muslim belong? Culture is somewhat clearer, relating to that which is learned, but there are many different aspects to culture particularly between culture of experience and that of heritage, both being important to the individual. Of even greater importance is the stereotype that assumes that culture can be deduced from appearance.

T.S. Eliot[2] referred to three types of culture; of the individual, of a group and of a whole society. Eliot's writing is particularly relevant as he tried to grapple, not always successfully, with the need for both uniformity and diversity in society. The assumption of a clear majority culture is itself misleading and perhaps wishful thinking. Is there a United Kingdom culture that is natural and innate to which others are strangers? There are

---

[1] Darwin C (1871) The Descent Of Man. p 214, John Murray, London.
[2] TS Eliot (1961) Notes towards the Definition of Culture, p 21, Faber and Faber, London.

many pressures that change social patterns and the hierarchy. For centuries, Celts, Picts, Scots, Danes, Italians, French, Germans and Scandinavians have moved to and from the country bringing with them their own customs and characteristics[3]. Blondness is thought to come from Northern invaders and we perhaps forget its Middle Eastern and Roman origins. Christianity is seen as the indigenous religion. The social whole is therefore neither uniform nor homogenous.

The last two centuries have seen influx first from Eastern Europe as the result of oppression and more recently from Asia, Africa and the West Indies as a consequence of Britain's commitments to its former Empire. Newcomers contribute to the richness of society but unfortunately they are identified as different and can become the object of xenophobia and racism.

The perspective of the individual reveals other pressures. A move to a new society, with fresh promise and a new start, means moving from the familiar to the unfamiliar, leaving kinships and probably learning a new language. It means facing the hostility and ignorance of others and of either adapting or resisting. It would be nice to think that adaptation could allow keeping the good of both cultures, but that would be rare. Even the practice of heritage culture in a different environment means being different from one's own parents in some way.

Psychologically, national customs, heritage and characteristics are a part of the means by which individuals form their personal identity. They constitute one or possibly several of the domains from which we derive our perception of self. The clearer, more stable and uniform the background culture the easier this process is.

For the mental health worker, cultural issues relate both to the development of the child within a cultural setting and to working effectively with people from cultures other than one's own. That should be an everyday part of practice as it is rare for a professional to sit down with a family whose culture is the same as his or her own. The family of a successful social worker whose parents were from Pakistan is likely to be very different from a family who are recent immigrants from the same country. A common heritage may provide an awareness of the need for cultural sensitivity but for all professional workers there is the risk of stereotyping.

Whatever the views and attitudes of individual cultural groups, all citizens have to live within the framework of the law of the land. There may be instances when the laws appear to run counter to the requirement of a particular culture but more often the task is to help those unfamiliar with the law to understand and use it.

In spite of all of the problems, the UK has had a good record of receiving strangers. Those who have come to its shores have added to the over-

---

[3] Winston Churchill (1956) A History of The English-Speaking People Vol 1, The Birth of Britain. Cassell and Company, London.

all culture and with few exceptions are eventually assimilated or accommodated into the society. Unfamiliarity, strangers, xenophobia, loss of kinships, language barriers, stereotyping, all come to one focus point, that of ignorance of each other's way of life. Helping both the threatened majority and the minority 'ethnic' group presents an ongoing challenge. One remedy for clinical services has been to have in clinical teams members from particular cultures. To a large extent that is unhelpful except for translation in emergencies. Taking a pointer from the literature on transcultural adoption, education and openness are constructive factors. Unfortunately the whole topic is all too often deemed to be too sensitive to talk about.

This book sets out to educate the reader, not so much to teach a culture but to teach about personal culture and to do so through the eyes of each writer. Here culture refers mainly to Eliot's second and third levels, the commonalties of religious and national cultural patterns. In this book the writers share their own insights into those patterns. Though factual information is given, it is more for the reader to share the experience of the personal view of the religions and heritage cultures and their place in British society, much in the same way that the therapist needs to share the experience of the client. Some of the texts will take the reader on an exploratory journey both to other places but also to other times. The health of Asian children and availability and adaptability of health and educational establishments are considered. A final chapter involves the reader in a dialogue about anxiety as to whether the law is flexible enough to cope with cultural diversity.

Opening doors and minds to other cultures and philosophies creates anxiety that something will be lost. However as Eliot put it, 'If Asia were converted to Christianity tomorrow it would not thereby become part of Europe'[4]. By the same token if the UK accepts a diversity of individual cultures including those from Asia it will not become part of Asia. Rather as with Kipling's Roman Centurion, the stranger ceases to be so and becomes a part of his new home: 'I've served in Britain forty years. What should I do in Rome? Here is my heart, my soul, my mind – the only life I know'[5].

H. Zeitlin
London
August 1999

---

[4] TS Eliot ibid p 122.
[5] Rudyard Kipling (1992) The Roman Centurion's song. Selected Poems, Penguin, London.

Contributors

Anna Bond

Anna Bond is a solicitor with the London Borough of Redbridge, heading the group which provides a legal service to the Social Services (including children and families) and the Education Service.

Ruma Bose

Ruma Bose grew up in India, where she first trained as a psychiatrist. She emigrated to the UK in 1982, where she continued to practise as an adult psychiatrist. She began her training in child psychiatry in Tower Hamlets which has the largest concentration of the Bangladeshi population in Britain. Since 1994 she has been a Consultant in Child and Adolescent Psychiatry there. She has a special interest in working with ethnic minority families and children in Britain, and has lectured and published on the subject. She is fluent in Bengali and in Hindi, and has travelled widely in India and Bangladesh. She is married and has two children.

Kedar Nath Dwivedi

Kedar Nath Dwivedi, MD DPM FRCPsych, is Consultant Child and Adolescent Psychiatrist, Northampton. He graduated from Varanasi and served as Assistant Professor in Social Medicine at Simla. He now runs the Midland Course in Group Work with Children and Adolescents. He is the editor of several books, including *Groupwork with Children and Adolescents*, *Therapeutic Use of Stories*, *Enhancing Parenting Skills*, *Meeting the Needs of Ethnic Minority Children*, *Depression in Children and Adolescents* and *Management of Childhood Anxiety Disorders*. He edits the *Transcultural Mental Health On-Line* and is interested in Eastern, particularly Buddhist, approaches to mental health.

Ali El-Hadi

Ali El-Hadi is consultant psychiatrist, Brookside Unit, Redbridge Health Care Trust and Honorary Senior Lecturer at the Academic Department of Psychiatry of St Bartholomew and the Royal London Hospital Medical College, London. He studied medicine at Cairo University, Egypt, and did his psychiatric training in Birmingham and London. He is also a tutor at the Institute of Family Therapy and Birkbeck College, London.

Queenie Harris

Dr. Queenie Harris is a Consultant Child and Family Psychiatrist at the Parkview Clinic, (formerly Charles Burns Clinic) Birmingham. She is also a Senior Clinical Lecturer in the Department of Psychiatry, Faculty of Medicine and Dentistry – University of Birmingham, and is a Recognised Lecturer, Board of the Faculty of Education and Continuing Studies, University of Birmingham. She came to this country in the early 1960s soon after qualifying in Medicine in South India. Her special interests are in Systemic Psychotherapy, Child Sexual Abuse and Transcultural Psychiatry. She is co-director of the Systemic/Family Therapy Training Programme in Birmingham.

Raj H Kathane

Raj H Kathane, MBBS, DPM, Dip Psychotherapy, MRC Psych, is a consultant in child, adolescent and family psychiatry in Luton. He was born in Nagpur, Central India, from where he graduated as a doctor. He studied psychiatry at the prestigious National Institute of Mental Health and NeuroSciences, Bangalore, and psychotherapy in Ahmadabad, where he headed an Infant Psychiatry Clinic. He came to the UK in 1979 and worked mostly in East Anglia. He was a consultant in Bedford for 10 years. He has lectured at local and national conferences to different professional audiences on varied subjects and also teaches family therapy. His thinking has been greatly influenced by ideas from general systems theory and Buddha's teachings.

Annie Lau

Annie Lau is a consultant child and adolescent psychiatrist, and Clinical Director of Child and Adolescent Mental Health Services at Redbridge Health Care Trust. She graduated from Saskatoon, Saskatchewan, Canada and worked at the Royal Ottawa Hospital before emigrating to Britain in 1978. She has published and taught widely in transcultural family therapy.

Konasale M. R. Prasad

Dr. Prasad graduated in medicine in India and did his postgraduate residency training in psychological medicine at the National Institute of

Mental Health and NeuroSciences, Bangalore – an apex Institution of Brain Sciences in India involved in research, training, policy formulations and providing clinical services. He worked as a Senior Resident in Psychiatry, Research Officer in Psychiatry and as an Assistant Professor of Psychiatry before coming to the UK. He has more than a dozen publications to his credit and has been awarded the Bhagwat Award (given by the Indian Psychiatric Society for Young Psychiatrists) and the World Psychiatric Association Fellowship for Young Psychiatrists.

Haroon-ur-Rashid

Haroon-ur-Rashid is a general practitioner in Tower Hamlets and a Board member of the local PCG. He graduated from Dhaka Medical College, Bangladesh in 1982 before coming to Britain in 1985. He studied at the London School of Hygiene and Tropical Medicine and the Royal Free Hospital and School of Medicine. He has a special interest in cross-cultural medicine and is one of the founding members of the Moitri Project in East London.

Shila Rashid

Shila Rashid is a systemic psychotherapist, trained at the Institute of Psychiatry and the Tavistock Clinic. She has been working for the past five years at the Redbridge Child and Family Consultation Centre, and more recently at Brookside Adolescent Psychiatric Unit. Her interest in mental health issues are varied, although she has a special interest in promoting practices that are sensitive to the varying needs of different ethnic minority communities.

Annapoorna Sharma

Dr. Annapoorna (Anna) Sharma is a consultant paediatrician at Parkside NHS Trust, the Central Middlesex Hospital and Honorary Senior Lecturer at Imperial College School of Medicine at St. Mary's, London.

Dev Sharma

Dev Sharma is an educational psychologist with the London Borough of Newham. He has extensive experience of working with ethnic minority families and children as an educational psychologist and a teacher. He is particularly interested in psychological issues that affect Asian children and families. He is currently working on a research project on the subject of stress among Asian adolescents.

Ramindar Singh

Ramindar Singh was, until recently, Head of Department, Department of Contemporary Studies at Bradford and Ilkley Community College. A former Deputy Chairman of the Commission for Racial Equality, he has researched and published on South Asian Communities and the education of ethnic minorities in Britain. His publications include: *Immigrants to Citizens: the Sikh Community in Bradford* (1992) and *Asian and White Perceptions of the Teaching Profession* (1988).

Farrokh Vajifdar

A Parsi Zoroastrian, Farrokh Vajifdar was born and brought up in India. He now carries out research and pursues further studies in the United Kingdom where he writes, lectures and is consulted on Indo-Iranian cultures. He is a Fellow of the Royal Asiatic Society (and a contributor to its Journal) and a member of national and foreign academic institutions. His special interests include: pre-Islamic Iranian languages and literatures on which he has published monographs, commentaries, reviews and translations from classical and modern studies.

Preface

This book is an attempt to portray a current perspective on South Asian children growing up in the UK in the 1990's. The authors were asked to cover not only the chapter content, but also where possible, to include aspects of experience from their professional lives. The book falls into three sections.

It starts off with Raj Kathane's chapter on 'Roots and Origins'. This provides an overview of ethnic and religious groups of the Indian sub-continent; immigration patterns to Britain, sociocultural characteristics of settled families, including employment and education; also tensions for these families at the interface with British cultural life. Annie Lau then takes up the theme of considering how traditional extended family values determine individual and family competence throughout the life cycle. Ruma Bose further considers the demands on traditional families as they struggle to accommodate to life in Britain. She gives an account of how the Bangladeshi community in Tower Hamlets 'evolved its own distinctive narrative and dynamics' in response to these demands – a process seen most clearly in young people who have to negotiate the demands of both worlds.

In the second section, various authors discuss the major religious communities to be found in South Asian families. Kedai Dwivedi and Konasale Prasad discuss beliefs and practices of the Hindu, Jain and Buddhist communities; and Ali El-Hadi, the Muslim community. Ramindar Singh and Farrokh Vajifdar go through basic religious tenets for Sikhism and Farrokh Vajifdar covers similar ground for the Jews, Christians and Parsis. Religious values are both explicit and implicit in shaping cultural beliefs and practices, and determine limits of expected roles and behaviour in 'normal family life'. A proper understanding of the South Asian communities needs to include these crucial influences that both shape and structure experience, and provide a sense of coherence.

The final section looks at issues in the public sector. South Asian children growing up in the UK encounter the outside world in the form of schools, medical services – GPs and specialist services, and sometimes they fall under the provision of the Children Act. What are the particular difficulties, opportunities and challenges, in these public sector areas? Anne Sharma, a paediatrician, considers health needs from a specialist paediatric perspective, and Haroon-Ur Rashid and Shila Rashid discuss the GP experience in Tower Hamlets. Queenie Harris, a child psychiatrist, looks at clinical issues confronting Child and Adolescent Mental Health Services. Finally a dialogue between Anna Bond, a solicitor, and Annie Lau, a child psychiatrist, considers issues that arise most frequently for social workers working with South Asian families, concludes this section.

Chapter 1
Roots and origins: ethnicity and the traditional family

RAJKUMAR H KATHANE

Introduction

In this chapter I discuss the main ethnic and religious groups of the Indian subcontinent, the region of the world that is called South Asia, and will touch upon some aspects of their lifestyle, practices and customs. I try to give some background information about the languages spoken, the names, the clothes and the food so that a Western reader will begin to understand 'Asian culture'. I then discuss the forces resulting in immigration from the Indian subcontinent to the UK, the patterns of immigration, patterns of settlement in the UK and the lifestyles of immigrant communities. I attempt to highlight the important differences between the immigrants' communities of origin and the emergence of new lifestyles that have been shaped as a result of mixing with Western and various other cultures, as well as changes that have occurred as a function of time. As will quickly become obvious, this is a vast subject and a chapter like this can only touch upon the main aspects. A serious enquirer will need to refer to numerous other sources of information that are available.

The Indian subcontinent is a vast region of the world and comprises the following countries (in alphabetical order): Bangladesh, Bhutan, India, Myanmar (old name Burma), Nepal, Pakistan and Sri Lanka. Facts and statistics about the countries of this region are given, and comparisons are drawn with the UK and USA, in Tables 1.1 to 1.6.

Ethnicity

Languages

The linguistic heritage of the Indian subcontinent is incredibly rich. There are at least 14 officially recognized languages and each language has at least five dialects, which are very distinct. In 1957 the internal provincial boundaries within the union of India were redrawn along linguistic lines,

Table 1.1. Land surface area in square miles, population in 1993 and population projection for the year 2000

Country	Land surface area (square miles)	Population 1993	Population 2000
Bangladesh	57,295	115,075,000	132,000,000
Bhutan	18,150	1,546,000	1,812,000
India	1,222,243	896,567,000	>1 billion
Myanmar (Burma)	261,222	44,613,000	51,567,000
Nepal	56,827	19,264,000	20,847,000
Pakistan	307,374	127,964,000	155,000,000
Sri Lanka	25,332	17,616,000	19,000,000
Total for Indian subcontinent	1,948,449	1,222,645,000	1,380,226,000
UK	91,256	58,080,000	59,520,000
England	50,343	48,068,400	
Scotland	30,418	5,100,000	
Wales	8,019	2,866,400	
USA	3,679,192	258,233,000	275,326,000

Adapted from: *Britannica Book of the Year 1994.* © 1994, Encyclopaedia Britannica, Inc. Printed here with kind permission.

Table 1.2. Countries of the Indian subcontinent, the UK and the USA: population density, urban–rural split, and per capita income (1993 figures)

Country	Population density per square mile	Population split, urban:rural	Per capita income in US$
Bangladesh	2,008	24:76	220
Bhutan	85	13:87	170
India	733	25:75	330
Myanmar	171	25:75	400
Nepal	339	9:91	180
Pakistan	376	32:68	400
Sri Lanka	695	22:78	540
UK	612	91.5:8.5	17,770
England	954		
Scotland	168		
Wales	357		
USA	70	75:25	23,150

Adapted from: *Britannica Book of the Year 1994.* © 1994, Encyclopaedia Britannica, Inc. Printed here with kind permission.

Table 1.3 Population statistics.

Population density per square mile: the following countries exceed Bangladesh's 2008:

Guernsey	2116
Bermuda	2895
Malta	2975
Gaza Strip	5085
Singapore	11,644
Gibraltar	13,227
Hong Kong	14,295
Monaco	40,666
Macau	54,782

Thus it can be seen that Bangladesh is the most densely populated large country. The following countries are at the lower end of the spectrum in terms of people per square mile

Canada	7.3
Libya	6.7
Iceland	6.7
Australia	6.0
Namibia	4.8
Mongolia	3.7
French Guyana	3.7
Western Sahara	2.2
Greenland	0.1

Here is a comparison with some of the EU countries.

Netherlands	954
Belgium	854
Germany	589
Italy	492
France	274
Spain	200
Sweden	50
Norway	34

China is the most populous nation in the world (1993 population: 1,179,467,000) and third largest in surface area (3,696,100 square miles) making a population density of 319 per square mile. Russia ranks number one in land surface area (6,592,800 square miles), and Canada (3,849,674 square miles) is the second. India is world's seventh largest nation by surface area.

Table 1.4 Per capita incomes of some of the richest and poorest nations of the world in US$

The rich countries: comparison of per capita incomes – US$ (1991 Census figures)

Spain	12,500
Australia	16,600
UK	16,800
Italy	18,600
Netherlands	18,600
Belgium	19,300
UAE	20,000
France	20,600
Canada	21,260
USA	22,600
Denmark	23,600
Germany	23,600
Norway	24,000
Finland	24,400
Guernsey	25,200
Sweden	25,500
Japan	27,000
Bermuda	27,800
Luxembourg	31,000
Liechtenstein	32,800
Switzerland	33,500
Jersey	34,000

Surprisingly the Kingdom of Saudi Arabia's per capita income was only $7,000.

The poor countries' per capita incomes in US$ (1991 census figures) were:

Afghanistan	220
Bangladesh	220
Zaire	220
Burundi	210
Sierra Leone	210
Cambodia	200
Uganda	160
Somalia	150
Ethiopia	120
Tanzania	100
Mozambique	70

Adapted from: *Britannica Book of the Year 1994.* © 1994, Encyclopaedia Britannica, Inc. Printed here with kind permission.

Table 1.5. Languages spoken and religions in the Indian subcontinent, UK and USA as at 1993

	Language	Religion
Bangladesh	Bengali 112,000,000 English 3,000,000 Urdu 200,000	Muslim 100,000,000 Hindu 14,000,000 Other 1,400,000
Bhutan	Bhutia 970,000 Nepali 340,000	Buddhist 1,000,000 Hindu 380,000
India	*Indo-Aryan Devnagari-based languages:* Hindi 403,000,000 Bengali 67,000,000 Gujarati 44,000,000 Marathi 68,000,000 Oria 30,000,000 Punjabi 24,000,000 Urdu 46,000,000 *Dravidian languages* Kanada 35, 000, 000 Malyalam 34,000,000 Tamil 58,000,000 Telugu 71,000,000 *Austro-Asiatic languages* Sino-Tibetan 2,000,000	Hindu 720,000,000 Muslim 100,000,000 Sikh 17,000,000 Roman Catholic 10,000,000 Protestant 8,000,000 Buddhist 6,000,000 Jain 4,000,000 Other 4,000,000
Myanmar	Burmese 30,000,000 Other Chinese based 13,840,000 *Of which:* Chin 970,000 Kachin 610,000 Karen 2,770,000 Kayah 180,000 Mon 1,080,000 Rakhine 2,010,000 Shan 3,780,000 Other 2,440,000	Buddhist 40,000,000 Christian 2,000,000 Muslim 1,700,000 Hindu 230,000
Nepal	Nepali 10,000,000 Other Indo Aryan 5,000,000 Austro-Asiatic 30,000 Tibeto-Burman 3,900,000	Hindu 17,000,000 Buddhist 1,000,000 Muslim 500,000
Pakistan	Urdu 10,000,000 Punjabi 64,000,000 Sindhi 27,000,000 Pashto 17,000,000 Baluchi 5,300,000 English 15,000,000	Muslim 124,000,000 Christian 2,000,000 Hindu 2,000,000 Other 100,000

Sri Lanka	Sinhalese 12,600,000	Buddhist 12,000,000
	Tamil 40,000,000	Hindu 3,000,000
		Muslim 1,300,000
		Roman Catholic 1,200,000
		Other 140,000
UK	English 56,000,000	Christian (all) 50,470,000
	Gaelic 80,000	Church of England 32,990,000
	Welsh 550,000	Protestants 8,710,000
	Other 1,000,000	Roman Catholic 7,610,000
		Other 1,160,000
		Muslim 810,000
		Hindu 410,000
		Jewish 315,000
		Sikh 230,000
		Atheist/non-religious 5,520,000
		Other 325,000
USA	English 251,000,000	Christian 223,000,000
	Spanish 19,000,000	Muslim 5,000,000
	French 2,000,000	Jew 4,600,000
	German 1,700,000	Buddhist 600,000
	Italian 1,400,000	Hindu 400,000
	Chinese 1,400,000	
	Bengali 40,000	
	Gujrati 110,000	
	Hindi 370,000	
	Total Indian 620,000	
	Malyalam 40,000	
	Punjabi 60,000	

Adapted from: *Britannica Book of the Year 1994.* © 1994, Encyclopaedia Britannica, Inc. Printed here with kind permission.

and provinces or states were formed according to the predominant language in each area. Of course these are not watertight compartments and there are zones, sometimes 50 or even 100 miles wide on each side of state borders, where the two languages of the adjoining states are spoken very freely.

There are two major groups of languages in India: the North Indian and the South Indian languages. There are four South Indian languages: Kanada, which is spoken in the state of Karnataka; Telugu, which is spoken in the state of Andhra Pradesh; Tamil, spoken in the state of Tamil Nadu; and Malayalam, which is spoken in the tiny state of Kerala. These four languages appear similar when written but have very different patterns of letters and are very different in speech. These languages are called Dravidian.

Although the script of the four South Indian languages is very different from the Devnagari script (which is the script of the languages used in

Table 1.6 Economic Base of Countries of Indian Subcontinent, UK and USA

	Agriculture	Construction	Defence and public administration	Finance	Manufacturing	Trade and restaurants	Transport and communication	Services
India	32%	6%	6%	8%	18%	12%	7%	6%
Pakistan	22%	4%	7%	6%	15%	15%	8%	7%
Bangladesh	36%		4.60%	2%	9%	8%	11%	22%
Sri Lanka	22%	7%	5%	5%	17%	20%	10%	3%
Nepal	55%	7%	6.60%	7%	–	6%	4%	6.60%
Myanmar	57%	1.60%	4%	0.20%	8%	23%	3%	–
Bhutan	43%	8%	11%	8%	9%	7.50%	7%	11%
UK	1.80%	6.20%	17%	24%	22%	14%	8%	6%
USA	2%	5%	12%	17.40%	19%	16%	6%	18%

Adapted from: *Britannica Book of the Year 1994*. Copyright 1994, Encyclopaedia Britannica, Inc. Printed here with kind permission.

North India), in fact these four languages are also heavily based on Sanskrit, using its words and grammatical structure.

There are several North Indian languages and these are all written using scripts that are based on the Devnagari script of the ancient Sanskrit language. These languages are: Marathi, spoken in the state of Maharashtra; Gujarati, which is spoken in the state of Gujarat; Bengali, which is spoken in the state of West Bengal; Punjabi, which is spoken in two or three North Indian states including Punjab, Harayana and parts of Kashmir; Marwadi, which is spoken in the north-western state of Rajastan; Behari which is chiefly a dialect of Hindi and is spoken in the north-eastern state of Bihar; and Oria, which is spoken in the Eastern state of Orissa.

Hindi is the commonest language spoken in India. It is spoken and understood by over 80% of the Indian population. It is India's national language and the widespread showing of Hindi films and their popularity all over India has made it possible for Hindi to spread, despite local resistance to imposition of Hindi as the national language. (India produces the largest number of movies in the world – probably five times as many as those produced in Hollywood. Bombay produces over 50% of these Hindi films.) Hindi and Urdu are very similar when spoken, and a combination of the two languages in which many Urdu words slip into Hindi is called Hindustani and is spoken and understood by even more people.

There are, however, significant differences between Hindi and Urdu: Urdu is written in Arabic script, which is similar to Persian, or Arabic, whereas Hindi uses Sanskrit script called Devnagari. In the Himalayan kingdom of Nepal, Hindi is used extensively. The languages used in the sub-Himalayan kingdoms as well as the north-eastern states of India are based on Chinese, but Hindi is also used. Bengali is used in Bangladesh, but has very distinct local dialects.

In Sri Lanka, two major language-based cultures operate – Tamil (which is identical to the Tamil spoken in the South Indian State of Tamil Nadu) and Sinhalese, which is a distinct language.

Names

There are three major name groups – Hindu and allied religions (Buddhism, Jain and Sikh), Muslim and Christian. I shall restrict myself mainly to Hindu names but will touch upon Muslim names.

Almost without exception, Hindu given first names have meanings and originate in the ancient language of Sanskrit. Until about 1950 children's given first names were often based on mythological characters such as gods and goddesses. The modern first names given since about 1950 still originate in Sanskrit and have meanings but are not based on mythological characters. Here are some examples of men's names: Ramesh (means the 'Lord of Rama' – Shiva), Prabhakar ('the one who makes Prabha or ray of light' – 'sun'), Subhash (meaning 'one who speaks sweetly'), Shyam (means 'dark coloured' and it is also one of the many names of Lord Krishna), Rajkumar (prince – 'Raj' means king and 'Kumar' means young or junior) and Balmukund (infant Krishna – Bal means 'child' or 'infant' and Mukund is one of the many names of Krishna), Ashok ('one who does not become sad or unhappy' – 'always cheerful'), Vijay (meaning 'victory), Prashant (meaning 'peaceful'). Some examples of women's names are Asha (meaning 'hope'), Usha (meaning 'dawn'), Nisha (meaning 'night'), Rekha (meaning 'line'), Sarala (meaning 'one who is "saral" or simple'), Maya ('illusion'), Jyoti ('flame', especially from the burning wick of a candle or oil lamp, or also light), Padmini ('arising from or of the lotus flower' – Padma means 'lotus flower'). Names are sometimes also place names – for example Vaishali is an ancient Indian city.

The rules governing middle names vary considerably in different parts of India. In the western states the middle name is almost invariably the father's first name. In the Hindi-speaking provinces of central and northern India, as well as Punjabi-speaking states such as Punjab, the middle name may be the name of the family deity and thus a grandfather; father and son may all have the same middle name and middle initial. In southern India the middle name is often the name of the village or town where the child was born, and in certain other South Indian states with matriarchal societies the mother's name is given as the middle name for the child.

The surnames or family names are, again, governed by several rules.

- Surnames may be related to the name of the village where the family originally came from (for example, Akotkar is the family that comes from the village of Akot, and Nagpure means the family came from the town of Nagpur). It is rather like having 'Liverpudlian' as a surname.
- Surnames may refer to an ancestral occupation. Some examples are Vakil (meaning a lawyer), Mali (meaning the gardener), Desai (businessman), and Lokhande (meaning the family who deals with iron or ironmonger).
- Surnames may depend upon the family's position in the village. Some examples are Patil (meaning the village elder – in the western state of Gujarat this is written as Patel), Deshmukh (meaning the elder in a much bigger village), and Deshpande (tax collector).
- Surnames that indicate education or learnedness. Some examples are Dwivedi (meaning the family in which the head of the family can recite, completely from memory, at least two Vedas – ancient scriptures written about 1500 BC); Trivedi (meaning the family in which the head of the family can recite Tri – that is three Vedas, the ancient scriptures); Tripathi (meaning that the family head can remember everything after listening to it only three times, and can recite it completely from memory); and Chaturvedi (they know four Vedas completely from memory). In Bengal, Chaturvedis are called Chatopadhyaya.

Most South Indian names tend to end with 'm' or 'n' – for example Ramanujam, meaning Anuj (brother) of Ram, or Ninan ('nain' means eyes).

In Punjab the distinction between men's and women's names is quite simple. Men's names have the suffix 'Singh' and women's names have the suffix 'Kaur'. Thus Jagjit Singh is a man's name, whereas Jagjit Kaur is a woman's name.

In all parts of India there is an almost universal practice that elders are never called by their name alone and a respectful suffix is always added. For example in the western state of Gujarat, for men the suffix 'Bhai' is added and for women the suffix is 'Ben' – thus a man with a name Arun is called Arun Bhai and a woman with a name of Meera will be called Meera Ben. The suffix 'Bhai' or 'Ben' simply means 'older brother' or 'older sister'. In the eastern state of Bengal, Didi, again meaning 'older sister', replaces Ben. In many of the northern states the suffix 'Lal' is added. For example, Jawahar becomes 'Jawahar Lal'. In the state of Maharashtra the suffix for men is '-pant' or '-rao'. A boy given the name 'Datta' will be called Dattopant when he grows older and attains an age of respectability (say 50 years), and a person called Vinayak in boyhood will be called Vinayak-rao. For women, the suffix '-bai' is added. For example the childhood name Radha becomes Radhabai in later age. In the four southern states the suffix for men is usually '-Appa' or '-Anna', both meaning 'older brother'. The suffix for women is usually '-Amma', usually meaning 'mother'. Another tradition, which is very rigidly followed, and has not changed with the passage of time, is that elders are addressed as 'uncle' or 'auntie or 'grandad' or 'grandma', even when they are not related to the person speaking. This respect depends upon the apparent age of the person being addressed. For example, if a child is speaking to a man who obviously appears to be at least the same age as his father then he will instinctively and automatically call him 'uncle'. If the child is speaking to a woman with grey hair who looks old enough to be his grandmother, the child will automatically call her 'grandma'. When speaking to elders, another suffix often added is '-Ji'. So, for example, the basic name Mohan becomes Mohan Lal (respectful) and eventually Mohan Lal-Ji (even more respectful). These rules apply even to complete strangers and in completely impersonal situations such as at railway stations. For example, a fruit vendor may attract the attention of a passer-by by calling him 'Badebhai' (meaning 'oh older brother'), or 'Cha Cha' or 'Kaka' (meaning 'oh uncle'), or 'Dadaji' (meaning 'granddad').

Like Hindu names, Muslim names also almost invariably have a meaning. Some examples of male names are Aftab (meaning 'the sun'), Aziz ('friend' or 'very close person'), Abdul (first name of Allah). Some examples of female names are Naeem ('the sweet one') and Noorjahan ('Noor' means 'light' and 'Jahan' means 'the world'). To indicate respect, the suffixes Khan (for men) and Begum (for women) are added. Another suffix, which was added during the days of the British Raj, is Sahab (meaning Sir); thus, for example, a person by the name Ali Akbar becomes Ali Akbar Khan (respectful) and finally Ali Akbar Khan Sahab (even more respectful).

It is worth noting that South Asian families coming from the Indian subcontinent adhere to these rules quite rigidly even when living in Western societies such as Britain or the United States. Children are always taught to address elders as uncle/auntie, or granddad/grandma. This is in stark contrast to what they are expected to do when they mix within the rest of British society. However, there is no indication that children resent it. Their own parents set them an example by following the code very strictly.

Elders (first generation immigrants) feel insulted and hurt, although they may not show or say it, if they are called by their first names without the appropriate or alternative suffixes. This has great significance in the National Health Service, where young nurses or doctors may have to address elderly Indo-Asian patients.

Another important cultural difference to bear in mind is that Indo-Asian first generation immigrants do not mind being asked their age at all. This is because, in their countries of origin, old age is considered graceful.

Clothes

Differences in clothing styles are much more conspicuous in women than men. Traditional women's clothes among people coming from the Indian subcontinent can be divided into three categories: *sari, salwar-kamiz* and *burkha.*

Sari is essentially a piece of cloth about 15 feet long by three-and-a-half feet wide with different types of floral or geometric designs printed on it. It is made in different materials, such as cotton, silk or synthetic man-made fibres. Sometimes threads of silver or gold (*zari*) are incorporated into ceremonial saris. Different styles of *saris* originate in different parts of India and are often described accordingly. These so-called 'homes of *saris*' are known as 'peth' and some examples are Benaras, Kota, Solapur, Calcutta, Nagpur handloom, and Paithani. There are also distinctive ways of wearing *saris* – for example 'simple round wrap', 'koorgi', 'Gujarati', 'Sri Lankan' and finally a 'nine yard' older traditional method. Sari is worn throughout most of India and by women of Hindu religion or those religions that are descended from Hinduism such as Buddhism, Jain and Sikh.

In the northern region of India, covering the states of Punjab, Uttar Pradesh, and going up to Kashmir in the north where the influence of Muslim culture is very high, another type of women's dress is seen prominently. This is called *salwar-kamiz*. It is a two-piece dress, *salwar* being the baggy trousers and *kamiz* (originally an Arabic word) meaning a shirt-like knee-length top. Depending upon the tightness of the fit of *salwar* it is often described in two or three different ways. *Chudidar* is the tightest fit and hugs the skin, especially from the knees down; *salwar* is a loose-fit and *sharara* is an extremely baggy fit. *Salwar-kamiz* is essentially a North Indian dress, however, because of the ease with which it can be worn, and with the disappearance of internal geographical boundaries within India, as a result of increasing ease of travelling, this has become very popular with women in other parts of India, especially the younger generation. Married women still tend to use the traditional *saris* in the other parts of India. It should be noted that, with passage of time and attitudes becoming less rigid, the dress code is starting to change.

Burkha, the third type of dress, is worn only by Muslim women. It is the black (or sometimes white) headdress that covers the entire body from toenails to the head, and covers all the face completely with a window of lace over the eyes so that women can see. This is in fact the Islamic women's dress being worn throughout the Islamic countries west of India – Pakistan, Afghanistan, and all the Middle Eastern Arabic countries, where it is called 'Abhaya'.

Besides the three main types of dresses mentioned above, regional variations can often be seen. For example, in the western state of Gujarat and the adjoining north-western state of Rajastan, women wear *lenga* (a loose shin- or ankle-length skirt), and a *choli* (a blouse) and often in combination with an *odhani* (which is a length of fine cloth material to cover the head and breasts for modesty).

In recent years, Western-style clothes, such as skirts, blouses, trousers, jeans and slacks, have become very popular – especially with the younger generation, usually until they get married. Many school uniforms tend to comprise skirts and blouses.

In the Himalayan states (such as Nepal and Bhutan) women's traditional dress tends to consist of indigenously woven and hand-made woollen skirts and blouses.

Men tend to wear Western-style clothes, like trousers and shirts, to work and outside homes, even when living in their countries of origin. Thus when they immigrate into Britain they do not need to make any major changes to their clothing styles. Men in North India might wear a *dhoti,* which is a white loincloth about 10 feet long with a shirt-top made in different styles. *Dhoti* was undoubtedly the commonest form of men's clothing until the beginning of the twentieth century, but under the influence of the British Raj, trousers (in India usually called 'pants') slowly replaced it. In modern-day India, *dhoti* is worn by manual workers and peasants working on the farms. It is almost never worn to work by educated modern men, although there appears to be a new trend leading to its resurgence, helped by politicians and similar people in the public domain.

In the southern Indian states, a variation of this is a shorter (six feet long), often more colourful version called *lungi.* This is still very widely worn in rural as well as urban areas. It is also worn in such distant regions as Bangladesh in the east and Punjab in the north. In the relentless heat of the Indian subcontinent, such simple apparel serves the purpose of keeping the person cool, hence its widespread use. Thus traditional men's clothes consist of a variation of a loincloth (length between 6 and 10 feet), which is wrapped around in different styles, a vest/shirt and often a head-dress like a cap or a turban.

Apart from the colour of the skin the most visible difference between ethnic minorities and the indigenous white population is to do with dress. Wearing of traditional clothes is an important element of self-identity and part of the way of life of the immigrant ethnic minorities, like eating their own foods, speaking their own language and observing cultural and religious practices. However, the host communities can often resent this, expecting them to adopt Western styles of clothing. Thus the style of clothing originating from the South Asian countries may often be considered as a sign of backwardness and the wearers are considered to be stupid or lacking in linguistic or job skills. As such, clothes become a form of stigmata (Modood, 1997). However, in a world that is rapidly shrinking through the availability of television and air travel, Western fashion designers may adapt clothing styles from other countries, including developing Third World countries, and then these clothes can be readily accepted by the indigenous population.

Food

India is a vast country, spanning nearly 2,000 miles from north to south and nearly 1,500 miles from east to west. There are a huge number of regional variations in food and it will be impossible to cover all of them and so I give only the briefest outline of typical Indian food and its variations.

There are obvious geographical differences. For example the population living in the coastal strips have a diet rich in seafood. People living deeper inland will depend on land crops. When the Mughals invaded India around 1200 AD, they brought with them many different styles of cooking and present-day Indian food has been greatly enriched by Mughal cuisine. There is often no distinction between lunch and dinner. It is not traditional to eat breakfast in the morning.

There are major differences between the north and the south. In southern India, rice and dishes made from rice form the staple diet. Some examples of this are the *idali* (a steamed rice dumpling, which is very light and fragile), *dosai* (also written as *dosa*) which is a large pancake made of rice flour and stuffed with freshly cooked vegetables. Coconut palms are in great abundance in Southern India and coconut products, such as coconut milk, coconut water and coconut oil, are therefore used extensively for cooking. Coconut has a very high content of saturated fatty acid therefore the incidence of coronary heart disease is very high in the coastal areas where its consumption is high. The same is true of *ghee* in the north of India.

In northern India the staple diet is wheat, sometimes barley and an indigenous crop called *jwar*. Cooking in northern India uses vegetable oil and ghee (clarified butter) quite extensively. Cow's milk is not used very widely; buffalo milk is used instead. Buffalo milk has nearly twice the amount of fat content as cow's milk in India. Butter and margarine are not used for cooking.

Cheese as it is known in the Western countries is generally not available or eaten in India, but local cheese called *panir* is made at home, particularly in the northern Indian states, and it is liberally used in cooking vegetables and meat dishes. Food often spoils very quickly in the hot weather and it is therefore almost always eaten when freshly cooked. With improving lifestyles and the wide availability of refrigerators, habits are changing and cooked food is often kept in the 'fridge'. However, this is not a universal practice.

Traditionally the Indian diet has mostly been vegetarian. However, since India's independence, eating habits and attitudes have changed considerably, with more and more people turning to non-vegetarian food. Hindus do not eat beef because cows are considered sacred, therefore the popular choice for Hindus tends to be chicken and goat meat. People generally do not prefer pork because pigs often live in extremely unhealthy conditions. Pork is also not eaten by Muslims because it is prohibited in their religion. Sweet dishes are made from many different ingredients, but largely fall into three categories: sweets made from milk, sweets made from pulses and wheat and sweets made from vegetables like carrots, onions and cauliflower. In Bengal sweets are mostly made from milk and in the northern states they are often made from dry nuts like cashew nuts or almonds.

A typical diet of a poor man, or a villager or a peasant might consist of a thick bread made from *jwar* flour with an onion, a few sprigs of garlic, one or two raw chillies, and some thick *dal* (cooked and mashed lentils).

'Eating out' is not a cultural norm in India, however with the pressure of modern day life and growing affluence it is becoming increasingly acceptable. Restaurants are becoming popular, especially in larger cities. However, a peculiar Indian institution is the roadside café called *dhaba,* a source of extremely inexpensive, fresh and excellent food, open 24 hours. These out-of-town shanty places are lifelines for lorry-drivers, tourists and the like.

Immigration patterns

Most Indians have come to Britain from the Punjab and Gujarat. Their languages include Punjabi, Gujarati, Urdu and Hindi. Many of those of Asian origin from east Africa are also Gujarati, mainly descended from Indians

Table 1.7. Population of the UK by ethnic group (1991 census data)

	All	Percentage born in UK	Percentage of total population
White	51,874,000	96	94.0
All ethnic minorities	3,015,000	47	5.5
Black	891,000	56	1.6
Indian	840,000	42	1.5
Pakistani	477,000	51	0.9
All	54,889,000	93	100.0

who migrated to east Africa as businessmen or to work in general construction. Those who came to Britain from Bangladesh speak Bengali. Muslims, Hindus and Sikhs are the most numerous, but the Asian community also includes Christians.

Black people came to Britain from the widely scattered islands in the Caribbean, which are now in the Commonwealth, as well as from Guyana and Belize. Nearly 60% of these came from Jamaica. This happened because there were better job opportunities in Britain than in their own countries. Most of the black immigration occurred in the 1950s and 1960s.

Immigration from India and Pakistan (including Bangladesh), which began later than that from the Caribbean, reached its peak in the 1960s. This was prompted by a desire for better employment opportunities – especially in the textile industry – and education.

In recent years the number of people coming from the Asian subcontinent has remained roughly constant, although there has been a rise in the number of people from African countries such as Ghana, Nigeria and Somalia as a result of an increase in asylum applications.

There was probably a slight increase in asylum seekers from the Punjab province of India during the period 1982–4 in the wake of the demand for an autonomous state of Punjab in India (Central Office of Information, 1997).

Until 1962, Commonwealth citizens had been free to enter Britain as they wished. In that year the government decided to limit the number of immigrants to a level the country could absorb, both economically and socially, and the first legislation to control Commonwealth immigration was passed.

Further restrictions were introduced in 1968 and entry from all countries is now controlled by the Immigration Act of 1971 which was amended in 1988 and the Asylum and Immigration Appeals Act 1993.

Most of the Asians of Indian extraction who came to Britain from Africa speak Gujarati or Punjabi. As a result of these complex origins, nearly half of the South Asians (that is people coming from the Indian subcontinent) understand more than one of the languages of the South Asian ethnic communities in Britain.

Of the immigrant population from India, 51% are Sikh, 33% Hindus, 7% Muslims, 6% Christians and 3% others. Amongst African Asians these figures are 58% Hindus, 19% Sikh and 15% Muslims. In other words 32% of the Hindu immigrant community came from India whereas 58% came from Africa. Among the immigrant Sikh population, African Asians are outnumbered by a ratio of 3:1 by Sikhs who emigrated from India.

Traditionally, people from the northern state of Punjab, the north-western state of Rajastan and the western state of Gujarat, are enterprising and engage in private business, and when they emigrated to Britain, wherever they settled, they tended to open up their own private businesses, whether corner shops, chemist shops, or catering businesses. On the other hand, people from certain other states, predominantly Bengal in the East (of which Calcutta is the state capital), Maharashtra in the West (of which Bombay is the state capital), and the four southern states of Karnataka, (of which Bangalore is the state capital), Kerala, Tamil Nadu (of which the state capital is Madras, now renamed Channai), and Andhra Pradesh (of which the state capital is Hyderabad), have traditionally engaged themselves in intellectual pursuits and remained in employment. As a result, when these people migrated, they were inclined to enter into service industries or be employed, whether as doctors, teachers, or scientists. Bengal is particularly rich in cultural and arts heritage – classical music, classical dance, poetry and literature being its forte.

Settling patterns

According to the 1991 census, ethnic minority communities were concentrated in the metropolitan and industrial areas: 45% lived in Greater London compared with only 10% of the white population. In nine London Boroughs ethnic minorities accounted for 25% of the population, the highest proportion (45%) being in Brent. The Bangladeshi group alone made up 23% of the population in Tower Hamlets. About 60% of the people from black ethnic groups lived in Greater London compared to only 41% of Indians and 18% of Pakistanis.

Outside London there are high concentrations of ethnic minority populations in Leicester and Slough (both 28%) and in Birmingham (22%). In Leicester the Indian group comprised over 75% of the ethnic minority population. Pakistanis are the largest component in Birmingham (32% of the ethnic minority population). The other areas of high-density concentration of ethnic minority populations are Yorkshire and the Lancashire textile towns of Bradford, Rochdale and Blackburn, and also Luton.

The ethnic minorities in Scotland number about 62,000, the greatest concentrations being in Glasgow, Edinburgh, Aberdeen and Dundee. The largest ethnic group in Scotland are Pakistanis (21,000).

Table 1.8. Percentage of people born outside Britain by ethnic origin and age (Spring, 1994)

Age group	All origins	White	Ethnic minority groups				
			All	Black	Indian	Pakistani/ Bangladeshi	Mixed/ other origins
All ages	7	4	54	48	59	54	56
0–15	3	2	14	15	7	16	18
16–24	6	4	40	24	28	52	51
25–34	9	5	65	40	77	83	74
35–44	10	5	94	84	99	98	94
45–59/64	8	5	98	99	100	100	94
16–59/64	9	5	73	59	78	79	76
60/65 & over	7	5	100	100	99	100	100

Source: Labour Force Survey (1994)

In Wales the majority lived in Cardiff and Newport. There are no precise figures for numbers of ethnic minority groups in Northern Ireland.

The 1991 census did not collect information by religious faith but only by country of origin, so there are no accurate figures available about people representing Hindu or Sikh or Jain religions. However, it is estimated that there are about 320,000 Hindus in Britain, originating largely from the Indian provinces of Gujarat and Punjab. The community is one of the most recent of the South Asian communities to develop in Britain. Some Hindus arrived directly from India in the 1950s and early 1960s, but most, although of Indian origin, came from East Africa in the late 1960s and in early 1970s. Some, again of Indian origin, have come from other parts of the world including Fiji and Trinidad. The largest groups of Hindus are to be found in Leicester, various areas of London, Birmingham and Bradford.

There is a large Sikh community comprising an estimated 400,000–500,000 people. Most came from Punjab in north-west India although a large minority had come via East Africa. Over 200 Sikh temples cater for the religious, educational, social welfare and cultural needs of the community. The oldest central temple in London was established in 1908 and the largest is in Hounslow, Middlesex.

Other religious persuasions include about 30,000 Jains, whose religion is of ancient Indian origin. A Jain temple called Deresar opened in Leicester in 1988.

Age structure, size of the family and household characteristics

Ethnic minority groups have a far younger age structure than the white population. At the 1991 census about one-third (32%) of the people belonging to ethnic minorities were under the age of 16, compared to 20% of the population of Great Britain as a whole. Only 3% of the ethnic minority groups were over the age of 65 compared to 16% of Great Britain's population as a whole.

Size of the family

Family sizes have fallen substantially in Britain over several decades. In 1994, according to the results of the fourth Labour Force Survey (LFS), only 4% of white families had more than three dependent children. Family sizes for African Asians were similar; Indian family size was slightly larger, but Pakistani and Bangladeshi families were significantly larger: 33% of Pakistani families and 42% of Bangladeshi families had four or more children and 8% of these had six or more children.

The households of ethnic minority populations coming from the Indian subcontinent tend to be more densely concentrated. For example, the 1991 census shows that 54% of all Pakistani households and 62% of Bangladeshi households had five or more residents, compared to only 7% of white households. Pakistani and Bangladeshi households also had the largest number of children. Bangladeshi households often have three or more children. Another perspective is that 29% of white households were single-person households compared with 31% of black households and only 7% of Pakistani/ Bangladeshi households.

Employment patterns and status

Data from the Labour Force Survey of Spring 1994 indicates that 5.9% of the working age population (aged 16–64 for men, and 16–59 for women) in Britain – that is nearly 2,000,000 people – were from ethnic minority groups. Of these, 560,000 were Indian ethnic origin, 530,000 were black and 440,000 were Pakistani or Bangladeshi in origin.

Overall 77% of ethnic minority men and 52% of women in Great Britain were economically active, compared to 86% of men and 72% of women in the white population; 73% of the black population and 71% of the Indian population were economically active compared with 79% of the white population. Only 49% of the Pakistani/Bangladeshi group was economically active.

The rate of economic activity among women of working age was 67% for blacks, 62% for Indians, and 26% for Pakistanis/Bangladeshis. This is possibly because of the different cultural attitudes towards marriage and towards women having jobs.

Table 1.9 shows that women from Pakistan, Bangladesh and India cannot be lumped together when considering their levels of economic activity. Women with Hindu, Sikh, Christian or non-religious backgrounds from India or East Africa were far more likely to have jobs than women from

Table 1.9. Economic activity of women

16-59 year olds, not in full time education	White	Caribbean	Indian	African Asian	Pakis-tani	Bangla-deshi	Chinese
Working full time	37	50	38	45	15	6	47
Working part time	27	16	15	19	5	1	24
Looking for work	6	16	8	6	8	8	2
House or family	27	13	36	26	70	81	21
Disabled/ retired	4	5	4	3	4	4	2
Weighted count	1091	666	517	299	340	105	147

From Modood (1997: 86)

Pakistan and Bangladesh. Looking at it the other way, Muslim women from India are far more likely to enter into the labour market and have jobs than Muslim women from Pakistan or Bangladesh.

Table 1.10 shows that the unemployment rate in the non-white population is significantly higher (21%) than that of the white population (9%). However, within that, these figures are lowest for people from Indian origin (14%) and highest for people from Pakistan/Bangladesh (28%).

Table 1.10. Unemployment rates (percentages) by ethnic origin, Great Britain, (Spring 1994)

Ethnic Origin	All	Men	Women
All origins	10	11	7
White	9	11	7
Non-white	21	25	16
Black	26	33	17
Indian	14	16	12
Pakistani/Bangladeshi	28	29	24
Mixed/Other	19	22	15

Source: Labour Force Survey (1994)

Further analysis shows that white people were more likely to work for private sector employers (62%) than those from the ethnic minorities (57%).

The majority of both white and ethnic minority populations work in the service sector. Black men and women are more likely to work in the public sector, whereas Indian, Pakistani and Bangladeshi men and women are more likely than average to be self-employed.

Growth in the ethnic minority population

In the period 1988–90, the total ethnic minority population in Great Britain was 2,580,000, which is an increase of 18% from 1981 (Jones, 1993: 19).

The LFS of 1990 shows that African Asian, Indian and Chinese men were more likely to be highly qualified than were white men; this is particularly the case among those aged 16–24 and especially among African Asians. A high proportion (relative to white population) of these groups is studying in full-time education, and this is now reflected in measures of educational attainment. These high levels of qualifications now appear to be having some effect in the job market.

The proportion of male employees from each of the African Asian, Indian and Chinese groups who are in the top job level category (professional, manager or employer) is now equal to or greater than the proportion of white men. This trend was also seen in the 1982 analysis called *Black and White Britain.*

From the evidence available in the LFS it appears that some ethnic minority groups have made progress overall in the job market in the 1980s in comparison both with the white group and with other minority groups (Jones, 1993: 153). Indian households had a housing profile that was much more like that of the majority population than any of the other minority ethnic groups. Their ownership level was higher, and more owned detached or semi-detached properties, but on this latter issue they were much closer to the whites than to the other three minority ethnic groups (largely due to their class distribution). In terms of car availability, they outranked all the other groups including whites. The incidence of overcrowding was low, despite larger average household size and a lower age profile than whites, and overcrowding was certainly much less in evidence than in the other South Asian communities. Amenity levels in general compared very well with those in the majority population (Karn, 1997).

Punjabi is easily the most commonly used South Asian language among the British Asians. A very large majority of Indians as well as Pakistanis and a third of the African Asians speak it. However, only 6% of Pakistanis can write Punjabi compared to 33% of Indians. There is little difference between the Punjabi spoken by Indians and Pakistanis. The written script called Gurmukhi is derived from Sanskrit and is unfamiliar to the Pakistani Punjabis. Pakistani Punjabis usually also speak Urdu and have made Urdu one of their national languages of Pakistan. Very few people of Indian extraction in Great Britain in fact speak Urdu (correctly pronounced 'Oordoo' with a soft 'd' as in 'the').

Services for immigrants

The Independent Commission for Racial Equality (CRE) was set up by the 1976 Race Relations Act to work towards the elimination of discrimination, to promote equality of opportunity and good relations between people of different racial groups, and to keep the operation of the Act under review.

The CRE supports and finances a network of 86 local Racial Equality Councils (RECs). These are voluntary bodies that promote equality of opportunity, good race relations and the elimination of racial discrimination. The councils are usually composed of representatives of statutory and voluntary bodies, including the churches, trades unions and ethnic minority organizations committed to racial equality. Many RECs have been involved in local initiatives to help victims of racially motivated harassment and violence.

Under the Public Order Act 1986 it is an offence to use threatening, abusive or insulting words or to publish or distribute material likely to, or intended to, stir up racial hatred. This also applies to behaviour designed to stir up racial hatred. The offence is punishable by a fine and/or imprisonment. In England and Wales a prosecution may be brought only by, or with the consent of, the Attorney General.

The European Community Council of Europe carried out an inter-governmental project to examine the approach to community relations by the different member states between 1987 and 1991. The report from this project stated that Britain had gone further than any other European country in introducing anti-discrimination legislation and in setting up institutional provisions to promote racial equality.

Another report commissioned by the then Department of Employment in Britain and published in 1992 concluded that Britain's law and practice combating racial discrimination in employment was the most advanced within the European Union (EU).

The Department of Employment had published a ten-point plan for employers to ensure equal opportunities.

Education

It would appear that the government believes that ethnic minority groups should be free to maintain their own cultural identity and has acknowledged the need to collect statistics on the ethnic origins, languages and religions of schoolchildren to ensure that the education provided meets

the needs of all pupils. Under the National Curriculum, foundation subjects at secondary level are offered in many modern foreign languages
including Arabic, Bengali, Gujarati, Hindi, Punjabi and Urdu.

Religious education is taught in all schools. All school syllabuses must
reflect the fact that religious traditions in Britain are mainly Christian
while taking account of the teaching and practices of the other principal
religions represented. The government also attaches great importance to
parental choice. In some areas specialist Muslim schools have been established and more recently a school has been established to offer education
in the traditional Hindu ways of life, and is attached to the Swaminarayan
temple at Neasden, north London.

The media

The British Broadcasting Corporation (BBC), Independent Television
Commission (ITC) and the Radio Authority aim to reflect the diversity of
cultures and languages in British society and provide programmes of
interest to all sections of the community. Guidelines exist for programme
makers stressing the need to avoid unnecessary reference to race or racial
origin, to ensure that coverage is objective and accurate and to guard
against stereotyped images.

The BBC has produced a variety of multi-cultural magazines and docu-
mentary programmes for television. These address different aspects of life
from the Asian countries, particularly India and the Hindu religion. Some
examples are *Sadhus – India's Holy Men,* – the great Indian epic
Maharabharat (a 93-part serialization), and *The Great Maratha.* More
recently a specialist television service for people from the East Indian subcontinent has become available and is called Zee TV.

In the past few years several local and regional radio stations have
sprung up, such as BBC Radio Leicester, and Radio WM (West Midlands),
which provide regular programmes for ethnic minority listeners – sometimes for as much as 18 hours per day. There are 180 independent commercial radio stations, 10 of which are 24-hour ethnic services owned and
operated by the ethnic minorities whom they serve. There are five stations
for Asian listeners (two Sunrise radio stations – one for greater London
and one for Bradford; Sabras Sound in the East Midlands; Radio Excel in
the West Midlands; and Asian Sound in East Lancashire).

There are a number of publications designed specifically for members
of the ethnic minorities. Such titles in English and other languages are
generally published weekly, fortnightly or monthly and include the *Asian
Age, Asian Times, Eastern Eye* and *India Abroad.* The rapid growth in
Internet services means that many newspapers from the Indian subcontinent are now instantly available to be read online on the Internet.

Employment: discrimination in the workplace

Of those who reported discrimination, 75% of the black Caribbeans and 50% of South Asians felt that it was because of their perceived race and colour (Jones, 1993). Very few thought it was as a result of their religion alone. However, 10% of Pakistani/Bangladeshi and the same number of Caribbeans felt that they were discriminated against because of their religion. The figure for Sikhs was about half of this and almost no Hindus felt that they were discriminated against on grounds of religion.

All immigrant ethnic minority groups agree that Asians experience the highest level of prejudice of any ethnic racial or religious group, and the Asians themselves believe that Muslims experience the highest level of prejudice.

Family life

Large numbers of Hindus, although not required to attend a place of worship regularly, attend Hindu temples for annual festivals. The first Hindu temple or Mandir was opened in London in 1962 and there are now over 150, a number of which are affiliated to the National Council of Hindu temples and to the Vishwa Hindu Parishad. This is an international organization. The Swaminarayan Hindu Mission in north London has the largest Hindu temple to be built outside India, together with an extensive cultural complex with provision for conferences, exhibitions and marriage ceremonies, and with sports and health clinics.

Shops owned by Indo-Asians, selling Indian groceries, pulses, spices, pickles, savoury and sweet items and 'Indian' vegetables and fruits (usually the produce of African or Caribbean countries) are now plentiful in almost all British towns. More recently large 'Indian supermarkets' have opened.

Similarly, Indian restaurants have become extremely popular in the UK. Although called 'Indian', most of these are owned by Bangladeshis and have on offer a Bangladeshi interpretation of Indian food. These are extremely popular with the indigenous white population, perhaps more so than with the immigrant Indian population. One often-quoted reason is the Indians eat authentic Indian food at home all the time anyway.

Indian take-away is the most popular take-away in the UK, having overtaken Chinese take-away and the traditional British fish and chips take-away. Samosas, bhajias, onion bhajias (often erroneously called bhajee) and chicken tikka masala are almost believed to be indigenous British dishes, and without these parties are now unimaginable!

The Labour Force Survey of 1994 shows that ethnic minority men were more likely than ethnic minority women to have a white partner. Mixed marriages, taken to include co-habiting relationships, are far more common now than in 1974. The ethnic minorities with the lowest incidence of mixed marriages are from South Asia. The percentages of each group who are the family heads in mixed marital relationships are as follows: 6% for Pakistanis, 7% for Bangladeshis, 9% for Indians, 3% for African Asians, 11% for Chinese, 24% for Africans, 27% for Afro-Caribbeans.

About 60% of people in occupational class 1 to 3 use a community language when speaking to younger family members, compared to about 75% of people in social class 4 to 6. In the Bangladeshi population this figure is much higher and does not vary between classes. Nearly all the younger generation (16–34-year-olds) sometimes use the language of their parents in talking with family members older than themselves. However, when talking with family members of their own age such as siblings, or talking with friends from other South Asian family backgrounds, they tend not to use the parents' native language, but prefer speaking in English instead. This marks a considerable decline in the use of South Asian languages in some communities. Over 50% of Indians and South Asians in the age range of 16–29 now use English as their main spoken language, compared with only about 20% of Bangladeshi young people in that same age range.

South Asian families tend to have very close emotional ties and try to replicate, wherever possible, the extended family structure from the countries of origin. They tend to keep in touch very regularly, using the telephone, letters or visits, with children living away because of university education, elderly parents living away or brothers, sisters and all extended family members such as uncles, aunts, nieces, nephews, or cousins. Social occasions such as birthdays or weddings, provide ample opportunities for replenishing family contact and warmth. It is not uncommon for elderly relatives, like parents, to be looked after within the family home of South Asian families and Hindu families. African Asians are no exception.

Until recently it used to be considered unacceptable to send elderly and infirm parents to be looked after in old people's homes or nursing homes. However, in the last few years there appears to be a trend for creating purpose-built warden-controlled accommodation and old people's homes where the elderly folk may go to live.

Importance of culture and religion

About 90% of Sikhs, Hindus and Muslims feel that their religion is important to them and to the way they lead their lives; however, Muslims seemed to feel that religion plays a very important role for them compared to the Sikhs and the Hindus, who feel that it is quite important. It seems that religion is more important to women than to men.

Most Hindu homes have their own private shrine or temple in one room, which may be set aside for this purpose alone or may also have other domestic functions. Deities may be worshipped on a daily basis or less frequently. Most members of the older generation tend to offer worship daily, working-age adults tend to offer this on important occasions such as festivals or important family dates such as birthdays, anniversaries and remembrance days. The younger generation – dependent young children as well as young adults – are told to offer prayers by their elders on these important dates. The place of worship may also be the venue for religious instruction and this may be offered at a general community meeting point.

Nearly 66% of Muslims attend a mosque at least once a week, 70% of Sikhs attend a temple (*Gurdwara*) at least once a week and less than 50% of Hindus do the same. Sikh women attend the most of all women; Hindu women are slightly less frequent and Muslim women rarely seem to attend.

At this juncture I should like to highlight a very important philosophical outlook that runs through all the 'Eastern' countries. It is the philosophy of 'God's wish' as an explanation of all that befalls individuals and the world, good or bad, and the notion that 'whatever happens, happens for good of everyone' – a view that is often used as a consolation. Thus when, after a lot of hard work, business becomes prosperous, children do well in exams, or a good marital match is found for a child, rather than attributing the success to one's own effort ('I did it'), people in the East are inclined to say 'that was God's wish, without which nothing is possible'. Similarly, when disaster strikes, a family member dies in an accident or things do not go according to plan, people are likely to say 'That was God's wish. We tried.' In Arabic and Urdu, 'Insha Allah' ('God willing') or in Hindi, 'Ram Bharose' ('in the hands of Lord Rama').

Although it could be argued that this attitude could lead to laziness, unwillingness to take personal responsibility or lack of enterprise, it is in fact not an alternative to lack of effort. These words are uttered after putting in hard work. Leaving the fruits of the toil in the hands of God enables a person to humble himself and to move away from an egocentric position. In times of crisis or disaster this philosophy provides a protective shield. It has been shown that it reduces the period of grief and mourning. Similarly, by not holding a human person responsible for things going wrong, the incidence of litigation and demands for monetary compensation are kept very low. After immigration and a full period of enculturation, this outlook may wear off – financial compensation may prove to be too strong and tempting a factor in the Western way of life to be ignored.

Hindu women who have migrated to Britain often wear Western-style clothes (such as skirts, trousers and blouses). In the 1960s and 1970s women tended to wear *sari* to work – and this was probably because of their inability to let go of their 'Indianness' and traditions. Attitudes

relaxed in the late 1970s and 1980s and many women then started to dis-
card the *sari* in favour of Western clothes. However, the late 1980s and
early 1990s have seen a resurgence of pride in being a Hindu or Indian
and this appears to have resulted in a return of *sari* among some women.
Many women, whether Punjabi, Hindu or Punjabi Sikh or other Hindus,
often prefer to wear *salwar-kamiz*. Only 1% of men and 12% of women
sometimes wear Asian clothes at work (Modood, 1997: 327).

Women usually wear traditional dress at home in the evenings and on
social occasions such as birthday parties, wedding receptions and religious occasions. Interestingly, even on those occasions men tend to wear
traditional Western clothes. The fact that a much larger number of women
than men always wear Asian clothes suggests that the 'projection' of
Asianness by means of clothes falls particularly on women.

Pakistanis and Bangladeshis are much more likely than Indians to wear
Asian clothes, and especially more than African Asians. Within the younger
generation, aged 16–24, less than 20% of women coming from Indian and
Asian Indian background always wear Asian clothes compared to 75% of
Pakistani women.

There are also age-related patterns in the wearing of Asian clothes. For
example, people under 35 wore Sikh turbans much less (16%), compared
to 37% worn by people over 35 years of age. Similarly in women under
the age of 35 only 35% wore *bindi* (a red spot on the forehead) compared
to over 70% in women over 35 years of age. This difference was even
more marked in women of African Asian origin. Significantly, these were
the very women who tend to wear Indian clothes to work much less often
than Hindu women from India. African Asian women wear Asian clothes
less than Indians, but they are more likely to wear items with a religious
significance.

Marriage

Attitudes of Hindus to mixed marriages are least disapproving, only 32%
not approving of it compared to 42% of Sikhs. Pakistanis were most disapproving. There is also a strong age factor, older people being more disapproving than the younger, but there were no significant differences
between the Indians and African Asians (in the age range 16–34) in disapproval of mixed marriages. Again Hindus of Indian or African origin
appear to have no gender differences in their attitudes.

The majority of the Asians from Indian subcontinent over the age of 35
have their spouses chosen by their parents. This practice is most common
among Pakistanis and Bangladeshis, but it seems that this 'arranged marriage' system is becoming less common among the young. Over 56% of
the Sikhs are also in arranged marriages, but only 36% Hindus. This practice is even less common among African Asians over the age of 35, and in
people younger than 35 it is now almost an exception. The tendency is for

young people to choose their own partner, although the marriages are usually entered into with blessing of parents on both sides (Stopes-Roe and Cochrane, 1990; Anwar, 1994).

Young Hindus from India and Africa often choose their own marital partners but the stark distinction between 'parents' decision' and 'my decision' is much less evident these days. Increasingly the parents are closely involved and the trend is for the parents to introduce a number of prospective partners out of whom the youngsters choose one by getting to know them well over a period of time.

Inter-racial marriages are happening with increasing regularity. These marriages tend to happen more between Hindus and white British. Marriages between Hindus and black British appear to be extremely rare. There does not appear to be any clear trend between Hindu boys marrying white girls or Hindu girls marrying white boys. Another more recently emerging trend appears to be for Hindus born and brought up in Britain to marry a partner from India. In these marriages the element of 'arrangement' is slightly higher, but the reason behind this trend is not very clear. Interestingly this trend also appears to be emerging in the United States. One possible hypothesis is to do with increasing rates of divorce in Asian marriages when both partners are brought up in the Western society. It is possible that as young people see around them the increased incidents of divorce, heartache, pain, destruction of family life, uncertainty and insecurity that separation and divorce cause, then eligible bachelors probably feel that a partner from India, with the more traditional values of respect for family life and greater tolerance, is more likely to provide a stable and secure family life. This trend needs to be watched and researched carefully.

Marriage and marital partnership

Patterns of marital partnerships in Britain have changed rapidly since the 1950s. In the 1950s men and women married early and remained married for the rest of their lives. By the 1990s both men and women tended to marry much later in age. Similarly the rate of separation and divorce increased significantly, as did the rate of remarriage for both sexes. Cohabitation increased rapidly, especially among younger people. Compared to the native white population, the black Caribbeans in 1982 were less likely to be living in a formal marriage (and more likely to be either single or living as married or divorced) (Brown, 1984). South Asians, on the other hand, were more often officially married than the white group as shown by the 1991 census. It is thought that the reason for this is the community's attitude to the nuclear family, which had been imported from their country of origin. It remains to be seen whether the changing patterns of British conventions will affect and change these attitudes in the South Asians.

Cohabitation

Cohabitation and separation/divorce were both more common among the black Caribbeans and white population than the Asian population.

'Partnering' includes people who have been legally married or those who had been married in the past but have separated, divorced or widowed, and also those who are currently living with a partner and are not married. Black Caribbeans had lower numbers of having been in partnership than the white or the South Asian populations, and up to the age of 40 they had smaller numbers of partnerships. There were only minor differences between the whites and the South Asians (irrespective of which country they originated from and which religious faith they followed), with the South Asians being slightly more likely to have been in a partnership than the whites.

There are very significant differences between the three ethnic groups in terms of cohabitation: 18% of black Caribbean couples live together as if they were married, compared with 11% of the white couples and only about 3% of the Asian couples. The rate of cohabitation is high for couples in their early 20s but rapidly declines as the age increases. Of course this pattern is probably caused by a combination of an age effect (people cohabit when young and they marry later), and a generation effect (meaning people nowadays are more ready to live together without marrying than they were a generation ago).

Mixed ethnicity partnerships

There are important sociological and religious barriers for mixed ethnicity partnerships. Mixed ethnic marriages form a very small proportion, of all partnerships in the population in Great Britain – only about 1% (Berrington, 1996). A common form of racism is for the dominant white group to object to 'miscegenation' if their daughters and sons marry someone from a non-white minority (Berthoud and Beishon, 1997: 29). On the other hand, if young people from ethnic minorities enter into mixed ethnic marriage or partnership it is often considered by members of their own community as a betrayal of the community identity. It is probably more important to discuss what difficulties are likely to be encountered by people of different sexes from different ethnic background as well as their children. The overall feeling is that mixed ethnic marriages are probably a good idea for a number of reasons: love should not be dictated by the colour of the skin, mixing of people is good for the common genetic pool, it is a sure sign of good relationships between different ethnic groups, and so forth. These, however, can lead to quite significant difficulties, which require special efforts if they are to be overcome. The difficulties arise because of language, religion, but most importantly because of different traditional ways of behaviour within family settings.

The partnerships involving Caribbeans mostly tend to be from the white population, but partnerships involving Caribbeans and Asians are very rare. Similarly there appear to be very few partnerships between different Asian groups, that is between Indians, Bangladeshis, Pakistanis, Sri Lankan, Chinese and so forth. There appear to be almost no partnerships between Pakistanis and Bangladeshis.

Identity

Hutnik (1991: 134) identified four strategies of self-identification: the dissociative strategy, the assimilative strategy, the acculturative strategy and the marginal strategy. A self-identification strategy is considered dissociative where categorization is in terms of ethnic minority group membership and not in terms of the majority group membership. It is considered assimilative where self-categorization primarily emphasizes the majority group dimension and denies ethnic minority roots. It is considered acculturative where individuals categorize themselves approximately equally in terms of both the above dimensions and it is considered marginal where neither dimension is important or salient to self-categorization. There may be a conscious decision not to choose an ethnic identity or a majority group identity. Here the self may be categorized primarily in terms of other relevant social categories such as being a student or a squash player.

It seems that roughly 30% of all South Asians, whether from India, Pakistan, Bangladesh or African Asians, use the dissociative strategy (this is again similar to the Caribbeans), about two-thirds of all South Asians use acculturative strategies, and assimilative and marginal strategies are used by a very insignificant minority. Within these groups, working-class Indians were more likely to be dissociative than other Indians, and Hindus from India were more dissociative than Hindus from Africa.

Sociological and ethnological research suggests that black Caribbean and British Asians are rather reluctant to call themselves 'British' in the British context, but find it easier to do so when they are abroad (Modood, Beishon and Virdee, 1994). Currently there is an ongoing debate about whether Asians think of themselves as black or whether this is a 'situational identity' (Drury, 1990).

Religion forms an important pillar in the formation of identity for all immigrant populations. It appears to be particularly important for those groups whose religions are in a minority in the host society, therefore Hindus, Muslims, Sikhs from the Indian subcontinent as well as African Asians place more importance on religion than, say, Christians who come from India or Christians among the African Asians.

Some concluding thoughts

In this chapter, I have tried to give some insight into the differences between Western (particularly the British) culture and the Indo-Asian culture, which influenced the present generation of South Asian children and young people in Britain today. These have been summarized by Viswanathan, Shah and Ahad (1997) as follows:

- Indo-Asian societies are more restrictive, unlike Western societies, which are more permissive and open.
- There is a more rigid hierarchical structure; obedience to elders and authority is expected and gender roles are rigidly defined.
- The culture is sociocentric rather than egocentric (whereas in modern, Western societies there is an emphasis on personal autonomy and individuality). Conformity and collectivity are expected.
- Privacy is not a priority, boundaries between family members, extended families, friends and neighbours are very 'porous' with everyone knowing everyone else's personal business.
- Behaviour is greatly influenced by shame – one is always mindful of what the neighbours might think and is aware of bringing shame to the family.
- Marriage is considered to be a strong alliance between families, extended families and even family friends, and not merely a contractual transaction between two individuals. Most marriages are arranged, the families playing an important role in mate selection and subsequent life. Public displays of romantic affection are frowned upon.
- There are extensive and complex extended family relationships and interactions. Three and even four generations often used to live under one roof under the guidance and authority of the eldest man. This has been giving way to nuclear families. Elderly parents live with their adult children until death.
- Patience, self-control, self-discipline and not yielding to passion are valued, and self–sacrifice (for the sake of family, friendships, country) is highly valued.
- There is a strong and overriding sense of obligation to the family, extended family and friends.
- The concept of self is extended to include the family and is blended with the identity of the family.
- There is heavy emphasis on high educational attainment and a preference for professional jobs (such as those of doctors, engineers, or lawyers).

It must be remembered that, under the pressures of modern day living, all of these characteristics are beginning to dilute or erode at differing paces and depending upon the urban/rural factor.

After immigration to a Western country, first-generation Indo-Asians continue to hold on to these value systems very strongly, but subsequent generations incorporate the values and rules of the new host society.

These children and adolescents need to go through a more complex process of identity formation than their counterparts in the white, Caucasian majority population. The close emotional bonds and clear rules within the family make the process easy and bearable.

The importance placed on high educational attainment by first-generation immigrants probably arises, at least in part, from their own sense of insecurity. This, in turn, arises from the poverty, consequent lack of opportunity and struggle for survival that they experienced in their childhood. They see that new opportunities have been made available through education. However, to the younger generations growing up in the West, with affluence, high standards of living, and social security systems that ensure that no one will die from want and that everyone gets enough, these ideas of their parental generation are becoming increasingly irrelevant. As a result, more and more youngsters are beginning to make choices that do not conform with their parents' preferences, and live like their other contemporary peer groups.

Another important point to keep in mind is that Indo-Asian families, especially the less educated, working class, first-generation immigrants, have a tendency to expect 'prescriptions' for their difficulties from their helpers (doctors, child psychiatrists, psychotherapist and so forth). They often find it difficult to grasp systemic, conceptual ideas – these may confuse them more than they help them. Use of such language can lead to a mistrust of the therapist, paranoid ideation and a breakdown of communication. At these times it is important to understand their fears and superstitions and to use very concrete language with simple words and short sentences. Behaviour modification has to be approached with caution as parents expect children to conform and they do not expect to have to reward a child for positive behaviour (Uba, 1994: 48).

Clinicians need to be mindful of the background that Indo-Asian families bring with them in order to be able to work effectively with them. At the same time it is important to avoid the pitfalls of generalizations and stereotyping. This is a very challenging and rewarding area of work.

References

Anwar M (1994) Young Muslims in Britain: Attitudes, Educational Needs and Policy Implications. The Islamic Foundation.

Berrington A (1996) Marriage Patterns and Inter-Ethnic Unions in: Ethnicity. In Coleman D and Salt J (eds) (1991) Census: Vol 1.

Berthoud R, Beishon S (1997) People, Family and Households. In Modood T, Berthoud R (eds) Ethnic Minorities in Britain, Diversity and Disadvantage. London: Policy Studies Institute, p. 29.

Brown C (1984) Black and White Britain. London: Heinemann.

Central Office of Information (1997) Ethnic Minorities. London: Central Office of Information, Publishing Services.

Drury B (1990) Blackness: A Situational Identity. Paper given at the Conference on New Issues in Black Politics, University of Warwick 14–16 May 1990.

Hutnik N (1991) Ethnic Minority Identity, A Social Psychological Perspective. Oxford: Clarendon Press.

Jones T (1993) Britain's Ethnic Minorities: an Analysis of the Labour Force Survey. London: Policy Studies Institute, p. 19.

Karn V (1997) Ethnicity in the 1991 Census. Vol. 4. London: Stationary Office.

Labour Force Survey (1994) HMSO London.

Modood T, Beishon S, Virdee S (1994) Changing Ethnic Identity. London: Policy Studies Institute.

Modood T (1997) Culture and Identity. In Modood T, Berthoud R (eds) Ethnic Minorities in Britain, Diversity and Disadvantage. London: Policy Studies Institute, p. 326.

Stopes-Roe M, Cochrane R (1990) Citizens of this Country: The Asian-British. Clevedon: Multi-lingual Matters.

Uba L (1994) Asian Americans: Personality Patterns, Identity and Mental Health. New York: Guilford.

Viswanathan R, Shah M, Ahad A (1997) Asian-Indian Americans. In Friedman S (ed.) Cultural Issues in the Treatment of Anxiety. New York: Guilford, pp. 75–195.

Suggested further reading

Anwar M (1979) The Myth of Return: Pakistanis in Britain. London: Heinemann.

Bahadur OL (1994) Book of Hindu Festival and Ceremonies. New Delhi: UBS.

Collinson C, Miller C (1984) Rites of Passage in a Multi-faith Community. London: Edward Arnold.

Gandhi M (1991) Hindu Names New Delhi: UBS.

Jaffrey M (1987) An Invitation to Indian Cooking. London: Jonathan Cape.

Jones, Trevor (1993) Britain's Ethnic Minorities: An Analysis of the Labour Force Survey. London: Policy Studies Institute.

Kanitkar VP, Cole WO (1995) Hinduism. London: Hodder Headline.

Sproul B (1991) Primal Myths – Creation Myths Around The World. New York: HarperCollins.

Chapter 2
Traditional values and the family life cycle

ANNIE LAU

Introduction

Professionals from a Western European ethno-cultural background working with South Asian children and their families are required, from time to time, to carry out a variety of need assessments within either a health, education or social services framework. These will then have an effect on the provision of services for the children. Often these assessments, which include diagnostic assessments, formulations and strategies for intervention, are conducted using concepts derived from a Western European cultural framework. For these assessments and interventions to be culturally valid and competent, however, the professional needs to be aware of, and informed about, the cognitive and orienting principles that provide guidelines for the determination of competence from the point of view of the Asian family, as well as the ethnic and religious community of which the child or young person is a part. Often these guidelines will be informed by principles and values determined or derived from religious belief, as interpreted by the particular ethnic group to which the child belongs.

This chapter provides a developmental framework for considering how traditional Asian extended family values determine both individual and family competence throughout the life cycle. These values also provide structure and context for individual and family developmental tasks, expectations of age and gender roles, kinship networks and relationships, and boundaries for appropriate behaviours within age groups. Other chapters in this book discuss particular religious affiliations to be found in families from the Asian subcontinent in the United Kingdom. This chapter includes examples of clinical material in which ideas discussed are applied in clinical practice with families referred to a Child and Family Consultation Centre. It also provides guidelines for culturally appropriate assessments and work with traditional South Asian families.

33

In order to understand Asian family values it is important to appreciate the central role of Hindu beliefs, which inform the world view of Asian Indian families (Almeida, 1996). These include the concepts of *karma* (destiny), caste (hierarchical organization of people into social orders) and *dharma* (living in accordance with principles that order the universe). The maintenance of caste was linked with ideas of purity and pollution (Nanda, 1990). Purity was linked with living a spiritual life, with abstention from 'bodily pleasures' like sex, drugs and alcohol. Caste is part of one's fate, or *karma*. A lack of purity affects the karma, not only of the individual, but the whole family; and not only in this generation, but future generations as well. Sexual purity in one's daughters affects not only the daughter's marriage prospects but also family's future and well-being.

Aponte and Hoffman (1973) wrote: 'Of course much of this will be defined by the culture, but the general rule of clear generational lines and adequate differentiation will hold. In an unhealthy family, or what Minuchin calls an enmeshed family, there is a blurring of the generation lines and a lack of differentiation.' This quotation is now quite old. The underlying assumption, however, that extended family values – dependability and interdependence being given a higher priority than values affirming individual right and choice – reflect a pathological state of being, group oppression, and psychological immaturity, that are still to be found often embedded in professional practice with South Asian children and their families. The model of adequate differentiation and clear generational lines as being the only acceptable form of healthy family functioning denies the validity of forms of family organization other than those of Western European nuclear families. Given the differences in moral imperatives in the two family models, it means that the professional using a Western Eurocentric model will fail to recognize the strengths and positive attributes of the Asian extended family, or to use those strengths in order to mobilize competent functioning along culturally congruent norms. Rather, individual and family functioning is often reinforced only if it conforms to Western European norms and values.

Bridging the gulf: acknowledging and working with difference

Leighton (1981) wrote that:

> Culture consists in the knowledge, values, perceptions and practices that are
> 1. shared among the members of a given society
> 2. passed on from one generation to the next.

The components of a culture are interrelated in such a way as to constitute a whole that governs the functioning of a society. Culture directs the behaviour of individuals within the group, enabling the group to survive.

The cultural and religious traditions of a group organize the perception of experience, give shape and form to myths and beliefs, and determine the limits of appropriate behaviour and family roles. The symbolic belief system of the group also provides explanations of health and illness, definitions of normality and deviance, and guidelines for how to be acceptably deviant within a recognized pattern. (Lau, 1990)

Culturally determined value orientations organize the individual's view of the proper relationship between self and context. In contrast with Western European ideals, which emphasize independence, self-sufficiency, assertiveness and competition, clear and direct verbal communication, Asian extended family values emphasize interdependence, harmony and co-operation in relationships. They place more emphasis on non-verbal and indirect communication by shared symbols. These ideas are also reinforced by the religious teachings of the main religions from the Asian subcontinent.

Family structure and organization

Value orientations determine structural relationships; hence family organization following the ideal of the pre-eminence of the group would be along extended family lines, with a primary emphasis on connectedness. Socialization processes throughout the life cycle will serve to inculcate and reinforce these values, especially in the upbringing of children. They will operate as protective factors for children who have been properly brought up.

Families will need to be located along a continuum between the traditional, hierarchical family with adherence to extended family values and the Western, contemporary, egalitarian family.

There are important differences between the traditional Asian family and the Western family in the construction of 'family' as a concept and the role of the individual within the family. The family is not bounded by the same boundary as the nuclear family unit; rather it tends to encompass grandparents, aunts, uncles and cousins. Life-cycle transitions are managed in the context of different rules with regard to authority, continuity and interdependence. Relationships are hierarchical between the sexes as well as between the generations. Authority is invested in grandparents or the most senior male members. The presence of the aged provides continuity and a link between the generations. Elder siblings usually have authority over younger siblings, and responsibility for their welfare.

The elaborate network of kinship relationships is determined through the male lineage (Ayakar, 1994). Kinship systems are highly structured: kinship terms delineate the individual's place in the family, including duties and expected obligations, within a system of mutual dependence. Traditionally, the conjoint home had the task of providing economic support to sons and their families; unmarried sisters; paternal aunts, and the parents.

Individual and family competence through the life cycle

It is important to clarify ethnocultural differences in competence throughout the life cycle, as this has implications for expected stage-specific individual and family tasks. The following discussion will consider expectations of the individual and family at various stages of the life cycle. It will also give examples of typical rituals from Jain families, as an example of how the religious structure of the ethnocultural group informs group norms and behaviours.

Preparation for parenting

As part of learning about adult roles, the adolescent growing up in a traditional Asian extended family in which three generations are present is continually exposed to childrearing practices considered normal and sanctioned by the group. The young girl learns about future adult roles from repeated observations and daily experiences of lived examples around her. This will include observed patterns of intimacy and relationships, and the attitudes and behaviour of her mother, grandmother, and other female kinfolk, with whom she has frequent and close contact. Her 'work experience' will also derive from 'supervised practice' in helping with the upbringing of younger siblings and cousins.

As a result, parenting does not come as a nasty shock to the young woman. Rather, within a well-functioning family, pregnancy is an expected and welcome event, for which her mother and female kinfolk will have prepared her.

In contrast, in the industrialized West, parenting, or the discovery of pregnancy, even within the context of a stable relationship, may be experienced negatively; as a career interruption, or a threat to a comfortable lifestyle, rather than a *raison d'être* (BBC World Service series, 'Help I'm Going To Be A Parent', 1995).

Producing a child, especially a male child, still signifies security for many a young wife in an arranged marriage, and an entry into full social status of the parental couple. In the traditional family the pregnant young wife will also be surrounded by a host of her female kinfolk whose task is to ensure that things go well and that, where necessary, the expectant mother can be relieved of tiring domestic responsibilities.

For Jain families, the birth of a child is celebrated after 40 days by a religious naming ceremony. Prior to this event the mother is allowed relief from family chores. She is also not considered 'pure' until after this period, during which time it is assumed that all remnants of the after-birth are evacuated. Jains have adopted a number of Hindu rituals; so a Hindu *pandit*, or wise man, is approached for an auspicious day for the naming event, which is an occasion for a family gathering and celebration. This event will include food, and often presents for the guests. The birth of a boy child is often more lavishly celebrated.

Infancy and early childhood

Given the importance of interdependence and family connectedness as goals for the socialization of the young, it should not be surprising that patterns of childrearing in traditional Asian extended families would be different. The child from a traditional South Asian family could sleep with its mother or grandmother for many years (Bassa, 1978). Indeed, co-sleeping arrangements may be preferred in these families although there may be adequate space for individual bedrooms. Parenting may be shared, and this provides the young child with a wider variety of parental figures and an increased range of models for age and sex role identifications.

Childhood stories, often with a religious underpinning, stress the importance of family, and reinforce family interdependence. (Lau, 1995). The growing child will be exposed to religious and cultural mythology, and these stories help to form the child's ego ideals. The child learns the overriding importance of being dependable, of being loyal to the group.

Altruistic self-sacrifice in the service of one's parents is one of the noblest achievements. This is exemplified by the following story from the Sikh tradition. Guru Gobind Singh (1666–1708) the Tenth Guru of the Sikhs, lived an exemplary life as a saint-soldier. His four sons all died in the cause of Sikh freedom. The first two sons, Ajit and Jujhar, aged 14 and 12 respectively, each rode out of the fortress of Chamkaur single-handed to challenge the Mughal army laying siege to the Sikh camp. The two younger sons, Fateh, 9, and Zorawar, 7, were captured by the Governor of Sirhind, and chose martyrdom rather than renouncing the faith of their people. There are similar stories from Muslim folklore. A common story relates how a young man carries his frail aged father all the way to Mecca on his back so that the old man could fulfil his religious duty of going to Mecca before he died.

Through regular participation in family rituals such as meals, outings, festivals, religious events, the child learns its place in the kinship system and the rules governing relationships and expected behaviour. For example, in a well-functioning South Asian extended family, the young child will have grown up noticing that respect for the grandparents will be shown not only by terms of address, but also by the fact that one often waits for the grandparents to be seated before the meal begins, and that as the elders they have an assumed right to the choicest pieces of food.

In Jain families, the main Jain festival of importance for the socialization of children is the *samvatsari*, or period of fasting of eight days. This takes place once a year at the beginning of September. The concept to be taught here involves self-discipline, and the principle of *ahimsa*, or non-violence, which extends to the prohibition against the taking of animal life. During this period, Jains are not allowed to eat anything that grows underground, for example potatoes, onions, and carrots, as they are likely to contain more living things; they have to count what they eat, and they must eat before sunset. On the last day there has to be a total fast: only boiled water can be taken and family members get together to ask for forgiveness for offences committed over the past year.

For Jain and Hindu families, the festival of Diwali (Deepavali) is equivalent in importance to Hannukah in Jewish families, and Christmas in Christian families. There are prayers in the evening to Lakshmi, the Hindu goddess of wealth. Special food is prepared, and children wear new clothes. Candles are lit at night after sunset and fireworks are set off. For Hindu families this is also an occasion where effigies of the demon Rawana are burnt in public parks, to celebrate the triumph of good over evil. This is, in fact, an annual event in Finchley, North London.

Middle childhood

The child starting school is taught to treat the teacher with the same respect as its parents, and that good behaviour in school will reflect well on the family name. An older child may be expected to take responsibility for a younger sibling or cousin, or to contribute to the family welfare by helping in the shop at the weekends. It will be a source of pride to 'behave so that your parents will be proud of you.' The child also learns that he does not have exclusive rights to the parents; rather, he may have to share his parents' time, attention and care-giving with other cousins. 'For an extended family system to succeed, love has to be re-directed across nuclear family boundaries' (Dwivedi, 1996).

Within the family boundary, the child will also learn manoeuvres for diffusing tension in the family. It is important to be sensitive to the feelings of others, and act to prevent confrontational situations from developing. One also needs to be aware of one's emotional reactions, and to be able to channel feelings of anger and disappointment constructively, so that one does not lose control. Containment of negative feelings is therefore to be preferred over open expression of anger or hostility, which would risk disharmony in the group. The child learns by example that it is normal and healthy to regard the wider family as an important emotional resource; a temporary refuge from one's angry parents, for example, or a place where one can practise strategies to use on one's parents. Worries can also be shared with a favourite aunt or uncle if one's parents are for any reason emotionally unavailable at the time.

An important ritual in the calendar is the *raki* celebration, observed by Hindu and Jain families. This is marked by an exchange of gifts between brothers and sisters in the month of August. The *raki* is a bracelet that the sister ties on her brother's wrist and Indian grocery shops carry a variety of colourful braided bands used for this purpose. In turn, the brother gives his sister a present. It implies the notion that the brother will always protect his sister from life's misfortunes and, for example, if his parents die, it would be his duty to look after his sister, including arranging her marriage. The custom of *raki* is continued after the parties are adults. In traditional families, a married sister will go to her brother's house by invitation, and bring sweets. Or she may send a card with a *raki* in it to her brother living in a different country.

Adolescence

The competent adolescent from a traditional South Asian extended family background is one who will have been prepared to meet his or her obligations to the family, which often include the obligation to look after one's parents and younger siblings. Within the family he or she will have been socialized to know the importance of being dependable. The competent adolescent will have a behavioural repertoire that includes respectful behaviour to one's elders, and strategies for tension diffusion and conflict avoidance within the immediate and wider family. Young people are taught to value concepts of tolerance, patience and sacrifice; this partially derives from the Hindu values of *dharma* and *karma*, and reflects the importance of accepting difficulties in order to be rewarded in the next life or reincarnation. An older brother or sister would be expected to help manage differences and childhood squabbles among the sibling (and wider cousin) group, and to maintain the peace, if necessary by the judicious exercise of authority. These skills prepare the young person for adult roles within a value orientation that stresses the importance of maintaining the integrity of the family group.

Other issues to do with individuation and separation, as well as distance regulation, will be negotiated in different ways from Western European families. Preparation for leaving home is an important difference for adolescents from traditional extended families (Lau, 1990). 'A culture that prescribes marriage, childbearing, and economic responsibility for extended family leaves little room for exploration' of areas taken for granted by Western families in the UK, including sexual experimentation, sexual orientation, career, work choices (Almeida, 1996). It is important to stress that preserving interconnectedness and interdependability is the important principle; hence 'leaving home' is low on the hierarchy of desirability.

The management of adolescent sexuality is an area that most often leads to conflicts in the traditional Asian family. From the time girls reach puberty, they are taught to be 'pure', and free expressions of sexuality are not encouraged. Where religious authority has been stamped on cultural tradition, the consequences of infringement of rules governing chastity are often severe. Islamic tradition has clear guidelines for both men and women. Men have to guard against being overwhelmed by sensual temptations. Women have to avoid attracting male attention, or arousing them sexually. There is a compulsory duty, from puberty onwards, of keeping certain parts of the body covered. These parts, *satr*, are, for men, the area of the body between the knees and the navel. For women, *satr* extends to the entire body except hands, feet and face.

Other Koranic social restrictions limit men's freedom of action, with the intention of guarding their sexual purity. Similarly, women should stay at home and not wander about displaying their finery and beauty. These social and religious restrictions regulating sexual behaviour and family life are also based on the belief that men and women have different roles, responsibilities and functions in society.

Marriage

In traditional Asian families, arranged marriage is very much the accepted norm. The two parties may vet each other, but under ritualized and supervised conditions, as sexual purity is considered extremely important, especially for girls. Intra-caste marriage is still important for Hindus; Jains prefer their offspring to marry within the same religious sect; and marrying within the particular religious group is important for Muslims, Jews and Christians. The dowry system still continues, albeit in modified forms, for the majority of South Asian families; for example, in a contemporary Jain or Hindu family, the boy's family may not formally ask for a dowry, but it will be important for family honour that the girl's family provide for some form of dowry, often in the form of money, jewellery, clothes, or even an apartment or house, depending on their financial capacity. Many families will therefore start to save for their daughter's marriage a few years before, while eligible families with potentially marriageable sons are being sought from the ethnic community.

Marriage in traditional families also raises differences in stage-specific family tasks. Where arranged marriage is an expected event in the family life cycle, the wider family has to provide a facilitating environment for stabilizing and nurturing the couple's relationship, particularly in the first year of marriage. There are also gender differences in the levels of adjustment required of the individuals concerned. The new wife moving into a joint household must invest emotionally in the relationship with her mother-in-law and sisters-in-law, and work out power relations within the female network. This includes submission to the authority of mother-in-law and elder sisters-in-law. Competence in these tasks, and conformity with the family norms and with the expectations of her husband's family, is vital towards ensuring her survival in the new family.

Case 1

A child of 6 months, belonging to a young Asian family, presented with feeding difficulties. The mother-in-law lived in the same household as the young couple. Exploration revealed that there was disagreement between the wife and her mother-in-law on feeding routines and weaning practices, arising from different family traditions. The power struggle between the two women had reached the point where the child was becoming distressed and confused, particularly as the young wife was working on a part-time basis and mother-in-law was involved with childcare.

Modes of communication

There may also be differences in expected communication modes. The Western-trained therapist's expectation of clear, direct verbal communication is often at variance with cultural rules where direct communication and confrontation are avoided because this may lead to loss of face within the family group (McGoldrick, 1982). In the East, a well-known ideal of maturity is the capacity on the part of the individual to tolerate psychological pain and discomfort without 'inflicting' this pain on others. This means that qualities like patience, endurance and self-containment are highly valued, as is silence, contemplation and introspection.

Children are praised for 'showing understanding', anticipating the needs of significant others and taking initiative. Thus a child is more praiseworthy if he offers tea to a parent on the parent's return from work, without being told to do so. A child who asks too many questions may well be asked to be quiet and to try to work out some answers by himself, after which he may then check out the logic of his reasoning with the adult. Western professionals unused to these concepts may well regard these processes as dysfunctional, reflecting a pathological passivity. Members of these families may then be seen as withdrawn, with poor communication skills.

Therapeutic goals

The therapeutic goals of the therapist and the family might differ. The preferred direction of change for families from traditional backgrounds will be towards greater integration of the family group, rather than increasing differentiation and separation of the individual from his or her family (Tamura and Lau, 1992). This has potential for conflict for therapists and their supervisors from a different value base. Acceptance of these differences in norms implies the use of different therapeutic strategies, with different aims, for example diffusing and containing conflict rather than amplifying it. Thus, a therapist who is working within cultural rules might put more energy into exploring possible areas of agreement, and finding the middle ground. Tamura and Lau (1992) provides case examples where differences in perception and cultural orientation emerged between the therapist, of Japanese ethnic origin, and a Western European supervisory team. This also led to differences in therapeutic strategy.

All parents, whatever their ethnic background, have similar expect-ations of what constitute the results of successful parenting. Indeed, in an address to the National Children's Bureau conference on 'Confident Parents, Confident Children' in 1993, Virginia Bottomley, the Secretary of State for Health, said all parents expected their children to grow up to be happy, healthy, literate, confident and law abiding. In a cross-cul-tural context, however, these categories are subject to definitions within the boundaries allowed by the ethno-cultural group. Bassa (1978), in making observations on Indian child rearing practices and identity for-mation, says, 'Self-fulfilment [i.e. happiness] is thus to be sought for and found within the family, not in a frantic search for love outside it'. For the traditional Muslim family, literacy will include being able to read the Koran as well as conforming to the requirements of the National Curriculum. Health may also be defined differently, with different explanatory models, as in the Ayurvedic traditions of India.

Family ritual maintenance

I have found it extremely useful to inquire about the extent to which fam-ily rituals are maintained in Asian families. Family rituals provide support, continuity with family, cultural, and religious tradition, and affirm mem-bership for participants. Life-cycle rituals mark and celebrate movement of the individual from one stage of his or her life cycle to another. Where this is a publicly celebrated event, like a naming ceremony for an infant, or the coming of age of an adolescent, for example bar mitzvah, the family is also making a public statement to the community. For Jewish parents, it is a declaration that somehow they have succeeded in holding together frag-ments for the next generation. They have also discharged their duty of responsibility for their child's religious education.

Family rituals, whether religious or secular, provide opportunities for family members to meet on a regular basis and to communicate. The pat-tern and regularity is important. Does the family eat together, watch TV together, and go out together? Is there a central family dinnertime? Are there holiday celebration rituals? Have the impact of immigration and the loss of supportive networks led to a loss of cultural rituals? All these fac-tors may have bearing on the meaning and significance to the family of the various problems that led to referral for a professional service.

Conflicts in mixed marriages

Intergenerational conflict in families with a mixed racial/cultural background may be compounded by the child's sense of confusion regarding
racial or ethnic identity. Where the parental subsystem has a poorly maintained boundary, with ineffective emotional containment, the child or
young person's frustrations may give rise to a wide range of deviant behavioural disturbances. There may be parental conflict over which family cultural traditions, rituals, values and loyalties are more important; cultural
differences in the expected roles of spouses, including kinship obligations,
may not have been resolved. The child or young person may end up being
triangulated in the parental conflict, or expected to make up for the losses
incurred by the parent of ethnic origin in the process of immigration. The
young person will end up being unable to resolve the racial diversity in
his/her background; it becomes a source of adversity instead of strength.

Refugee families

Families with a refugee background will need to be handled with particular understanding for the traumatic stresses that have been part of the
family's recent experience, and allowances should be made for apparently
uncooperative behaviour. Adults will, to a varying extent, carry features of
post-traumatic stress disorder, particularly if they have been raped or tortured. My own experience suggests that one can expect a long engagement process, as often these families find it difficult to trust authority and
establishment figures, given their previous highly traumatic experiences.
Bereft of personal networks, crises in daily living, such as inability to heed
the final written demand for payment, may lead to the supply of electricity
being cut off from the household. Health visitors often report being frus-
trated because people never seem to be home when they call. It is unfortunately all too common that as soon as a refugee family is housed in this
country, supports are withdrawn and services that may make a difference
to the family's adjustment, such as counselling, are not offered. The
adults' unresolved losses, for example personal networks and family,
social and financial status, and a sense of helplessness and an inability to
take control over their own affairs, often leads to a depressive withdrawal
from the children and their psychological needs. Where language is a
problem, and this is often the case, it means the parents are inadequately
involved with their children's school life. They are then unable to support
their children's needs for integration with an appropriate peer group,
which would enhance a sense of belonging.

Case 2

A Sri Lankan refugee mother and her son were referred by a pediatric
department. The referring problem was the mother's apparent inability to

wean her son successfully. At the age of 2 years he was not gaining weight properly, with an inadequate intake of solids. It was found that the mother had a great deal of difficulty allowing her son to grow up. She was beset by overwhelming fears that he would grow up to abandon her; hence she was unable to separate from him and set proper boundaries.

Eliciting the lady's migration history enabled an understanding of the family predicament. She had suffered several traumatic losses in her family, as they had been part of a militant Tamil Tigers group involved in civil unrest in Sri Lanka. Thus, two sons and two brothers had died in the fighting; her 17-year-old daughter was missing; she had been abandoned by her 'husband', with her son – all that was left of her extended family. She had been brought to the UK as a domestic for a Kuwaiti family, who lost their money in the course of the Gulf War, and she then had to seek asylum in the UK. Within this context, she was depressed and unable to resist her son's temper tantrums and clinging behaviour.

Guidelines for family assessment

- What belief systems and values (including religion) influence role expectations, define and set limits of appropriate behaviour?
- What are the gender issues that need to be addressed?
- What are the structures relevant to authority and decision-making in the family? Are there formal kinship patterns? What important relationships have important supportive and homeostatic functions? What is the relevant family network to be worked with?
- What are the stage-specific developmental tasks at different life-cycle stages for this family? How does this family negotiate life-cycle transitions, continuities and discontinuities with the past and present? What are traditional solutions and mechanisms used for conflict resolution and to what extent does the family use them?
- How is the living unit organized to enable essential tasks to be performed?
- What activities, including family rituals of ethnocultural and religious origin, maintain and support structural relationships? What traditional networks supported and enabled traditional family tasks to be performed? Which of these networks or rituals have been lost?
- What is the family's migration history? What are significant stresses and losses arising from the family's own immigration experience, from the environment of origin, or from adaptation to host country? What racial or cultural factors confer advantage or disadvantage in the host culture?
- The clinical hypothesis must take into account the meaning and function of the disturbance for the family, the cultural group, and the wider community.

Therapeutic interventions must engage the authority structure of the family and be congruent with the family's world view. It is important to enable the identified client and his or her family to work out the correct balance of separation/attachment consistent with family and societal norms. The focus of treatment should be on family issues, even when one is dealing with individual clients (Almeida, 1996). As Asian families are concerned with issues of past legacies (*karma*) and future life-cycle impact, it is important to frame the problem within a context that enables the issues to be owned by the family. The author finds a developmental formulation, with an elaboration of the family tree and family history, often to be helpful in engaging the family elders in the task of agreeing a common agenda and goals.

Existing therapeutic techniques and methods can be successfully used in work with Asian families, providing the therapist is sensitive to the importance of respecting cultural rules and is prepared to modify his or her clinical approach. This may mean more flexibility in working with subsystems such as the group of sisters-in-law, rather than with the whole family. Asian families respond more readily to therapists who are directive and assertive (Rao, 1986; Almeida, 1996) as this conforms to traditional expectations of the learning process.

The author has also found the use of structural family therapy techniques, with their emphasis on problem-solving in the present, useful when working with Asian families. Working with stories and metaphor is also consistent with an indirect, non-confrontational style sometimes preferred by Asian families (Lau, 1988; Peseschkian, 1986). Wolin and Bennett (1984) link the importance of maintenance of family ritual to the continuity of family heritage. All these strategies attempt to mobilize family strengths and assert competencies within an ethnocultural context.

The management of intergenerational conflict can often be facilitated if family members can be helped to see themselves as families in transition between cultures, and that the issues are very similar to other families in a similar situation (normalization). It may be helpful to identify what has been positive for everyone in the process of acculturation, and what religious, cultural and family values have contributed to family well-being. What, then, are the choices that are available to enable family members to benefit from being in the UK, and which position the family most effectively to benefit from the opportunities? What are the hopes and dreams of the adults for the young people? And what of the reciprocal aspirations of the young people for the future? Which good parts of family culture and which values do they want to keep? Maintaining a boundary around future goals often helps the family move on from a situation of escalating conflict, and return to an area of negotiation and compromise.

Acknowledgements

I would like to acknowledge Mrs Nayna Choraia as my source of information on material from the Jain tradition. I am also grateful to Dr Shirsalker for reading the manuscript.

References

Almeida R (1996) Hindu, Christian and Muslim Families. In McGoldrick M, Giordano J, Pearce JK (eds) Ethnicity and Family Therapy (2nd edn). Guilford Press: London.

Aponte H, Hoffman L (1973). The open door; a structural approach to a family with an anorectic child. Family Process 12: 1-144.

Ayakar K (1994) Women of the Indian Subcontinent. In L Comas-Diaz, B Greene (eds) Women of Color; Integrating Ethnic and Gender Identities in Psychotherapy. New York: Guilford Press.

Bassa DM (1978) From the Traditional to the Modern; Some Observations on Changes in Indian Child-Rearing and Parental Attitudes, with Special Reference to Identity Formation. In EJ Anthony, C Chiland (eds) The Child in his Family – Children and Parents in a Changing World. Chichester: Wiley.

Dwivedi KN (1996) Culture and Personality In Dwivedi KN, Varma VP (eds) Meeting the Needs of Ethnic Minority Children, London: Jessica Kingsley.

Lau A (1988) Family therapy and ethnic minorities. In E Street, W Dryden (eds) Family Therapy in Britain. London: Open university Press, pp. 270–90.

Lau A (1990) Psychological problems in adolescents from ethnic minorities. British Journal of Hospital Medicine 44: 201–5.

Lau A (1995) Ethnocultural and Religious Issues. In C Burck, B Speed (eds) Gender Power and Relationships. London: Routledge.

Leighton AH (1981) Culture and Psychiatry. Canadian Journal of Psychiatry 26(8): 522–9.

McGoldrick M (1982) Ethnicity and family therapy: an overview. In M McGoldrick, JK Pearce, J Giordano (eds) Ethnicity and Family Therapy. New York: Guilford Press, pp. 3–30.

Nanda S (1990) Neither Man nor Woman: The Hijras of India. Belmont CA: Wadsworth.

Peseschkian N (1986) Positive Family Therapy. Berlin, Heidelberg: Springer-Verlag.

Rao AV (1986) Indian and Western psychiatry: a comparison. In Cox JL (ed.) Transcultural Psychiatry. London: Croom Helm, pp. 291–305.

Tamura T, Lau A (1992) Connectedness versus separateness: applicability of family therapy to Japanese families. Family Process 31: 319–40.

Wolin S, Bennett LA (1984) Family rituals. Family Process 23: 401–20.

Chapter 3
Families in transition

RUMA BOSE

Several authors have described the tremendous cultural diversity of the South Asian presence in Britain (Ballard, 1994). Differences in lifestyles, religion, language, caste affiliations, rural or urban origins and migration history are based on differences in the regional roots of the communities in the Indian subcontinent. As members of the different communities in Britain continue to identify with and feel closest to members of their own communal group, it is clear that there is no such entity as the 'Asian community'. However, when South Asians are juxtaposed with other ethnic groups, such as West Africans or the English, it becomes apparent that, despite their heterogeneity, South Asians in Britain represent a distinct ethnic presence, with their cultural and ancestral roots in the Indian subcontinent, a common history of British colonization of the subcontinent, and similarities in their post-migration experience in Britain.

In writing a chapter on South Asian families, one must acknowledge some common elements and it is possible to look at trends without promoting simple generalizations about all Asians. Eade (1992) has criticized much of the earlier writing on ethnic minority groups in Britain, which conveys an impression of bounded cultures with stable and unchanging 'essences'. South Asian cultures in Britain, as in the subcontinent itself, are alive, responsive and interactive and embody several views and lifestyles.

All societies and cultures change over time through sociopolitical upheavals, contact with other cultures, and economic and geophysical changes, but no culture change is as abrupt as that experienced by those who move to a different country. As South Asian migration in Britain is a recent phenomenon it is too early to describe firm patterns in the changes in family life. Yet as those of the second generation are becoming parents themselves, significant changes are evident in family organization and values following migration. The South Asian cultures in Britain are in a flux, reflecting changes following migration, changes in Britain, events in their country of origin, and events globally, in an increasingly interconnected world. Issues pertinent to the first generation, such as the maintenance of ties with the homeland, the myth of return, and dislocation, have less relevance for the young who are growing up in a bicultural, sometimes multicultural, world and see themselves firmly rooted in Britain. Their ties to the land of their ancestral origin have a different meaning from those of their parents. For the young the major issues pertain to their life here, such as race, the emergence of British South Asian cultures at the level of the individual and the family and the community, identity, and their place in British society. This chapter will describe trends within families with a focus on the experiences of the young growing up in a bicultural world in Britain.

Gardner (1995) highlights a major problem in the study of migration: the different levels at which it functions. It can be viewed from both an individual and a structural perspective. The meaning that an experience has for an individual, or a family, may be different when described at a social level in a global context. For example, South Asians experience loss of power and status, as a minority group – especially as a non-Western minority group from developing countries. Yet in relation to their families from their place of origin, they have increased economic power, status and influence. However, to exclude one level at the expense of the other is an academic exercise removed from the continuities of experiential reality, where the social forces that prevail within a society and across societies are simultaneously experienced and re-invented at an individual and family level. Therefore, although the chapter is concerned with the effects of migration at the level of the family, it will also refer to descriptions at a societal level. This is necessary for an understanding of the historical, economic, sociocultural and political forces that influence and direct change at a micro-level. Although the focus is on families who are in Britain, Gardner's (1995) work has demonstrated how connections are maintained and sometimes even strengthened within the family spread across the countries, with far-reaching consequences on the social and cultural life of the societies at both ends of the interconnected world.

A detailed analysis of families in all South Asian Communities is beyond the scope of this chapter, and any attempt to provide such an analysis would risk lapsing into generalities. In developing a framework for exploring change, this chapter will focus on the Bangladeshi community in Tower Hamlets in London with whom the author has worked extensively. It is hoped that an analysis of the changes and issues relevant to the Bangladeshi families in Tower Hamlets will provide a structure for exploring and understanding the experiences of the other South Asian groups, maintaining a sensitivity to the diversity and the unique experiences of the different communities.

A great number of studies on the psychosocial consequences of migration describe general processes applying to individuals (Kovacs and

Cropley, 1975; Chataway and Berry, 1989), and families (Sluzki, 1979) and whole societies (Goldlust and Richmond, 1982). A few authors have highlighted the emotional and psychological complexity of the experience, underscoring the heterogeneity of meaning for individuals and families (Lock, 1990; Turner, 1991). In recent years the presence in Britain of ethnic minority groups from the non-European countries has stimulated considerable interest among psychiatrists and family therapists. It has challenged notions of what were thought to be universally applicable 'norms' in human relationships and behaviour, both normal and deviant, and consequently notions of the appropriate interventions used in dealing with problems (Tamura and Lau, 1992). More recent papers have focused on the dimension of power, and the unequal relationship between the observer and those whose culture is being observed (Littlewood, 1992; Krause and Miller, 1995; Maitra and Miller, 1996). This applies equally to the study of families in transition. A framework for describing families in transition must include the relationship between the receiving society, the community, and its country of origin – all of which serve as powerful determinants of how change and problems are perceived and expressed and, in turn, how communities resist and create strategies and narratives. This is particularly important in the study of minority groups in the West, who have experienced colonization in the past and whose cultures continue to be seen as alien, peripheral or developmentally primitive, with 'deficits'. Without this perspective in mind, trends and difficulties will be perceived as originating exclusively in the community, and the onus of coping with problems will be placed entirely on the family or community.

Turner's (1991) paper highlights another major pitfall in studies on migration and change. Earlier studies describing the processes and stages of change were largely based on the underlying assumption that changes were towards assimilation. The focus on acculturation often missed the fact that individuals and families have to contend with real losses of traditional networks, support systems, disadvantage and, for many, racism. For example, children in a village in Bangladesh are exposed to the company of other adults, older siblings, and other children from a very early age. This enhances interactive language and social development (Kotolova, 1993). In a nuclear family in Tower Hamlets, a young child will require greater attention from the parents to compensate for the absence of this stimulus of the traditional social nexus in the child's life. Just focusing on acculturation will overlook the struggles that the parents have to contend with in adapting to the demands of their new circumstances in a manner in which they had not been required to do previously.

Similarly, problems are sometimes ascribed to 'cultural differences' when they may be an expression of the losses experienced in the new circumstances. In the previous example, parents may be described as being verbally understimulating, and their limited verbal interaction with the child may be attributed to 'cultural differences' in child rearing. It would be more helpful to recognize the new demands placed on them without their traditional network, which would normally complement these functions in a child's development.

Bangladeshis in Tower Hamlets

Bangladeshis in Tower Hamlets come mainly from small land-owning rural families in Sylhet in the north-east of Bangladesh. Most are Sunni Muslims. Adams (1987) describes how an unusual administration system of land tenure under the British in Sylhet allowed a large number of people to own land directly without an intermediary, as was required elsewhere in Bangladesh. This promoted a sense of autonomy and economic control among many Sylheti families, who could then invest in young adventuring men willing to travel on merchant navy ships to further the family's assets. Some of the pioneers 'jumped' ship to work in the East End of London in the 1930s and 1940s. There has been a small, established Sylheti community in the East End since the days of the East India Company, further strengthened in the 1920s by a few ex-seamen who settled in London after their services in the First World War (Adams, 1987). The post-war boom in the UK in the 1950s and 1960s drew a new wave of single men from the recently independent subcontinent to work in the factories in London and the industrial north. Through a process of chain migration and the distribution of job vouchers to kinsmen and fellow villagers, heavy migration from the subcontinent drew mainly from a few concentrated areas, one of which was Sylhet. The men, who came alone with the intention of returning home after they had sufficient savings, made periodic visits to Bangladesh to see the family, marry and raise children. Regular remittances to the joint family ensured that the wife and children and their share of the land were looked after by kinsmen, who also benefited from the new income. Changes in immigration law in Britain made it increasingly difficult to travel freely to Britain, precipitating the process of family reunion, whereby wives and children came over to join the men. Only dependent members of the nuclear family were admitted under British immigration law. The subsequent recession in industry left many of the men out of work, and stimulated them to search for new livelihoods such as in the Indian restaurant business and the garment trade in the East End of London.

The process of family reunion, which started in the late 1970s for the Bangladeshi community, is now almost complete. Most school-age children in the community were born here and Tower Hamlets has the largest concentration of Bangladeshis in Britain. The presence of a large Bangladeshi population has ensured the continuity of a familiar world through the Bangladeshi shops, mosques, the Bengali press and a lively community network. It has promoted a sense of group cohesiveness and solidarity in the face of the severe racial hostility and the disadvantage that the families experience. The community is diverse in terms of both class and exposure to urbanization prior to migration, and this adds to differences in experience following migration. Although the Bangladeshi population in London is mainly from rural Sylhet, a sizeable minority has educated, urban origins, and is employed in professional jobs in the UK such as in medicine or chartered accountancy.

In describing the cultural ideals that underpin a community's life and that orientate constructs of selfhood, social organization and child-rearing practices one risks conveying an impression of homogeneity within a group and a sense that the essence of the group is unchanging. However, to fail to describe these cultural ideas would make it difficult to describe what is being changed at a psychosocial level and its significance to those within the group. To understand the meaning of a new experience for a group, one would have to know its own definitions and the cultural ideals that motivate and organize that group, recognizing that there will be variations in experiences and several interpretations and reinterpretations of the ideals.

In common with other South Asian groups, Bangladeshi's constructs of selfhood include relatedness with significant others, and cultural ideals that emphasize interrelatedness, mutual obligation and dependence. In taking an action, an individual has an obligation to consider the interest of the family, and in social events the views of others are given great importance in the family and society. Studies on kinship patterns in Bengal (Inden and Nicholas, 1977; Aziz, 1979) describe the centrality of the kin (*atio svajan*) as the social unit of life, and the primacy of the family's interest over the individual. *Atio svajan* translates as 'one's soul, one's own people' and encompasses all those related agnatically and affinally, however genealogically or geographically distanced. Patrilineally linked descendants of a common male ancestor constitute the *ghushti*, which provides a strong sense of belonging by common ancestry within the larger nexus of *atio svajan*. Descent is patrilineal and relationships are organized hierarchically along the lines of age and gender. There are specific roles and responsibilities that accompany specific relationships. It must be stressed that relationships are not dry and deterministic but are underpinned by love and mutual obligations. For example, the older brother is addressed as *boro bhai*, which has a complex significance, without an equivalent in English. It embodies respect, intimacy and hierarchy in a role that has an obligation to look after the younger. In turn, the one addressed as *boro bhai*, feels *shena/maya* (love for someone younger) with an expectation that his authority will be respected. This is an ideal and there are variations in the strength to which it is adhered. An understanding of the organizing ideal is necessary in order to understand the meaning of the experience for the community when exposed to a different world-view in Britain, where the individual is emphasized, and the individual's interests, independence and egalitarian relationships are the ideals.

In rural Sylhet, the structure of the family unit is patrilineally linked households grouped in close proximity (homesteads, *bari*) and daily life is shared intimately with close kinsfolk. Very few families in Tower Hamlets are 'joint families' in the sense of parents and married sons or brothers living together in one household or in close proximity. Immigration laws allowing the entry of only dependent members of the nuclear family, and council housing policies favouring nuclear households, have led to the demise of the joint family structure in Tower Hamlets. For most of the first generation, however, the ideal of 'jointness' and the primacy of the kin in the social order, have endured, even though the structure of the joint family no longer exists.

This ambience of the joint family is no less important than the structure that operationally defines a joint family (Kakar, 1981; Anwar, 1976). Chain migration has ensured that most families have other relatives in the UK, with whom close ties are maintained by visits, contacts at social and religious gatherings and through mutual commitments of obligation and assistance. The primacy of the family in life and the experience of mutual interdependence are communicated to the children growing up in Britain, even though they have not experienced the participation of the wider family in their daily life. Equally important is the maintenance of ties with the family left behind in Bangladesh. Those of the first generation look upon the family in Bangladesh and *desh* (land of ancestral roots, village) as a source of containment at times of crises and a means of the renewal of the core cultural ideals. A spiritual quality is attributed to contact with one's *desh*. For those growing up in Britain, contact with Bangladesh has less of a spiritual meaning, but Bangladesh continues to be perceived by many young people as a land that is beautiful, good and restful, although remote from the concerns of their lives here. At times of crises with their children, especially older children, parents often consider sending the child to the extended family in Bangladesh in the hope that the contact with the family and the social and physical environment of the *desh* will have a healing influence. It is also believed that the social and cultural influence of the family and society in Bangladesh will give the child a clearer sense of what is the correct and desired behaviour, away from the 'corrupting' influences in Britain. This practice has brought many parents into conflict with authorities in Britain, who may misunderstand the intention of such action, which is perceived as an attempt to control the child by repressive sanctions in a society where the family has greater authority. Reports by young people who have returned after a period in Bangladesh following a crisis, suggests varying responses. Some gained a clearer sense of direction, others found the social order excessive and for many it was an opportunity to experience the family and the *desh* at first hand, although it may have offered little in resolving their difficulties in Britain.

In a study of Bangladeshi families in Tower Hamlets the author (Bose, in press) found that, although the primacy of the family was emphasized by most parents of the first generation, many expressed a wish to continue to live in nuclear households apart from their married brothers. It was often explained as something to which they had simply become accustomed, and they would therefore find it difficult to live jointly again. Their experience of living apart was reinforced by the structure of the social institutions in Britain where the nuclear unit is emphasized, for example when dealing with social, educational, housing and health benefits. The availability of State help has reduced the need for interdependence in the wider family. Close kin are sometimes separated over wide distances, reducing their availability at times of crisis. This is of some consideration when working with families. Although most people are closely connected with members of the wider family, the involvement of the family in resolving the crises cannot be assumed. There is a tradition of sons looking after their parents in their old age and both parents and young people remain strongly committed to living with or looking after their parents, and see this as one of their key responsibilities.

In a traditional Bangladeshi household, women spend most of their time with other women, as do the men with menfolk. The presence of other adults in the home reduces the time that married couples have for each other. Newly arrived wives in the nuclear households in Britain found the absence of women in the family difficult. Closer relationships with women in neighbouring flats, and with daughters who are now grown up, has lessened the loss for many (Bose, in press). The absence of other adults in the family has necessitated a renegotiation of roles for many couples, with a redistribution of responsibilities in daily living and a need for more direct communication with each other. In Bangladesh, traditionally a man takes a lead in the public sphere although the women may have considerable influence over the decisions made at home. In Tower Hamlets, women are seen shopping at pavement stalls, working as machinists from home and organizing Arabic classes for children in the absence of an Islamic school in the neighbourhood. The increased participation of women beyond the traditional roles has been accompanied by a lively debate in the community about what are the correct social codes of behaviour for women. These concern matters such as *purdah* (veiling), whether worn or defined as a state of internal purity, the responsibilities of a working mother in Islam and the special role of women in keeping the family's honour.

Marriage continues to be arranged by elders in the family according to traditional ideas about what constitutes a good match, with emphasis on the reputation and the matching of families. Both parents and most young people adhere to the traditional arrangement. In choosing a prospective bride or groom, the initial decision is usually that of the parents, but both parents and the young recognize that everyone's approval and agreement is important for the best outcome, indicating a niche for individual choice in the midst of traditions where marriage ties are made between families.

It is increasingly the practice that couples meet socially, albeit in the company of others, before the final agreement. It must be emphasized here that most young people do not have major differences with their parents over the traditional arrangement, and recognize the primacy of the family in the key stages of psychosocial development. Difficulties can occur, however, if preparations begin too early for a girl who does not feel psychosocially ready for marriage. Brides are sometimes brought from Bangladesh, as they can be relied upon to preserve traditions more correctly. Although some young men who have grown up here are happy to marry women from Bangladesh, young women who have grown up in Britain indicate a stronger preference for husbands from Britain in the expectation that they will be able to communicate better, and because their British ways will be familiar and cause less difficulties with the in-laws. After marriage, a British Bangladeshi bride may not live with her in-laws, but her relationship with them will be close and of great importance, for after marriage she acquires the Gushti membership of her husband and becomes one of his family.

It is children who are exposed most fully to the bicultural world. Young children are unable to articulate their bicultural experience as well as their older siblings. By the age when they start school, Bangladeshi children have already been socialized into a world where the emphasis is on relatedness and getting on well with siblings and peers, and where there is an awareness of the importance of the family in every event. For the older child, parents direct socialization by firm emphasis on what is acceptable behaviour and what is not, and the use of social pressure: 'What will others say?' 'This is what is expected now as you are older.' 'You must behave well as the younger ones will learn from you.' Delegation of age-appropriate responsibilities instils a firm sense of what is socially expected at different ages and from relationships – for example, siblings are told always to 'play together and never let the smallest one cry'. The use of stories, Islamic teachings and examples of those who show model behaviour are relied upon to emphasize the point. Children participate in every aspect of social and family life, with ample opportunities to interact, observe, and learn the norms of social behaviour and relationships. Withdrawal of attention/love by parents, as a means of socialization is not approved. Young children whose behaviour is less socialized are expected to improve with time and age when their understanding develops, or as a result of the use of firm discipline for older children. This contrasts with interventions used in school such as the emphasis on analysis of a situation, assertion of one's views, reasoning and psychological methods such as the fostering of empathy. Children learn both ways and respond appropriately in the different contexts. Their experience may resonate with that of the older siblings who are able to articulate how they move between the different worlds that they inhabit. Older children describe responding differently in different situations, such as at home and outside. At home they know that, although they may have different views, their parents' views must be respected. Love, obedience and looking after the well-being of parents in their old age is considered the highest duty of children towards parents in recognition of all that parents endure to bring up children well. Most young British Bangladeshis describe this as a positive aspect of their culture that they wish to retain. Differences with parents are to be negotiated strategically without open confrontation, which may appear disrespectful. Outside home, self-assertion is valued, and used to achieve one's ends. Young people do not experience their different behaviours in different situations as a disjunction, or as a passive response to different contexts, but as an adaptive necessity, best understood by their peers who are in a similar situation. This was borne out in a meeting I had with a group of young women in a run-down, decaying community centre with meagre facilities and little furniture or resources. The group had continued to meet since the women's last years in school, despite the depressing state of the building, as they valued the opportunity to meet and informally discuss their experiences at home and in university.

Most first-generation Bangladeshi parents have had little formal education themselves, but education is highly valued by them and is often described as the main reason for continuing to live in Britain, despite the hardships. Education is seen increasingly by parents and young people alike as the way out of the rag trade and the loss of status following migration. For the first generation of parents their lack of English has meant that they are unable to help their children with schoolwork or participate actively in parent–teacher meetings. Children who are lucky enough to have older siblings are in a better position. Although the children are fluent in Sylheti, a distinct dialect of Bengali, only a few can read Bengali. Sylheti uses the script for standard Bengali, which is unfamiliar to most parents, who therefore cannot teach written Bengali to their children. This has implications for their children's access to the knowledge of Bengali history, stories and cultural heroes. Wilson (1978), writing about black children in America describes how the lack of black heroes in stories, and the lack of black history in school, disadvantages black children, who do not learn about black heroes with whom they can identify in the critical years of their psychosocial development.

Bangladeshi parents are unfamiliar with the teaching methods used in modern education but have come to understand that their children are being taught by very different methods in school from those they experienced themselves. Despite the disadvantage, the educational performance of the Bangladeshi girls in Tower Hamlets in certain schools has shown impressive improvements testifying to the complexity of the issues that determine outcome in education. The high value placed on education, the fact that girls spend more time on books as they are not allowed out freely like their brothers, their advantage in investing in further education in a new world, which offers them new possibilities, the fact that some leading girls' schools in Tower Hamlets have addressed the special cultural and religious needs of their pupils and parents, and the presence of Bengali teachers in these schools, have all contributed to the positive results. The educational achievement of the Bangladeshi girls in another neighbouring borough where the community is smaller and scattered has caused concern and may indicate the role of the local factors in influencing broad parameters such as outcome in education.

In traditional Muslim Bangladeshi society, socialization into adult roles begins from the age of seven or eight years, when children are believed to be capable of moral and religious responsibilities. This age is significant from the religious point of view as it is the stage when the child is believed to begin to differentiate between good and evil (Gil'adi, 1992). The preparation of girls for marriage and keeping a home, and of boys as wage earners who will represent the family in the outside world, begins early. Girls acquire their skill through participation in the care of the younger siblings and helping their mother with household chores. This is also another facet of the interdependency of roles and relationship in families. Mothers in Britain do not expect that their daughters will learn these tasks as early as they had learned them themselves, recognizing that their daughters are growing up in a changing world where formal education has taken precedence in the formative years. However, the very fact that Bangladeshi parents may have expectations of children that are contrary to the modern notion of childhood as a long period of learning when there are no expectations of participation in family responsibilities evokes a judgement that parents are exploiting the children, especially girls, in roles that are exclusively an adult's in British society. In families where it is a real problem for a girl, often the marital relationship is poor and the mother overburdened and depressed with the sole responsibility of caring for several young children. The difficulties for the girl are often compounded by overcrowding with lack of space for doing homework. In Tower Hamlets, the creative use of homework clubs in women's centres and schools has offered an alternative for young people preparing for examinations.

A major issue for the young is that of fulfilling the role of interpreters and translators for their parents. Older children describe it as something that they did reluctantly because it reverses traditional roles in families, giving the child more power than the parent. Others, despite this distressing aspect, recall that it has given them a real understanding of what their parents have had to grapple with, without knowledge of English and of British ways.

Adolescence in the West is marked as a period of rapid physical growth and sexual maturity, with moves towards solidifying an identity and establishing autonomy from the family. Writers from the Indian subcontinent have commented on the absence of adolescence as a well-defined developmental stage in the traditional social constructs of development (Ramanujam, 1992). Puberty is recognized as an important developmental stage towards sexual maturity and some kindling of interest in the wider world, but without the emphasis on the constructs of separation and autonomy attributed to adolescent development in the West. In a traditional rural society, after emerging from childhood, one passes through the stages of preparation for adult roles and responsibilities. Das (1992) describes how the transition occurs in girls through role preparation, menarche, and increasing emphasis on the protection of their honour and reputation until marriage.

Children growing up here are exposed to Western expectations of adolescence, through their education in school, the influence of books and media, peer culture, and the educational structure, which mirror the prevailing constructs of stages of development. For a Bangladeshi girl growing up in Tower Hamlets, her transition to adulthood is complex, marked by multiple roles and expectations, which are both hers and her parents, and which she is expected to fulfil. A girl's behaviour at this stage is of critical significance for her *izzat* (honour) and that of the family's. Daughters become the repositories of the family honour and are looked upon as symbols of the family's prestige (*izzat*). What is important is her reputation within the community. If she is seen to behave, dress, move and mix 'wantonly', her honour and consequently that of her family will be questioned. This has implications for her future marriage, and that of her siblings, as the family's *izzat* depends on her.

For Bangladeshi parents, their daughters' desire for greater participation with peers and involvement with the outside world at this stage, heightens their anxiety about the potential risks to their reputation, especially if the outside world is seen to be alien and dangerous. Parents may respond by restricting the time that their daughters spend outside the home, even with friends. School holidays and the time when the daughter leaves school can precipitate a crisis, as school may be a girl's only source of peer contact outside the home. The absence of younger aunts, older cousins and siblings in a large family network, in contrast to the situation in the villages in Bangladesh, increases the need for friends for peer company in Britain. Contrary to popular assumption in the West, a young girl may have more freedom of movement in a village in Bangladesh, where the boundaries of the 'inside world' are the boundaries of the *bari* homestead, which are wider than the boundaries of a flat in Tower Hamlets. For the girl in Bangladesh, the homestead is inhabited by familiar kinsfolk, and the outside world is not the dangerous 'other' but an extension of the familiar world that shares the family's values.

Young girls in Tower Hamlets have responded with inventive solutions such as the youth community centres, visits to libraries, and after-school clubs, which combine an opportunity for peer contact with activities that earn parental approval. On leaving school, young girls and their parents are keen for them to work in local establishments with a good reputation in the community. The parents' anxiety is lessened if they know that their daughter is busily engaged at work. This may also underscore her competence and add to her reputation as a bride in a changing world in the community in Tower Hamlets where the benefits of women working are becoming increasingly valued. Other women choose further education, which offers new possibilities and also gains approval. Although further education is valued by most parents, it can engender anxiety in some about their daughter leaving home, and the postponement of a daughter's marriage may hold up the marriage of her younger sisters. Some young women adopt the headscarf – a symbol of Islamic veiling – the use of which asserts her internal purity and places on her the responsibility of observing the Islamic code of behaviour. It gains her the trust of her parents and others in society, and earns her the freedom to move more freely in her new role in the outside world.

This is not the only reason why so many of the young have turned to Islam. In a society where their identity as Bangladeshis is looked down upon, an Islamic identity and a sense of belonging to the universal Islamic community (*Ummat*) offers a positive identification with a powerful alternative. For both parents and the young, Islam confers certainty in an increasingly changing world where modernization is overtly equated with Westernization. In Britain, discovery of and contact with Muslims from other countries has stimulated an appraisal of what is Islamic in origin, what is not, and what holds Muslims together worldwide. In rural Bangladesh there is no separation between 'culture' and 'religion', which are experienced seamlessly in everyday life. Many of the young in Britain who have not experienced social and cultural life in Bangladesh, however, make a sharp distinction between traditions that are Islamic in origin, and those whose roots lie in the pervasive culture of the Indian subcontinent, shared by Hindus, Muslims and Buddhists alike. What is not desirable in the new context of British society, or in contact with other Muslim communities, is readily disowned as being 'cultural in origin' and 'belonging to the Indian subcontinent'. For example, inequalities in gender role in Bangladeshi society are attributed to 'culture', whereas a woman's rights in the Islamic marriage contract are emphasized as an illustration of the equality of women's position in social institutions. This delineation brings young British Bangladeshis closer to both other Muslims and to their British counterparts. It is an example of how communities continually reinterpret, re-evaluate and realign themselves in response to the demands of their new contexts.

For boys growing up in Tower Hamlets the transition from schoolchildren to young adults is uncertain. Along with their white English counterparts in the East End of London, they have few jobs to aspire to and the seduction of drugs is pervasive. Their lack of working fathers as role models, many of whom are elderly now, makes it difficult for them to find well-trodden paths into adult roles and responsibilities. Young men not wishing to take up the unskilled jobs that their fathers did have turned to higher education as a means of moving out of poverty and low status. Although a few have succeeded, others are less convinced that their education in the East End will help them in an increasingly competitive world where inequality and discriminatory attitudes will disadvantage them. They have come to share the aspirations of the others in British society, but fear that they are denied the means to achieve them. For the generation of young people who have grown up in Tower Hamlets, their experience of racial harassment has changed over the years. Initially this was an everyday occurrence and even walking down the main street was hazardous. Since the ratio of Bangladeshi to English families has changed in the Bangladeshi-populated neighbourhoods, racially motivated attacks have become less frequent. Young people describe covert discrimination as more distressing. This includes poor expectations from teachers, being 'overlooked' in groups, and less enthusiasm from career officers about their futures and plans.

The young Bangladeshis are pioneers in a world that their parents have not experienced. Whether dealing with racism in school, or finding a model of behaviour in their new roles as students in a British university or as British Bangladeshi brides, they are the first. The peer group with whom they share their experience serves as a reference group for sharing their dilemmas, and trying out new roles and new strategies in a rapidly changing world.

The young are often asked about their identity. A study published by the Centre for Bangladeshi Studies (1993) describes the variations in experiences and the composite nature of 'identities' depending on the context in which the young person defines himself or herself. Although there are several strands to their definition of identity – Black/British/Bangladeshi/ Muslim/Sylheti/Asian – what few would doubt is that they see their future in Britain and that they have a distinct identity that they wish to emphasize (Gardner and Shukur 1994).

I have avoided presenting an overview of all Asians and all generation, whilst developing an understanding of how communities change in response to their unique histories and the new context. The story of Bangladeshis in Tower Hamlets demonstrates how the community is evolving its own distinctive narrative and dynamics, which cannot just be understood from a structural perspective. In adapting to their changing world, they have redefined their experience and used their own distinct cultural resources. These cultural resources have underpinned their explorations whilst at the same time they are being interpreted and re-invented. This process is most clearly seen in the young, whose experiences are rooted in both worlds.

References

Adams C (1987) Across Seven Seas and Thirteen Rivers. London: THAP Books.
Anwar M (1976) Between Two Cultures: A Study of Relationships between Generations in the Asian Community in Britain. London: Commission for Racial Equality.

Aziz KMA (1979) Kinship in Bangladesh. Monograph Series I. International Centre for Diarrhoeal Disease Research, Bangladesh.

Ballard R (1994) Introduction: The Emergence Of Desh Pardesh. In Ballard R (ed.) Desh Pardesh. London: Hurst & Co.

Bose R (in press) Impact of Migration on Bangladeshi families in Tower Hamlets. Immigrants and Minorities.

Centre for Bangladeshi Studies (1993) Routes and Beyond: Voices of Educationally Successful Bengalis in Tower Hamlets. London: Centre for Bangladeshi Studies.

Chataway C, Berry JW (1989) Acculturation experiences appraisal, coping and adaptation. Canadian Journal of Behavioural Sciences 21: 295–309.

Das V (1992) Reflections on the Social Construction of Adulthood. In Kakar S (ed.) Identity and Adulthood. Delhi: Oxford University Press.

Eade J (1992) Ethnicity and the Politics of Cultural Difference: an Agenda for the 1990s? Unpublished paper given at a workshop on 'Ethnicity', St Anthony's College, Oxford, May 1992.

Gardner K (1995) Global Migrants Local Lives. Oxford: Clarendon Press.

Gardner K, Shukur A (1994) 'I'm Bengali, I'm Asian, and I'm Living Here': the Changing Identity of British Bengalis. In Ballard R (ed.) Desh Pardesh. London: Hurst & Co.

Gil'adi A (1992) Children of Islam. Concepts of Childhood in Medieval Muslim Society. Oxford: Macmillan.

Goldlust J, Richmond AH (1982) A multivariate model of immigrant adaptation. International Migration Review 8: 193–225.

Inden RB, Nicholas RW (1977) Kinship in Bengali Culture. Chicago: University of Chicago Press.

Kakar S (1981) The Inner World. Delhi: Oxford University Press.

Kotalova J (1993) Belonging to Others. Cultural Construction Of Womanhood in a Village in Bangladesh. Dhaka: University Press Limited.

Kovacs ML, Cropley AJ (1975) Alienation and assimilation of immigrants. The Australian Journal of Social Issues 10(3): 221–31.

Krause IB, Miller A (1995) Culture and Family Therapy in Mental Health. In Fernando S (ed.) A Multi-Ethnic Society. A Multi-Disciplinary Handbook. London: Routledge.

Littlewood R (1992) Psychiatric diagnosis and racial bias. Empirical and interpretive approaches. Social Science and Medicine 34: 141–9.

Lock M (1990) On being ethnic: the politics of identity breaking and making in Canada, or, Nevra on Sunday. Culture Medicine and Psychiatry 14: 237–54.

Maitra B, Miller A (1996) Children, Families and Therapists. Clinical Considerations and Ethnic Minority Cultures. In Dwivedi KN, Prakash V (eds) Meeting the Needs of Ethnic Minority Children. London: Jessica Kingsley.

Ramanujam BK (1992) Toward Maturity. Indian Clinical Setting. In Kakar S (ed.) Identity and Adulthood. Delhi: Oxford University Press.

Sluzki CE (1979) Migration and family conflict. Family Process 10(4): 379–90.

Tamura T, Lau A (1992) Connectedness versus separateness: applicability of family therapy to Japanese families. Family Process 31(4) 319–40.

Turner J (1991) Migrants and their therapist: a trans-context approach. Family Process 30: 407–19.

Wilson AN (1978) The Developmental Psychology of the Black Child. New York: Africana Research Publications.

Chapter 4
The Hindu, Jain and Buddhist communities; beliefs and practices

KEDAR NATH DWIVEDI AND KONASALE MR PRASAD

The word 'religion' is derived from the Latin word *religare* meaning 'to bind', to bring together humans and God. It constitutes a common set of beliefs, customs, traditions, practices and, of course, a way of thinking. During the evolution of the human race it has given a sense of direction and the stamina to face and see through the daunting problems of survival. No wonder religion has remained a potent driving force despite the sledgehammer blows of great thinkers like Marx and Freud and the ascent of science. Religion has stayed the test of time.

Unfortunately, contrary to its intent, religion has divided mankind into almost immiscible sects and groups. Religion has nevertheless given a sense of identity and has provided the cohesive power for human migrations and settlements in strange geographical locations. The growing paranoia of immigrant populations about the loss of identity and of native populations about the 'dilution' of their culture can sow the seeds of reactive psychopathology and mental illness among the vulnerable. There is therefore a need to know the customs, beliefs, practices and attitudes of such populations, which originate from core religious beliefs.

India has been the cradle of many great religions, such as Hinduism, Buddhism, Sikhism and Jainism. Hinduism, Buddhism and Jainism are many millennia old. Modern Western interest in Indian thought began in the nineteenth century. In 1840, Lord Macaulay, the Governor of India, ordered the translation of Indian Classics. Thus, Max Müller published the *Sacred Book of East* in 50 volumes. German philosophers like Schopenhauer, Stcherbatsky and Poussin were greatly influenced by Indian philosophy, and philosophers like Heidegger, Keith and MacDonald resemble Indian thinkers in many ways. Psychotherapists like Jung, Erich Fromm, Fritz Pearl, Ronald Laing and others have also been greatly influenced by Indian thought, particularly Buddhism.

Historical perspective

From the historical point of view the development of the ancient religions in India can be divided into following stages.

- period of the Indus Valley civilization (5000 BC to 2500 BC);
- vedic period (2500 BC to 1200 BC);
- upanishadic period (1200 BC to 600 BC);
- period of the Heterodox schools (800 BC to 200 AD);
- revival of Hinduism (200 AD onwards).

The Indus Valley civilization was one of the most extensive of the three earliest civilizations, the other two being Egyptian and Mesopotamian. It was a community-oriented culture of town dwellers with a central government, wide roads, temples, swimming baths, a drainage system and so on. Excavations in Mohanjo-daro and Harappa in 1918 by John Marshall, a railway employee in India, revealed statues of proto-Shiva in yogic postures surrounded by wild beasts. In the Indus Valley civilization, which was the original indigenous Indian civilization, the Yogic culture had notions like that of individual soul, cycle of birth and rebirth, the layered nature of consciousness and the goal of release from the cycle of birth and rebirth. Then came the Aryans, perhaps from the Russian plains. The Indus Valley civilization ended suddenly as the nomadic Aryans massacred, enslaved and drove away the indigenous people of the Indus Valley towards the south of India. The Aryans established an affluent rural culture in the North. They were a very poetic and nature-oriented people and worshipped the sun, fire and other natural forces. They composed the four vedas (Rigveda, Yajurveda, Samveda and Atharv-veda) and established the social structure of Varnashram (four social classes and four stages of life).

Brahmanas, the commentaries on the vedas, appeared in 2000 BC and *aranyakas* – teachings of forest living such as meditation – appeared in 1500 BC. The Aryans had a notion of a world soul or God and had ideas about afterlife and the rituals that can influence the afterlife.

After a thousand years of affluence, people became more philosophically concerned with questions such as that of ultimate reality. The *vedic* period was thus followed by the *upanishadic* period of intense philosophical deliberations. Is there an ultimate reality? Do space and time bind it or is it beyond space and time? And so on. Theories of *brahma, karma* and of non-duality were established and *upanishads* began to be composed. The culture became more 'self' oriented. The extensive upanishadic literature beautifully linked the concept of the individual soul (from the yogic culture of the Indus Valley civilization) with the cosmic soul (of the vedic culture). It also described the nature of the layered consciousness and clarified the endless cycle of birth and rebirth on the basis of the Karmic theory. The Karmic theory is a the theory of cause and effect, volitional actions and their consequences, not in the sense of someone dishing out consequences but in the sense of seeds turning into fruits given the right conditions and right amount of time. Usually there is a long backlog or a waiting list of Karma that have been performed already and are still in the queue waiting to turn into consequences, maybe for many lifetimes. This is because many actions (*karma*) can be performed in a short time but their consequences can last for a very long time.

Then heterodox schools emerged that challenged the vedic authority. For example, the Ajivikas (eighth century BC) challenged the karmic theory and proposed a fatalistic theory. They suggested that everything that happened in this universe was predestined and unfolded like a coiled string according to the blueprint already there. The implication was that there is nothing one can do to influence the future, therefore there is no sense in being ethical or moral for the sake of the future. Their slogan 'eat, drink and be merry' clearly threatened the upanishadic theory of *karma*. Jainism (seventh century BC), on the other hand, proposed that the soul is like a magnet that attracts iron fillings or impurities. The purpose of life has to be to purify the soul through austerity, suffering and penance. This was a dualistic theory and advocated renunciation and humility to liberate the 'self' from matter. This attitude was quite the opposite of that of the Ajivikas. Then the Buddha (sixth century BC) taught the middle way between the two extremes, that is, between the hedonistic, irresponsible, indulgent lifestyle of Ajivikas and the austere and painful lifestyle of Jains. His theory can be described as a stream theory (as opposed to string theory or the magnet theory), where things are changing, impermanent, interactive, systemic and interdependent in complex ways. Buddhism proposes that all phenomena are transitory in nature and thus attacks the notion of ultimate reality and self.

The sixth century BC is also known as the Axial Age because of the emergence in the world of many great philosophers during that period. These include the Buddha (563–483 BC) in India, Ezekiel (exiled in 579 BC) in Tel-Abib, Confucius (551–479) in China and Heraclitus (535–475 BC) in Greece. The Buddha proposed the theory of eternal flux of change. Ezekiel was a prophet and the book of Ezekiel is in the Old Testament. He influenced Judaism and the rebuilding of Israel. Confucius was a great humanitarian social reformer who studied the mind, world peace and the provision of social order. Heraclitus was very similar to the Buddha: he came from a royal family but gave the luxuries to his brother, practised solitary meditation and produced similar conclusions to Buddha. He too denied the reality of 'being' and understood it as 'becoming', eternal flux of change.

Buddhism spread to several countries in the Far East and Middle East. However, in India its influence gradually declined, which led to the revival of Hinduism in secondary literary forms. It began in the second century AD. This literature included philosophical, mystical and popular aspects and is grouped under six headings

- *smrities* or epic stories such as Ramayan, Mahabharat;
- *sankhya* or knowledge, for example by Kapil;
- *yoga* or similar practices, for example by Patanjali;
- *nyaya vaisheshik* or epistemology, for example by Gautam;
- *meemansa* or rituals;
- *vedanta* or philosophy, for example by Shankar.

Today the followers of Indian religions worldwide form the second largest religious group in the world, next only to Christianity. According to the 1992 figures there were 1,883,022,000 followers of Christianity versus 1,069,545,000 followers of Indian religions (*Hutchison's Encyclopedia On-Line*). In this chapter, we discuss the beliefs and practices of three of these religions: Hinduism, Buddhism and Jainism. These religions have many common features. The differences are subtle and require a good grasp of the major tenets of the religions.

Hinduism

Hinduism must be the most complex of all religions. The primary aim of Hinduism is to become one with God. In Hinduism, the idea of oneness of God with many life forms is one of the most fiercely debated issues. Whether such a reunification really occurs has also been debated both at an intellectual and an emotional level. To resolve this, several schools of Hinduism emerged. Almost all the schools accepted the authority of the *vedas,* which are the fountainhead of Hindu religious principles. Some schools did not accept the authority of the *vedas* and splintered out as separate religions, namely Buddhism and Jainism.

There are three major schools in Hinduism. They are

- *advaita* (monism or non-dualism);
- *dvaita* (dualism – soul and matter); and
- *vishishtadvaita* (special monism – qualified by space and time).

Each of these schools has an *acharya* (great teacher) advocating the respective schools. They were Sri Shankaracharya (788–820 AD), Sri Madhvacharya (1238–1317 AD) and Sri Ramanujacharya (1017–1127 AD), respectively. In addition to these, there are many other schools as well, such as Nimbark, Gawpad, Vadarayan and so on. These cannot be dealt with here.

The fundamental doctrine of monism propounds that the god (*Parabrahman*) alone is true, the material world around us is false (illusion) and that god and the life (*jiva*) are the same (Swami Adidevanada, 1993). God is conceptualized as an absolute form of energy (*chaitanya*) with an absolute existence, absolute knowledge and absolute bliss (*sat-chit-ananda brahman*). God is therefore formless and beyond the perception of ordinary senses, requiring us to acquire transcendental consciousness to be aware of God. The material world is said to have a relative existence. Moving from such a relative existence toward the absolute existence to become one with it (self-realization – *mukti*) is the goal of all living creatures (Adidevananda, 1993).

Special monism proposes that there are three divisions of the single major principle: energy (*chaitanya*), inertness or non-energy (*achaitanya*) and God (*Ishwara*). God encompasses the states of energy and inertness. However, it conserves both the distinction and non-distinction for the material existence. God is conceptualized as a conglomeration of various superlatives. In its subtle existence, God is the refined manifestation of energy and non-energy, whereas in its crude manifestation it is the material world around us. Life in bondage with material world is not liberated. Therefore, detaching oneself from the material world is essential for liberation and to become one with God. Everyone is able to obtain *mukti*. Except for some features, *atman* and *paramatman* are very similar. Disposing of these subtle differences leads one to *mukti*, which can be attained through *karma-yoga, gnyana-yoga,* or *bhakti-yoga* (Adidevananda, 1993).

The dualism school puts forth nine principles about the relationship between God and life. They are as follows (Adidevananda, 1993):

- God (Sri Hari) alone is superincumbent;
- the world around us is true;
- the distinction between God and life is true;
- all life forms are followers of God;
- there are distinctions even amongst the living beings;
- the experience of true happiness is liberation;
- immaculate devotion (*bhakti*) is the instrument for liberation;
- there are three different types of evidence for the existence of God; and
- all *vedas* propound God.

Some scholars consider Hinduism to be a set of superstitious beliefs, and, primitive rituals. Jagmohan (1998) considers this confusion to be due to 'the failure to perceive the phenomenon in its historical perspective and the inability to separate the pure from the fake, the profound from the profane, and the lofty from the low'. He grades Hindu thoughts and practices at three levels. The core Hindu philosophy is level I. The fundamental philosophy is oneness and principles of unity, viz., unity in the diversity of humans, of nature, and, of religion. Level II consists of the beliefs and practices, which are not contrary to its basic philosophy. They came into existence to meet the religious needs of the common folk who could not grasp the intellectual content of its core and who had to depend on temples, images of gods, goddesses and their symbols. In level III are all the spurious rituals, rites, cults and superstitions and practices, such as *sati* (Jagmohan, 1998). The critics tend to look at the contents of level III only.

Hindu thought is based on the law of *karma*, transmigration of souls and rebirths. The word *karma* means duty or work. *Karma* does not only include deeds but also the individual's thoughts and experiences. What we undergo currently is influenced by what we did in the past, and what we do in future is determined by what we are doing now. Lord Sri Krishna gives a lofty message in the *Bhagavadgita* regarding *karma* – we have rights over our deeds but not over the fruition (Sri Mad'bhagavadgita, 2, 47). Though it looks meaningless in our result-oriented world, it preaches that one of the highest morals is working for the sake of work (*karma-yoga*). If we cannot complete the *karma* in one birth, it necessarily has to be carried forward to the next birth. *Atman* (the soul) carries these fine impressions in the form of *sanskaras* to the next birth. Life after birth is compared to a human being changing clothes when one set is worn out. In between the two births, *atman*, which carries a subtle body, spends time in either heaven or hell before it enters a new body. This cycle of birth and death (*punarapi jananam, punarapi maranam*) continues until we clear all the *sanskaras*. Once the *sanskaras* are cleared, the soul (*atman*) becomes one with the Great Soul (*paramatman*) or the God (self-realization – *mukti*). In contrast with the teachings in Christianity and Islam, transit through 'heaven' and 'hell' is transient and determined by the quantity and the quality of *sanskaras* accumulated. Hinduism does not believe in unlimited consequences of a limited cause. The goal of human beings is not just to avoid 'hell' and reach 'heaven' but to become one with God. Many rituals and ceremonies are prescribed for the atonement of sins and for clearing of *sanskaras*, aiding people to become closer to God.

Many ways of achieving this are described exhaustively. They can be classified broadly into four groups. Each such group is called a *yoga* meaning 'to bring together'. The most difficult path is reasoned faith, which is encouraged throughout. It is prescribed as a vehicle for higher forms of spiritual life. An extreme degree of inquisitiveness making reasoned distinction of what is God and what is not, and, finally accepting God to the rejection of all else (*neti neti*, not this, not this) is called *gnyana-yoga* (true knowledge). *Karma-yoga* is described above. *Bhakti-yoga* involves total devotion and utmost submission to God. The fourth method, otherwise known as *Raja-yoga*, is through conquering the internal world. It is also called *ashtangayoga*, meaning the yoga consisting of eight steps: *yama* (morality), *niyama* (disciplined effort), *asana* (posture), *pranayama* (breathing exercises), *pratyahara* (control of sense organs), *dharana* (concentration), *dhyana* (meditation) and *samadhi* (transcendental state of mind).

What creates a profound impact on the Hindus is the fathomless meaning of the festivals and rituals. The festivals bring together people and communities. They herald a healthy social life with a spiritual background. The festivals are determined astrologically, based on the positions of the stars, planets and zodiac signs. The ancient sages had developed a dependable calendar and reliable astrological calculations to predict the position of these celestial bodies to determine the days and months of these festivals. This is still being followed by the Hindus.

The nature and importance of these festivals varies according to the regions and the caste or *varna*. However, many festivals carry the same degree of significance across the length and the breadth of India. Some of them are the festival of lights (called variously *deepavali*, *divali*, and so forth) and the worship of the goddess Durga (its name varies in different areas of India: *durgastami*, *vijayadashami*, *navaratri*, and so forth). Both of these are symbolic of the victory of good over evil.

The latter festival is celebrated in some parts of India with a wonderful display of dolls and toys, where children take part with great fervour and involvement. These festivals involve inviting relatives and friends followed by feasting and sharing the joy and the sorrows of the families involved. The festival of lights involves lighting lamps all over the house, everywhere in the towns, cities and villages. It also involves burning crackers, which is a delightful experience for children and adults as well. During this festival, friends and relatives exchange gifts as tokens of love and continued bonding and support to each other's families. *Holi* is a festival of colours. Residents of a locality or village, friends and relatives throw colours on each other, forgetting differences in the social class. This festival is symbolic of the rebirth of the God of Love (Kamadeva) who was earlier burned to ashes when he tried to entice Lord Shiva to marry Parvati.

There are regional differences in emphasis with regard to these festivals. All Hindus, with some regional differences, celebrate the three festivals described above. Some festivals are specific to certain regions. For example, the festival of *pongal* or *sankranti* is celebrated mainly in the southern part of India. It is a festival that follows the season of harvesting. It involves distribution of sweets, worshipping bedecked livestock and in some places a competition of bullock carts. Children and adolescents actively take part in this festival. The Hindu New Year called variously *ugadi* (meaning the beginning of the new era), *gudipadva*, and so on, is celebrated in many parts of India.

Jainism

During the sixth century BC, India was going through a phase of religious tumult and renaissance. This period is also considered to be a time of social and intellectual ferment in India. Jainism and Buddhism, two great religions of the world, emerged almost simultaneously during this phase of religious renaissance in India. The values of non-violence, tolerance and self-discipline that were preached by them have become deeply ingrained as the cornerstones of the Indian ethos and inspired many great leaders of the world, such as Gandhi.

The word *jain* means a person who conquers or one who overcomes. It means a person who conquers his or her own internal desires and drives or who has overcome such worldly desires. As described earlier, this religion originated as an offshoot of Hinduism in revolt against certain *vedic* precepts such as the prescription of violent rituals such as animal sacrifice to appease God. Quite obviously, the cornerstone of Jainism is the practice of non-violence, sympathy, compassion and right ways of living.

The original proponents of Jainism are the great masters and monks, called *tirthankaras,* meaning 'builders of the ford' (Lin, 1998). According to Jainism, *tirthankaras* were born as ordinary mortals but attained perfection through an intense and prolonged spiritual pursuit. They are also known as *arihants* or *jina* and are the gods of the Jains. The preaching of Mahavira Jaina who was the last of the 24 *tirthankaras* is recorded in a sacred book by 12 of his disciples. Mahavira lived in the sixth century BC. He achieved enlightenment at the age of 42 after severe penance for 12 years. For the next 30 years of his life, he preached the great truths he had encountered during his enlightenment.

At the very heart of the preaching of Jainism lies the objective of liberation from the cycle of birth and death, which is full of miseries. This is known as *nirvana* or *moksha*. As in Hinduism, it preaches that every living being is in bondage with the material world (karmic atoms) that are accumulated by one's own past deeds. These are the root causes of human vices such as, anger, hatred or violence. These vices, in turn, lead to further bondage to the material world. An ordinary soul cannot find an escape from this. Mahavira preached three ways to escape from this cycle of life. They are the right faith (*samyak-darshana*), right knowledge (*samyak-gnyana*) and right conduct (*samyak-charitra*) (Bavisi, 1998).

Jainism stresses four great virtues:

- amity, love, and friendship (*maitri*);
- compassion (*karuna*);
- appreciation, respect and joy (*pramoda*);
- equanimity and tolerance (*madhyastha*);

The Jains follow strict guidelines, called five great vows, as a part of *samyak-darshana*. These are:

- non-violence (*ahimsa*);
- truthfulness (*sathya*);

- not stealing (*astheya*);
- chastity (*brahmacharya*); and
- not receiving gifts, or non-attachment (*aparigraha*).

In fact, these five principles form the *yama*, or the first step of the *raja-yoga* (Swami Vivekananda, 1978) described earlier in the section on Hinduism. Jains attempt to follow them as far as is possible. These principles are strictly observed by those committed to the spiritual life, such as monks and nuns, whereas the common people follow them according to their abilities (Bavisi, 1998). Within Jainism there are two sects – the Digambaras (those who consider that the sky is their cloth, thus remaining naked) and Shwetambaras (those who believe in wearing only white clothes). The former sect practices an extreme form of renunciation where even clothes are renounced.

Jains emphasize right thinking because of a logical presumption that all actions are true reflections of internal thoughts. In order to have complete control over actions, it is essential to exercise control over the thought process. Jainism recommends meditation on 12 Bhavanas (thoughts) (Bavisi, 1998):

- Impermanence of the world (*anitya bhavana*). It is fruitless to be attached to the worldly things because everything in the world is transient. Therefore, it is essential to strive for freedom of the soul.
- Being unprotected in the world (*asarana bhavana*). Nobody offers absolute protection against death, disease and so forth to anyone in this world. Taking refuge in the principles of Jainism and the great personalities like *tirthankaras, arihants,* is suggested as the best protection.
- Impermanence of relationships (*samsara bhavana*). All of us go through a continual cycle of births and deaths with the transmigration of soul, which is full of miseries and pain. It is we who establish these relationships and undergo the sufferings. This thought helps one to detach from earthly belongings.
- Solitude of the soul (*ekatva bhavana*). Here, one thinks that the soul is in its journey in solitude towards freedom. The soul is responsible for its actions and suffers the fruits (both good and bad) on its own. This makes one feel responsible for oneself.
- Separateness (*anyatva bhavana*). Jainism preaches that one's soul is separate from this world whereas the body is made up of matter that belongs to the world. As a corollary to the principles of the impermanence of the world and the impermanence of relationships, one should not develop attachment with worldly objects.
- Impureness of the body (*asuchi bhavana*). One is encouraged to think about the impureness of the body as it contains blood, meat, faeces, urine and so forth. But it is emphasized that the soul is completely

pure and, therefore, it is important to concentrate on that which is all pure.

- Influx of *karma* (*asrava bhavana*). The soul is eternally receiving the influx of *karma* every time one enjoys or suffers through the senses (*indriyas*). One should aim at releasing oneself from the bonds of *karma*. So, it is important to be watchful of what one does.
- Stopping the influx of karma (*samvara bhavna*). From the above it is clear that one should stop thoughts that cause the accumulation of *karma*.
- Shedding of karma (*nirjara bhavana*). Here, the emphasis is on getting rid of the karma that have already been accumulated by austere measures.
- Transitory nature of the universe (*loka bhavana*). Related to the notion of the impermanence of the world, this thought makes one understand the real nature of the world.
- Unattainability of *nirvana* (*bodhi-durlabha bhavana*). It is very difficult to attain *nirvana*. One should not, therefore, lose any opportunity to attain it.
- Religious thoughts (*dharma bhavana*). When everything in the world is misery, it is essential to think about taking shelter in the religion, scriptures and so forth.

These thoughts are to be meditated upon all the time to lead a life of renunciation and right knowledge.

Professor Lin (1998) writes that 'one of the most important activities of the *tirthankaras* was the search for an understanding of the universe'. Jains developed a cosmographic schema of the universe, sketching it into three regions: heavens at the uppermost regions, a middle-world where humans live followed by eight hells, one below the other, each more horrible than the last.

The important festivals of the Jains are Lord Mahavira's birthday, the *ayambil oli*, the *dashalakshana vrata, paryushana* and *divali* (Malaiya, 1997). There are many other festivals that overlap with the Hindu festivals but the Jain festivals have their own unique and profound meaning. For example, *divali* for the Jains is the day when Mahavira attained nirvana. It is supposed to have started when King Chetaka of Vaishali was told by confederate kings 'since the light of intelligence (*vardhamana mahavira*) is gone, let us make an illumination of the material matter' (Malaiya. 1997). The *dashalakshanavrata* (meaning a festival with ten virtues) is observed for 10 days in the Indian month of Bhadrapada, which falls around August–September every year. Bharilla (1997) observes that it consists of strict pursuit of 10 virtues, namely, supreme forbearance, supreme modesty, supreme straightforwardness, supreme contentment, supreme truth, supreme self-restraint, supreme austerity, supreme renunciation, supreme possessionlessness and supreme celibacy. Another unique festival in Jainism is *paryushan*. The central idea emerges from a simple algorithm of happiness requiring peace, which in turn requires forgiveness as essential component. It is celebrated as an eight-day festival where it is stressed to 'maintain purity of the body and the soul and subdue the carnal cravings' (Surishwarji, 1998). The final day is reserved for the actual 'act of forgiveness and craving for pardon for having hurt others'.

Buddhism

The Buddha

When Queen Maya dreamed of an elephant, this was analysed by a dream analyst who diagnosed her as being pregnant and predicted that she would give birth to a son who would either become an emperor or a monk. The baby was born in the Lumbini garden (now in Nepal) in 563 BC and was called Siddharth Gautam. His father, King Shuddhodan, not wanting his son to become a monk, arranged a very protected life for Siddharth in the palace. However, when he did go out he happened to see (despite the attempts by the administration to hide such realities of life) a sick man, an old man, a dead man and a monk. This created an urge in him to go for a search of the deathless. At the age of 29, he left his palace, his wife Yashodhara and son Rahul and visited the forests in search of the truth. He studied under different teachers and practised techniques for self-realization. These did not satisfy him fully. He therefore discovered his own method and achieved Buddha-hood at the age of 35 at Gaya in India. He began teaching at Varanasi in Pali, travelled widely and died at the age of 80 in 483 BC at Kushi Nagar.

Some of the basic principles in Buddhism are as follows.

The Four Noble Truths

The Four Noble Truths of Buddhism are:

- *dukha* (suffering, anguish, and conflict) is universal and omnipresent. Birth, decay, disease, death, meeting the unpleasant and losing the pleasant are nothing but *dukha*;
- there is a chain of causation leading to *dukha* (see below);
- by removing the cause, *dukha* can be eliminated;
- following the eightfold Noble Path (see below) can lead to the elimination of causes and that of *dukha*.

This model is based on the existing medical model of symptom (or clinical features), disease (diagnosis or etiology)), strategy (prognosis) and management (treatment).

The theory of dependent origination

The theory of dependent origination – the theory of the causal chain (12 *nidanas*) leading to *dukha* is that

- *avidya* (ignorance) leads to
- *sanskar* (conditionings, volitional tendencies), which lead to
- *vinyan* (a stream of consciousness), which leads to
- *nama-rupa* (psycho-physical formation), which leads to
- *satayatan* (six sense modalities – optic, auditory, olfactory, taste, proprio-visecero-ceptive, and mind or ideational), which lead to
- *phass* (*sparsh* in Sanskrit, contact or meeting together of attention, sense door and stimulus), which leads to
- *vedana* (sensation and pleasant, unpleasant or neutral feeling), which leads to
- *tanha* (*trishna* in Sanskrit, craving, desire, thirst for pleasant and repulsion to unpleasant), which leads to
- *upadan* (clinging, attachment to phenomena, ego, life, ideology and so forth), which leads to
- *bhava* (the process of becoming the stream of conditioned existence), which leads to
- *jati* (rebirth, disease, decay, death, meeting the unpleasant, losing the pleasant), which leads to
- *dukha* (suffering).

Thus, the Buddhist paradigm suggests that the root cause of our suffering is ignorance.

The Eightfold Noble Path

The Buddhist practice is aimed at enlightenment and consists of several components. These are interdependent in the sense that one helps the other (Dwivedi, 1990).

- *sila* (*sheela* in Sanskrit) is morality. Buddhists should follow at least five precepts which include abstaining from killing of any sentient beings, stealing, sexual misconduct, speaking any falsehood and from using any intoxicants. Monks and nuns have more than two hundred precepts to follow. The Buddhist precepts can be divided into three subgroups as follows: (a) right speech, (b) right action, (c) right livelihood.
- *samadhi* (concentration of mind). There are 40 objects that can be used for meditation. The commonest technique used however, is *anapan,* which involves focussing attention on one's breath as described

later in this chapter. It involves the following three steps: (a) right effort, (b) right mindfulness, (c) right *samadhi*.

- *panya* (*pragnya* in Sanskrit) is Wisdom: (a) right thought, contemplation or aspiration (*sankappa*); (b) right view or understanding (*ditthi*).

The Buddhist texts explain and elaborate these components in detail.

The two dimensions of Buddhism

Buddhism has two fundamental dimensions: a dimension of wisdom, philosophical maturity, understanding, insight, freedom from subjectivity, and so forth, and the other of compassion or spontaneous activity in accordance with the needs of living beings.

Wisdom

Wisdom is a product of experiential realization of the following:

- *Anicha.* All phenomena are transitory in nature and therefore impermanent. Everything is in a melting pot, in an eternal flux, in the process of becoming.
- *Anatta.* There is nothing substantial. Therefore there is no ultimate reality, no God, no soul.
- *Dukha.* Since all phenomena are incomplete, unsubstantial and unsatisfactory, their non-awareness leads to *dukha* or suffering.

The experience of selfhood or personhood is a product of five groups (*khandhas* or aggregates) of transitory phenomena. These are:

- *rupa* (form, matter);
- *vedana* (feeling);
- *sankhar* (*sanskar* in Sanskrit) (volitional tendencies);
- *sanya* (perception);
- *vinyan* (consciousness).

The sense of 'self' is a product of illusory mental processes (Dwivedi, 1994a, 1994b). These mental events, according to the Buddha, take place in terms of *khanas* or mind moments, there being 17×10^{21} such *khanas* within the wink of an eye. It is the rapidity of the mental processes that creates the illusion of continuity, the sense of 'I', the sense of solidity of relationships, feelings and so on. Today one can illustrate this with the example of a fan or a cartoon film. When we see a stationary-ceiling fan, we see three distinct blades, which can create the illusion of merging into one in a fast moving fan. Similarly, when we watch a cartoon film we see beings and their movements although these are only still drawings that are projected rapidly onto the screen.

Attachment to this sense of self, self-grasping or self-cherishing is therefore natural and inherent in our lives. We are always busy taking things personally, flagging ourselves up with self-expression, self-assertion, autonomy, independence and heading towards narcissism. It is this natural tendency, produced by illusory processes, that is the root cause of all our suffering, but it is not easy to cut through these illusory processes. In order to become disillusioned or enlightened, an extra effort is needed to resist this very strong current.

There is an emphasis in Buddhism on experiential knowledge, understanding and wisdom about the above. Meditation is aimed at developing this knowledge. Moral living helps to develop the concentration of mind that is essential for the development of knowledge.

Compassion

Compassion comes about by the understanding of universal nature of suffering and processes involved. This can be further cultivated by practice of four *brahma viharas* (or sublime dwellings):

- *metta* (loving kindness);
- *karuna* (compassion);
- *mudita* (sympathetic joy);
- *upekkha* (equanimity).

Phases of Buddhism in India

A large number of schools of Buddhism arose after the death of the Buddha. Revival of Hinduism also led to an interchange of ideas and practices between Hinduism and Buddhism. Roughly speaking, Buddhism survived in India for 1500 years (from the fifth century BC to the tenth century AD) until the Muslim invasion and passed through three important stages, each of roughly 500 years.

The *hinayana* tradition or the Old Wisdom School aimed at individual enlightenment or salvation and emphasized the value of disciplined monastic life. After 200 years of Buddha's *nirvana* it split into *theravada* in the east of India and *sarvastivada* in the west of India. They differed in their systematic elaboration of analytical psychology or *abhidhamma* (*abhidharma* in Sanskrit) – see below.

The *mahayana* tradition aimed at universal enlightenment or salvation and emphasized the value of household life. This liberal attitude was criticized by the Hinayanies as a symptom of laziness whereas *mahayana* criticized the *hinayana* tradition for rigidity. After 400 years the *mahayana* divided into different schools. Two major *mahayana* schools were the *madhyamika* school, which emphasized the notion of nothingness and 'void' and the *yogachar* school, which emphasized the value of practice and depths of experience.

The *vajrayana* or 'thunderbolt' tradition, or *tantra* emerged as an esoteric shortcut.

Tipitaka

The canonical Buddhist scriptures consist of many volumes. They are referred to as Tipitaka, meaning 'three basketfuls'. The *pali tipitaka* contains scriptures of one of the *hinyana* schools, the *theravadins*. Today it can be obtained in the Roman script as well on a CD ROM. It is divided into three groups.

- *sutta pitak* of Buddha's sermons;
- *vinaya pitak* of rules of Buddhist order;
- *abhidhamma pitak* or further systematization of Buddhist psychology.

Like the periodic table of elements in chemistry, *abhidhamma* analyses all the subjective phenomena into elemental categories (*dhammas*), such as

- *rupa* or matter (28 elements);
- Chitta or mind or mental states (89);
- Chetasika or factors associated with Chitta (52).

The process of perception (*chitta*) takes 17 *khanas* or 'mind-moments' (a measure of time, as described above). When an object strikes through the sense door, the *bhavanga* (unconscious) is stirred for two *khanas* and in the second *khana* the unconscious is cut off. The third *khana* is that of attention, the fourth of sensation, the fifth of assimilation, the sixth of discrimination and the seventh of determination. Cognition takes place in the eighth to fourteenth *khanas* and registration in the fifteenth and sixteenth *khanas,* followed by a *khana* of rest before the next chain of perception begins.

The scriptures of other *hinayana* schools are partly preserved in Sanskrit and Chinese, but a large number of them are lost. The oldest catalogue (518 AD) of Chinese *tipitaka* mentions 2113 works, of which 276 are still in existence (Conze, 1960).

The spread of Buddhism

After the death of the Buddha, a conference was held in Rajagrih in India under the chairmanship of Kashyap to recite all the Buddha's teachings. The second conference was held after a century in Vaishali and the third conference was held in the third century BC in Pataliputra under the chairmanship of Tissa during the reign of Emperor Ashoka. Ashoka came to the throne in 270 BC. He was the grandson of Chandragupta Maurya, the Emperor of India, who combined a large number of states and defeated the Greek forces. Ashoka became a Buddhist, patronized Buddhism and was instrumental in its spread in India and abroad. In the history of the world, he must have been the most compassionate and efficient ruler. He established huge public hospitals not only for human beings but also for animals, postal services, highways and so on. He sent missionaries to Sri Lanka, Burma, Egypt, Syria and elsewhere, which led to establishment of Buddhism in these countries and others. Buddhism reached China in the first century BC, Korea in the fourth century AD, Japan in the sixth century, Tibet in the seventh century and Mongolia in thirteenth century.

Nalanda was one of the greatest universities in India from the second to the ninth centuriues AD. According to the Chinese traveller, Miuen Tsiang, who visited India in the seventh century, the University of Nalanda had 8500 students and 1500 were resident in the university. The students came from India, Japan, Korea, China, Mongolia and elsewhere and were free to choose any lectures from 100 lectures delivered every day.

Zen is a Japanese term derived from Chinese *chan,* Sanskrit *dhyan,* or Pali *jhan* meaning meditation. Zen is a way of transcending the intellect, of leaping from thinking to knowing and of directly experiencing the One Mind. Its origin is traced to the incident when Buddha, instead of speaking in front of his audience, held a golden flower in silence. Only Mahakashyapa, famed for his austerity, understood the meaning of the Buddha's action and smiled. Thus, Mahakashyapa is known as the first Indian Patriarch of the *zen* school and Bodhidharma of Kanjivaram, Madras was the 28th Indian Patriarch. He took *zen* to China across the sea in 520 AD and became the first Chinese Patriarch. It reached Japan in the twelfth century.

In about 500 AD, the development of *tantra* in Hinduism furthered the growth of a magical form of Buddhism (tantric Buddhism), which expected full enlightenment from magical practices. It became very influential in Nepal, Tibet, China, Japan, Java and Sumatra. Tantra has two major schools: right-handed (school of secrets) and left-handed (*vajrayana*). *Vajrayana* was founded by the second Nagarjuna (600–650 AD). The tantric practices include spells, gestures, dances and meditation on the *mandala* of deities – involvement of all aspects of our being (body, speech and mind). By the seventh century, Tantra was established in India both in Hinduism (Shaivism) and Buddhism. Tantra uses passion as a vehicle of salvation. By the tenth century the *kalachakra* form of Tantra developed in India with the notion of primordial or *adi* Buddha. Padma Sambhava, a Professor from Nalanda University, took Tantra to Tibet and established Red Cap Buddhism in 749 AD. Milarepa (1052–1135) expounded the teachings through mystic songs. The yellow cap school (with the Dalai Lama as its spiritual head) was founded in Tibet in the fifteenth century as an adherent of *madhyamika* school. The black cap school in Tibet was a combination of Buddhism and the traditional Bon magic of Tibet.

Meditation

The Buddhist texts describe different levels of absorptive states. Stage I consists of initial and sustained attention, rapture, bliss and singleness of mind. Stage VIII consists of singleness of mind, equanimity and neither perception nor non-perception. These are relevant to extremely advanced meditators. For an ordinary student a number of techniques are available to assist him or her to begin meditation. The objects for meditative awareness are often classified in four groups:

● body (parts, posture, movement, etc.)
● *vedana* (sensations, feelings, etc.)
● mental states (mood, mode of thoughts, etc.)
● mental objects (thoughts, etc.)

In the UK, there are a number of centres from different schools of Buddhism that offer training in meditation.

The *vipassana* technique (based on the *theravada* school) taught at the International Meditation centre in Wiltshire, is taught through standard residential meditation courses. Each course is of 10 days duration. One begins by undergoing the formalities such as taking the precepts and practising *Anapan*. This involves focusing attention on one's breathing. The focus is on the actual sensation of the air touching the nostrils and any sensations arising at the focusing point. This helps to cultivate a calm and penetrative mind. From the fifth day onwards such a developed mind is used experientially to examine the mind–body phenomenon and develop wisdom, knowledge and understanding as described above. One starts obtaining glimpses of illusory processes that create the impression of permanence, solidity, agency and entity. It is like appreciating the fact that the movement or continuity seen on the cinema screen of a cartoon film is nothing but an illusory outcome of rapidly projected still pictures. This helps one to better manage one's feelings and relationships (Dwivedi, 1989, 1992, 1993a).

Religious influence on social structures

According to the Indian ideology, our natural tendency of attachment to the sense of self (self-grasping or self-cherishing) produced by the illusory processes is the root cause of all our suffering. However, it is not easy to cut through these illusory processes and an extra effort is needed in every aspect of life, ranging from meditative practices to getting on with extended family life. The natural tendency of love is to flow towards one's own husband, wife, child and so on. This can easily break an extended family into nuclear families. An extended family can survive only if this love is redirected across nuclear boundaries by transcending narcissistic tendencies.

In such an extended family system it is possible to find parents who will offer affection, food, play materials and so on to the children of others in the extended family before offering them to their own. They may even refer to another's child as their child and their child as another's child. The ideology that 'love grows in hiding' also takes away the pressure to show or prove one's love.

In Indian culture, the parenting of young children tends to take place in such a way that the growing child deeply experiences the dependability of parents, extended family and the community (Roland, 1980). There is therefore an atmosphere of indulgence, physical closeness, common sleeping arrangements, immediate gratification of physical and emotional needs and a very prolonged babyhood. In their latency period, children are then helped to heighten their sensitivity to other people's feelings and to improve their capacity for containing and regulating their own feelings. In contrast with the Western value system, self-expression or expression of opinions that define and heighten the sense of one's self is not seen as a desirable goal. This attitude of aiming to transcend 'self-cherishing' is derived from the well-formulated philosophical system that lies at the heart of such a culture's wisdom (Dwivedi, 1994c, 1996a, and 1996b).

Thus, sensitive child-rearing practices can mediate greater inner emotional strength, supportive social structures and help-giving networks, and can offer better protection against mental health problems in children and their families (Kallarackal and Herbert, 1976; Hackett, Hackett and Taylor, 1991; Roberts and Cawthorpe, 1995).

In Britain

The majority of Hindus in Britain are of Indian origin. Many had initially migrated mainly from Gujarat in India to East Africa and then came to the UK. Families that have migrated to the UK may find it difficult to celebrate many of the traditional Indian festivals such as the festival of colours, the festival of lights, *pongal/sankranti* and so on. However, many towns and cities have Hindu Associations, temples, and community centres and try to organize celebrations of some of the Indian festivals, and also weddings, cultural programmes, language and religious classes, recreation, sport and leisure activities and so on. The Swami Narayan temple of marbles in London was recently built and is exquisitely artistic as well as a place for worship. The Krishna consciousness movement is essentially a Western movement and has a membership mainly of Western Hindus. However, Hindus of Indian origin also support it.

The majority of Jains in the UK are also of Indian origin, many of whom have migrated from East Africa. Some Jain temples and associations have also been formed. In contrast to Hindus and Jains, the majority of Buddhists in the UK are of Western origin or from Sri Lanka, Burma and the Far East. There are some Buddhists of Indian origin as well, mainly from the Ambedkar movement. Many towns and cities have Buddhist Societies. These are usually umbrella organizations and the membership may include people interested in any school of Buddhism. Their meetings often include a short period of meditation and talks. Several of these, such as the Buddhist Society of London, run extensive courses on Buddhism. There is a UK Buddhist Studies Association, a Network of Engaged Buddhists and the Friends of Western Buddhist Order. The Buddhism Psychology and Psychiatry Group (BPPG) is chaired by one of the authors (KND).

In addition to the Buddhist Societies there are many Buddhist centres for systematically learning and practising meditation. These centres usually belong to a specific school of Buddhism and may have resident monks and/or nuns. Some examples are Amarawati Buddhist Monastery and Chithurst Buddhist Monastery in the Thai tradition; the International Meditation Centre, the Vipassana Trust and the Birmingham Buddhist Vihara in the Burmese tradition; and the Jamyang Buddhist Centre, the Kagyu Samye Ling Centre, the Holy Island Centre and the Tibet Foundation in the Tibetan tradition. Many of these and others have formed the Network of Buddhist Organizations. There is a Dharma School in Brighton. The Pali Text Society works on Pali texts for their translation and publication. There are several journals available on Buddhism as well, such as *The Middle Way, Buddhism Now* and *Tricycle*.

Helping families

In helping ethnic minority families it is essential for the professionals not only to be aware of their culture but also to be sensitive to it. Mental health professionals may unwittingly set up culturally insensitive services for ethnic minorities and wait for them to come. When the services are not taken up by the ethnic minority families, the professionals wonder why (Sue and Sue, 1990).

In a multicultural society, there are people belonging to cultures that may be many thousands of years old living side-by-side with people belonging to cultures that are just a few centuries old. Their cultural differences can manifest in many different ways. Virtually all aspects of human behaviour are influenced by culture. For example, in Indian culture, food is not just food: emotions are also grounded in it and the attitude towards food and feeding are influenced by the well-established ideologies around the theory of *rasa, karma* and of non-self-cherishing (Dwivedi, forthcoming). The medicinal values of traditional Indian foods have also been explored by the ancient Indian medical system (*ayurveda*) and are again being studied with the help of modern science, with very encouraging results (Dwivedi, S., 1996; Rai and Dwivedi, 1988).

Another example would be to picture a family therapy session with an Indian family with a therapist conditioned by the Western value systems. The therapist will naturally look for overt affectionate behaviour within the session as evidence of love between the family members. However, the family may be conditioned to express their deep love for each other by hiding it, especially in front of onlookers! Similarly, in an assessment of parenting, the parents and the professionals may have very different values attached to commercial play materials or transitional objects (Dwivedi, 1996d).

Children from the ethnic minorities are exposed to stresses that can affect any child, such as financial matters, health issues, demanding school-work, distressing life events, relationships with others, and social conflicts (Dwivedi and Varma, 1997a, 1997b; Dwivedi, 1998; Stewart-Brown, 1998). The children from ethnic minorities can also experience two other sources of stress, one related to their dislocated family background and the other to racism (Dwivedi, 1993b). In a culture where the emotional support from one's extended family, especially in times of stress, is an essential ingredient of any coping strategy, the fact of migration and dislocation deprives many ethnic minority families from that healing support. Racism, leading to poor wages, night shifts, long working hours, overcrowding and bad housing, increases the risk of health problems and impact on children's psychological development (Braun, 1997). Racism also undermines their culture, identity and self-image. It may leave children and their families feeling hopeless when they experience bullying and racial abuse in schools, playgrounds and other places. Racism denigrates and dehumanizes communities, lowering their self-esteem, and increasing their sense of worthlessness and depression (Fernando, 1991). Ahmed (1986) has highlighted that in the very fabric of British society there are subconscious assumptions about the superiority of Western childrearing practices and denigration of others. Ethnic minority cultures are often described in ways that make them seem bizarre or backward (Mares, Henley and Baxter, 1985). Many professionals, having been conditioned in such a value system, may see relationships, for example, in an Indian extended family, as rather 'oppressive' and stifling. Split off, abusive aspects from Victorian cultural times may be projected on to such families, and professionals may become passionately involved in rescuing Asian youngsters from their so-called 'primitive' and 'oppressive' family values. Self-poisoning by a number of adolescent Asian girls, for example, as a product of projective identification, symbolizes the acting out of the view of the dominant group that the minority is 'harmful or poisonous' (Goldberg and Hodes, 1992).

The professionals may also act as if the minority communities never had anything like psychotherapeutic approaches until Western science came along and invented it (Sue and Sue, 1990). Many cultures have an extensive body of therapeutic knowledge and practices to deal with problems involving relationships, feelings and mental health (Dwivedi, 1980,

1997). For example, the Indian literature of 500 BC contains a very sophisticated, coherent, advanced and systematic treatment of the nature of consciousness, not found in modern Western science until the nineteenth century (Reat, 1990). De Silva (1984) has compiled an interesting account of many of the therapeutic interventions available in the Buddhist literature.

References

Adidevananda, Swami (1993) Brahmasutragalu, a commentary in Kannada, Mysore, India: Sri Ramakrishna Ashrama.

Ahmed S (1986) Cultural racism in work with Asian women and girls. In S Ahmed, J Cheetham, J Small (eds) Social Work with Black Children and their Families. London: Batsford, pp 140–54.

Bavisi B (1998) Jainism: Fundamentals of Jainism. http://www.angelfire.com/co/jainism

Bharilla H (1998) Dashalakshanurata. http://www.jainworld.com/phil/dasl.htm

Braun, D.(1997) 'Parent education programmes'. In K.N. Dwivedi (Ed.) Enhancing Parenting Skills. Chichester: John Wiley

Conze E (1960) Buddhism. Oxford: Bruno Cassiror.

De Silva P (1984) Buddhism and behaviour modification. Behaviour Research and Therapy 22(6): 661–78.

Dwivedi KN (1980) Indian notions in counselling situations. BAC Counselling News 32: 10–14.

Dwivedi KN (1989) Medical benifits of concentrated mind. ODA News Review 2(6): 16.

Dwivedi KN (1990) Purification of mind by vipassana meditation. In J Crook, D Fontana (eds) Space in Mind. Shaftesbury: Element, 86–91.

Dwivedi KN (1992) Eastern approaches to mental health. In T Naidu, A Webb-Johnson (eds) Concepts of Mental Health in the Asian Community. London: Confederation of Indian Organizations (UK), pp. 24–30.

Dwivedi KN (1993a) Emotional development. In KN Dwivedi (ed.) Group Work with Children and Adolescents. London: Jessica Kingsley.

Dwivedi KN (1993b) Coping with unhappy children who are from ethnic minorities. In VP Varma (ed.) Coping with Unhappy Children. London: Cassell, pp. 134–51.

Dwivedi KN (1994a) Mental cultivation (meditation) in Buddhism. Psychiatric Bulletin 18: 503–4.

Dwivedi KN (1994b) The Buddhist perspective in mental health. Open Mind 70: 20–1.

Dwivedi KN (1994c) Social structures that support or undermine families from ethnic minority groups: Eastern value systems. Context 20: 11–12.

Dwivedi KN (1996a) Culture and personality. In KN Dwivedi and VP Varma (eds) Meeting the Needs of Ethnic Minority Children. London: Jessica Kingsley.

Dwivedi KN (1996b) Race and the child's perspective. In: R Davie, G Upton, V Varma (eds) The Voice of the Child: A Handbook for Professionals. London: Falmer Press.

Dwivedi KN (1996c) Children from ethnic minorities. In V Varma (ed.) Coping with Children in Stress. Aldershot: Arena Publishers.

Dwivedi KN (1996d) Meeting the needs of ethnic minority children. Transcultural Mental Health on-line (http://www.priory.com/journals/chneeds.htm).

Dwivedi KN (1997) (ed.) The Therapeutic Use of Stories. London: Routledge.

Dwivedi KN (eds) (in press). Post traumatic Stress Disorder in Children and Adolescents. London: Whurr.

Dwivedi KN, (forthcoming) Cross Cultural Issues in Feeding Problems. In A Schwartz, A Southall (eds) Getting the Whole Picture, Different Perspectives on Childhood Feeding. Oxford: Radcliffe Medical Press.

Dwivedi KN, Varma VP (eds) (1997a) Depression in Children and Adolescents. London: Whurr.

Dwivedi KN, Varma VP (eds) (1997b) A Handbook of Childhood Anxiety Mangagement. Aldershot: Arena Publishers.

Dwivedi S (1996) Putative use of Indian cardio-vascular friendly plants in preventive cardiology. Annual National Medical Academy of Medical Sciences (India) 32(3/4): 159–75.

Fernando S (1991) Mental Health, Race and Culture. London: Macmillan.

Goldberg D, Hodes M (1992) The poison of racism and the self poisoning of adolescents. Journal of Family Therapy 14, 51–67.

Hackett L, Hackett R, Taylor DC (1991) Psychological disturbance and its association in the children of the Gujarati community. Journal of Child Psychology and Psychiatry 32: 851–6.

Kallarackal AM, Herbert M (1976) The happiness of Indian immigrant children. New Society 26 February: 422–4.

Jagmohan S (1998) Restore the lost dynamic of Hinduism, Indian Express, 02 January 1998, Indian Express Group of Publications.

Lin P. Jainism (1998) http://www.intranet.csupomana.edu/~plin/ews430/jain1.html

Malaiya YK, Jainism: Principles, Traditions and Practices (1997) http://www.cs.colostate.edu/~malaiya/jainhlinks.html

Mares P, Henley A, Baxter C (1985) Health Care in Multicultural Britain. Cambridge: Health Education Council and National Extension College.

Rai PH, Dwivedi KN (1988) The value of 'Parhej' and 'sick role' in Indian Culture. Journal of the Institute of Health Education 16(2): 56–61.

Reat NR (1990) Origins of Indian Psychology. Berkeley CA: Asian Humanities Press.

Roberts N, Cawthorpe D(1995) Immigrant child and adolescent psychiatric referrals: a five year retrospective study of Asian and Caucasian families. Canadian Journal of Psychiatry 40: 252–56.

Roland A (1980) Psychoanalytic perspectives on personality development in India. International Review of Psychoanalysis 1: 73–87.

Stewart-Brown S (1998) Evidence based child mental health promotion: the role of parenting programmes. In KN Dwivedi (ed.) Evidence Based Child Mental Health Care. Northampton: Child and Adolescent Mental Health Service.

Sue DW, Sue D (1990) Counselling the Culturally Different. New York: John Wiley.

Surishwarji, Acharya Sri Rajyash (1998). Festivals bring people closer, The Hindu, 21 August 1998, pp 24.

Vivekananda, Swami (1978) Raja-Yoga or Conquering the Internal Nature, Advaita Ashrama, Calcutta: Advaitaaa Ashram.

Chapter 5
The Muslim community: beliefs and practices

ALI EL-HADI

Muslims worldwide and in the West:

Today it is estimated that there are one billion Muslims in the world. There are 44 Muslim nations – one in four nations in total. There are large Muslim minorities in non-Muslim countries such as China and Russia. In Britain there are 1.5 million Muslims. There are 6 million in Western Europe. There are 1000 mosques in Britain and the same number in France.

The Muslims in Britain are predominantly Asian immigrants from Pakistan, India, Bangladesh and East Africa. Much smaller groups come from the Middle East, Turkey, Malaysia and Indonesia. The majority of Muslims in Britain are permanently settled here. A minority are a floating population of university students.

During the last three decades big social changes have taken place in the British Muslim community. So, whereas in the 1950s and 1960s the majority were men who came to work, now there is a preponderance of families. The average Muslim family is still larger than its British counterpart, but there is evidence that this is changing (McDermott and Ahsan, 1986).

Faced with the diversity of Muslim societies, writers suggest categorizations such as Moroccan Islam, or Pakistani Islam. For Ahmed (1988) such categorization is an easy way out, a distortion, and a gross simplification. In his view 'Muslims are the same everywhere and yet their societies are different everywhere'.

For Al-Azmeh (1993) there are as many Islams as there are situations to sustain them, and the presumptions of Muslim cultural homogeneity and continuity do not correspond to social reality. Therefore, Muslim reality in Britain is composed of many realities, some structural and some organizational and institutional. Said (1993) believes that European Islam has been

represented as a cohesive, homogenous, invariant force, an 'otherness' –
enough to be conceived of as a historical enemy.

> It is very much the case today in dealing with the Islamic world – all one billion
> people in it, with dozens of different societies, half a dozen major languages
> including Arabic, Turkish, Iranian, all of them spread over about a third of the
> globe – American and British intellectuals speak reductively and, in my opinion
> irresponsibly of some thing called 'Islam'.

Kabani (1989) gives a more personal account of growing up in a
Muslim society:

> I am keenly aware of the privilege I enjoyed in a region where the majority is
> very poor. Yet I believe that what I have in common with less fortunate women
> from Morocco, or Pakistan or Bradford transcends class difference and is
> greater than what separates us.

South Asian perspective

South Asia is home for 40% of the total Muslim population. As an area it is
dynamic, and crucial to Islam worldwide. South Asian Muslims have
played a crucial role in modern Islamic renaissance. Influential thinkers
such as Iqbal, Azad and Mawdoodi are South Asian. Renowned authors
such as Faiz Ahmed, the Urdu poet and Salman Rushdie are also south
Asian. In the field of sport there are household names such as Imran
Khan, and the Khan brothers.

In India, Islam faced an interesting challenge in its encounter with
Hinduism – a polytheistic and ancient religion. This was unlike the
encounter with Christianity, another monotheistic religion, in Europe and
the Middle East, which led to clear divisions. In South Asia the clash
remains inconclusive. So whereas Islam's relationship with Christianity
has been marked by clear confrontation, as is evident in Europe and some
parts of the Middle East, the encounter with Hinduism led to mutual synthesis, adaptation and accommodation. Evidence for this can be found in
numerous instances where a building changed from a temple to a mosque
and vice versa. In one case, that of a mosque in Delhi, as the plaster
peeled, elephant heads and lotus flowers, usually found in Hindu temples, were revealed.

In India the Mughal Muslim Empire spanned three centuries
(1526–1857). Some historians regard the Mughals as the ideal Muslim
rulers. It is likely that they also saw themselves as champions of Islam
judging by their titles – for example, Jahangir's title Nur al-din, light of
religion, Shah Jahan's title Shihab al-din, star of religion and Aurangazeb's
Muhyi al-din. Evidence of synthesis between Islam, the new religion, and
Hinduisim, the established one, can also be found in rituals such as death

rituals. Further evidence is the way ideas about and beliefs in migration of the souls, astrology and caste became part of daily life. Such ideas are quite foreign to Islam.

Several factors led to the demise of the Mughal Muslim Empire in the eighteenth century. Some also led to the demise of other empires like the Ottoman Empire, and the Saffavids – for example, size and poor communication. Another factor – one that perhaps characterizes Muslim societies – is a struggle between two seemingly opposing forces. One can be described as orthodox, legalistic, formal, whereas the second is informal, mystic and syncretic A perennial struggle and a dilemma facing Muslim rulers is a choice between Islamic purity or orthodoxy and syncretism and the inclusion of other religions and ideologies. Evidence of this conflict can be seen today, as a choice between drawing firm boundaries around Muslim societies or including other, non-Muslim groups in the definition of the nation. Pakistan's recent history is a testimony to this in the conflict between President Zia, representing orthodox forces, and Prime Minister Bhutto representing syncretic forces. Some writers believe it is a mistake or an oversimplification to view such forces as contradictory. They believe that they represent different aspects or faces of Islam.

The essence of Islam

Unlike most Western societies, where religion has been relegated to the place of worship only, in Muslim societies Islam has continued to pervade all aspects of life.

Kabani, writing about her Muslim upbringing, said 'it affected the way I viewed my parents and the neighbours, determined what we ate and drank, how we washed , how we dressed, how we spoke, how we saw the world, especially the non-Muslim world of the West' (Kabani, 1989).

Western writers view this as the inability of Muslims to accept the human origin of their religion, as ' Islam has not been secularized'. For some, this is seen as a source of great mystery. For a Muslim the choice is between being a Muslim or being 'nothing'.

The word 'Islam' in Arabic is derived from *istislam*, which means 'submission' – so, in other words, it means submission to God. It is also related to another word *salam*, which in Arabic means 'peace'. In essence Islam's central message is about peace, universalism, and brotherhood. The Islamic saying in Arabic *la ikrah fi al din* means 'there shall be no compulsion in religion'. Another relevant saying here is *lakum dinukum wa leydini*, which means your religion is for you and mine for me. Balance is an essential concept in Islam. It is the balance between *deen*, religion, and *dunnya*, world. Central to the Muslim ideal are the concepts of *al-adl*, equilibrium and *al-ahsan compassion*. There are two key elements in Islam – one book, the holy Quran, and one life, that of the Prophet Muhammed. Such simplicity might reflect its appeal.

The Quran

The Quran is a collection of divinely inspired utterances and discourses. It has some 300 pages divided into chapters called Suras. 'The Quran' in Arabic is literally the 'discourse' or 'recitation'. The general tone is sombre and meditative, it is written as a dialogue between God and humanity. The different and successive messages reflect different moods, they carry warnings, advice, and exhortations. A recurring theme of the advice in the Quran is to do with *ilm,* (knowledge): it exhorts Muslims to use their minds and think. Most Muslims uncritically accept the Quran as 'the speech of God'. They dismiss any suggestion of possible contemporary literary influence. Some writers have commented on the similarity in style with the special elliptical quality of Bedouin speech known as *I'jz.* In response they argue that the Prophet, who was 40 at the time of the first revelation, was in fact illiterate. For some this further enhances the miraculous character of God's message.

It is tempting to see that the criticisms and attacks by Western orientalist writers on the authorship of the Quran are matched by idealizing descriptions of it by Muslim writers, as an 'inimitable symphony', the very sound of which moves men, and women to tears and ecstasy. For Muslims the power and sublimity of the Quran remains unchanged over centuries.

The five 'pillars' and obligatory duties of Islam are:

- *Al tauhid,* faith in one God.
- *Al-Salawat,* the daily prayers, five times a day.
- *Al-Siam,* fasting during the month of Ramadan.
- *Zakat,* annual redistribution of wealth to the poor section of society.
- The *Haj,* the pilgrimage to Makkah, a ritual emphasizing unity among Muslim Ummah.

The Prophet was born Muhammed Ibn Abdullah in 570 of the Benu Hashim of Quraish in the Caravan city of Mecca, in the Arabian Peninsula, now Saudi Arabia. The tribe of Quraish was the ruling tribe, enjoying wealth and power. They considered themselves aristocrats. His father, Abdullah, died before his birth; his mother Aminah died when he was six. He was left in the care of his grandfather Abdul Mutallib who died when he was eight. As a result he was left in the care of his uncle, Abu Talib.

Some writers believe that such childhood experiences – poverty and deprivation – may explain the Prophet's personal qualities – gentle affection for the weak and the underprivileged in society. In fact little of historical significance is known about his early life, apart from some accounts that are more of mythological than theological significance. Examples are encounters with holy men who recognized his spiritual destiny. Not surprisingly the figure of the Prophet has attracted both scathing attacks and idealization. It is difficult to find a fair and a realistic view of him. Orientalist Western writers from Voltaire to Gibbon and Dante have described him as 'amoral', 'debauched', a camel thief, and an antichrist. In contrast to this, Muslim writers describe him as the 'ideal man'. For example a Pakistani newspaper's editorial appeared on his birthday with headlines 'The Prophet: man or a miracle?' One researcher has found 2713 biographical books about the Prophet in Pakistani languages. Recently Western views and perceptions have become more realistic, even positive. One study placed him in the 100 most influential persons in history. I think the recent controversy surrounding Rushdie's *Satanic Verses* highlights Muslims' sensitivity to Western criticisms of the figure of the Prophet, his life and family. The Prophet's name, Muhammed, is probably the most popular name in the world. Muhammed, in Arabic, is derived from the root *hmd* meaning 'praise', so it means 'the praiseworthy'.

In time the Prophet's sayings and traditions, *Hadith,* came to be accepted as the truth by Muslims. The Imam Bukhari collected 7300 *hadiths* in 97 books. Collecting *hadith* became an Islamic science. The problem is establishing the authenticity of a *hadith.* There are an estimated one million known *hadiths.* The Prophet's actions and customs are called *Sunna.* Muslims are sometimes referred to as *Ahlesunna* or *Sunni,* which translates to the followers of *Sunna.* The *Sunna* includes a very wide range of Muslim responses and actions, from abstaining from alcohol and pigs' meat, colouring a man's beard with *henna,* to having green clothes and flags. For Sunni Muslims, the Prophet's actions are complemented by the actions of his companions, the first four Caliphs, who are called companions (*Sahaba*). For Muslims, the Prophet's and his companions' behaviour provides a template for correct Muslim behaviour in everyday life. This is seen by some as a way of dispensing with the need for priesthood. The Prophet was emphatic: 'There is no monkery in Islam.' However this does not mean that every action of Muslims is fixed forever. There are *hadiths* that advocate that Muslims use rational choice based on *Ijthad* (independent judgement), *shura* (consultation) and *ijma,* consensus.

For Muslims, there are significant points or lessons from the Prophet's life that highlight central Islamic values such as the universality of humanity transcending tribe, clan or race. An example is his marriages outside the clan, a central source of attack by Western critics who see them as debauchery. Some of his wives were neither kin nor of his social group. Maria was a slave girl. This was a way of forging alliances above tribalism. Another example is the Prophet's choice of Bilal, a black slave, for a very prestigious position of the first *muezzin* (the caller to prayer) of Islam.

The Islamic world view

The centrality of the Quran

The political vision of Islam is certainly an egalitarian or a socialist one about equality, tolerance and social justice. The Muslims' view of the world is moulded by their scripture – the Quran. Unlike Christian and Hebrew texts, which were translated into Latin, the Quran was not. For devout Muslims, the Quran is the 'speech of God' who chose to communicate his words in Arabic, so to translate it to another language is almost blasphemous. Therefore non-Arabic-speaking Muslims can only approach the Quran through Arabic, which remains to a large extent the main language of intra-Muslim communication. In comparison, to Christians the word of God was manifested in Christ's person, not in the language in which his speech was revealed. The Quran, as God 's revelation to mankind, is as central to Islam as Christ is to Christianity (Ruthven, 1984).

The final version of the Quran was not completed until a few years after the Prophet's death, during the caliphate of U'thman, the last of the four caliphs. For Arabic speakers, both Muslim and non-Muslim, the Quran is the perfection of the language. Arabic calligraphy, of mainly Quranic text, is a highly developed art form. One can hardly fail to notice posters, stickers of Quranic verses in Muslim homes, cars and shops in Britain. For Ruthven the Quran was designed for oral transmission. Indeed, public recitation of the Quran remains a central part of many public and social events, such as funerals, feasts and celebrations in Muslim communities. The professional Quran reciter, Muqrai, is a popular and respected figure – some have become very wealthy. Records and cassette recordings of popular Muqri are on sale in shops worldwide.

For Muslims, the sonorous, rhythmic prose of the Quran recitation by a Muqri is a source of aesthetic pleasure similar to the pleasure people experience from music or painting. Memorizing the Quran, the whole of its 120,000 words, is something to which good Muslims aspire. In the now growing number of Islamic schools in Britain, *mudrassh,* memorizing the Quran, is a central part of the curriculum. Most pupils, are non-Arabic-speaking school-aged children from Asian and African backgrounds.

Learning the Quran is central to learning Arabic. The organization of the Quran as a text, the lack of sequentiality in the chronology of the narrative, makes it accessible to almost everyone in Muslim society. Some believe that this is another way in which Islam managed to dispense with the need for priesthood.

Instead there is the *ulama,* a class and a group with superior knowledge of the Quran and its interpretation. For the average reader, many passages are obscure and cannot be understood without reference to the substantial body of interpretation *tafsir,* which is mostly derived from the *hadith* and oral traditions. In time, this body of literature became a source of law. So any of the prohibitions or prescriptions contained in the Quran can be given the force of law only by studying the occasion of the revelation.

A good example here is the prohibition on wine. There are three different Suras dealing with the subject of wine drinking and they seem to be contradictory. Only by tracing the chronology of the revelations on the subject, which is derived from the *hadith* literature, would it be possible to determine the injunction prohibiting the drinking of wine. The *tafsir*, like the Quran, contains a body of Arabic, Biblical, and Talmudic folklore. It also incorporates a wide range of popular culture, which makes it accessible to the Muslim masses and explains some cultural assumptions held in common with Christians and Jews. The Islamic ban on representational art perhaps drove the imagination into the footnotes. This could explain the development and proliferation of *tafsir*. This is akin to the development of Western painting as an imaginative evocation of biblical texts.

The Muslim God, *Allah*

For Muslims, God, Allah, is the God of the whole world, the 'creator of everything', the 'absolute sovereign' on earth. Only Allah has the power to create, destroy, save people's lives, or in any other way to control the fate of human beings.

Any attribution of magical or supernatural power to a lesser deity is regarded as *shirk* (disbelief) and *zaan* (conjecture). This is contrasted with *ilm* (knowledge). All *ilm* proceeds from Allah and leads back to him. The idea of God's 'uniqueness' challenges Christianity's idea that God could have a son. The God of the Quran is rather more abstract than that of the Old and New Testaments, and fatherhood is explicitly rejected. Allah is supra-personal rather than impersonal. Unlike the God of Greek philosophy, who stands aloof from mankind, Allah deeply involves himself in human affairs. The Quran uses numerous adjectives to describe Allah. The most frequent are two related adjectives: *al Rahman,* and *al Rahim,* which translate as 'the merciful', 'the compassionate'. This invocation *Besmallah,* in the 'name of God Al Rahman, Al Rahim' precedes most Suras in the Quran. Muslims use it before eating, embarking on a journey and other daily activities. According to the Quran, Allah's knowledge encompasses everything; in contrast man's knowledge can only ever be partial. Islam views the universe as firmly in the will of a divine caretaker who both stands apart from it and participates in the creation.

Quranic verses clearly command Muslims to be tolerant towards Jews, Christians, Hindus and Buddhists. This in part explains the relative tolerance accorded to other religious communities under Islamic governments.

Allah is both the creator of the universe and its ruler. Man's position in the cosmic system created by Allah is unique. He is an earthly creation, created out of dust and given domination over the earth and its creatures as God's 'vice-agent' Khalifa.

The Quranic' account of the fall of Satan, *Iblis,* is similar to the Bible's – he is punished for refusing to prostrate himself before Adam and Eve. The tale of Adam and Eve is also similar to the account in Genesis, but with a different emphasis. The act of disobedience is not dwelt upon.

Unlike the biblical account, where the expulsion from paradise is associated with a sense of shame and disgrace, Adam is immediately forgiven. His act is not seen so much the cause of 'original sin' but more as a consequence of his humanity.

While Allah is both omniscient and omnipotent, man is paradoxically endowed with free will and freedom of choice. Intellectually this has been a difficult issue for Islamic theology to resolve. Attempts by a rationalist sect, the Mu'tazillis, in the eighth and ninth centuries, to resolve it by limiting God's omnipotence were rejected.

Al-Ashari and followers attempted a synthesis by redefining man's free will as having the capacity to acquire, through an act of acceptance, the actions that God had created for him.

A devout Muslim's stand is one of both respect towards and fear of Allah. He or she should be able to 'marvel' at and celebrate God's wrath. As Islam implies an act of submission, a Muslim is expected to submit to Allah's governance. Such an act of surrender involves giving up autonomy on behalf of the individual self. The subjective experience of such surrender is called *iman* or faith – it is a voluntary act of existential commitment to God. There are two main negative values in the Islamic world view: *kufr* (disbelief) and *jahl* (ignorance). The Quranic text uses the term *kufr* to describe those who deny or conceal the truth as revealed to them through Allah's messages. In common and colloquial Arabic, the term *kafer* is used to refer to Christians, Jews and pagans. The concept of *jahl* (ignorance) is seen as the root cause of *kufr*, its opposite is *ilm*, which means 'knowledge'. A person who is in a state of *jahl* is typically arrogant, quick tempered, hot blooded, or someone who surrenders himself to violent passions. A state of *jahl* implies an inability to achieve mastery over one's passions, which distorts judgement. A *jahil* (a person in a state of ignorance) is incapable of recognizing the truth of God's signs and is given frequently to stepping over the boundaries of behaviour set by God. Such values form the ethical vision of Islam, and are given a positive legal content.

The Quran only sketches out certain rituals and rules of social behaviour. However, scholars and lawyers of the first centuries of Islam elaborated rituals observed by contemporary Muslims and rules used by them, and they have become the basis of *Sharia* law.

Islamic moral values and beliefs

The Islamic notion of 'good' is *alma'ruf* meaning the known, the opposite of *almunkar*, the unknown. The Islamic ethical vision integrates this notion of the known or familiar way of doing things as positive and socially approved. The opposite, the unknown or the unfamiliar way, is socially disapproved – it is seen to be outside established customs. The notion of the 'known' or 'familiar' is developed and evolves into the concept of the ma'ruf which forms the basis of *fiqh*, jurisprudence, the essence of which is a simply socially conservative morality, which emphasizes the observance of the paths of ancestral morality, not straying into contemporary or modern ways.

In common with Christians and Jews, Muslims believe in life after death and the Day of Judgment. Some of the Quranic Suras and sayings of the Prophet give a remarkable description of the last hour, the Day of Judgement. In keeping with the belief in divine law, if God is the original legislator, he must be the final court of appeal. The verses describe the horrors of hell graphically, as well as the joy of heaven, which is extensively described as a place of palpable luxuries and sensuous joys.

Such accounts attracted criticisms from medieval Christian writers for their explicit eroticism. In response, Muslim commentators point out that the descriptions are allegorical. Both Islamic ethics and the belief in divine law binding human behaviour militate against the split or division of the world into ordinary and spiritual. The Islamic message is life-affirming in its concern with the details of daily living; it integrates the ordinary with the transcendental. Socially and politically, Islamic ideals involve a commitment to the cause of human freedom. It is an existential view that aims to liberate human consciousness from attachment to objects and possessions. It discourages tribalism and nationalism and advocates Islamic universalism. This is consistent with the view of the 'Divine' as a unifying reality.

Generally, the rules laid down in the Quran – for example, to do with marriage and social conduct – are more like guidelines. They reflect the wider social and geographical context of the eighth century Arabian peninsula. Such rules are not appropriate to present day life in, for example, Western Europe. It is consistent with the vision of Islam that they must be adapted or modified to suit the individual Muslim cultural and social context. Matters such as dress codes and rules regarding diet are good examples. In recent times, what has been described as 'Islamic revival' among Muslim communities in the West has been characterized by undue emphasis on such things as the rules of dress. This reflects insecurity, particularly among young Muslims, about their identity. Al-Azmeh describes such behaviour as taking on an aspect of psychodrama, with the creation or invention of a 'culture' bordering on the exotic with too much emphasis on such things as dress and exhibitionistic piety (Al-Azmeh, 1993). Unfortunately this has created a false impression of Islam as a religion of legalism backed by a harsh medieval punishment, obscuring the central message of Islam. Such a message is much broader and has a universal appeal – that man is not the Lord of the universe. It is about the limits of human knowledge and permissible human behaviour – that it is for different societies and different generations to decide for themselves how to define such limits. The Quran contains only guidelines to such limits; it cannot define them absolutely (Ruthven, 1984).

Family life and social behaviour

On the whole, Muslim societies are still organized along traditional lines and in keeping with socially conservative values. Muslim communities in the West, certainly in Britain, reflect the prevailing social attitudes in the societies or countries where British Muslims originally came from, such as Pakistan, India and the Middle East. However, there are noticeable changes among second-generation Muslims, who have been involved in a process of defining themselves and their identity as British Muslims. They have been adapting the practices and customs handed down by their parents, the first generation immigrants, to suit their new and different Western, British context. The results are very diverse and varied social forms and lifestyles, which defy any attempt at describing in general terms. So the following is an account of some of the broad aspects of family and social life.

Muslim societies are organized by a different set of social values from those that are central to Western industrial societies. Such values can be loosely described as 'interdependence' and 'connectedness', rather than 'independence' and 'individuality'. Family and kinship relationships are central to social organization; greater emphasis is placed on family ties and loyalty, rather than individual autonomy.

Case example 1

Shahid, an 18-year-old, was referred by his GP with complaints of depression and difficulty getting on with his parents. He had been studying for A levels at the time of the referral, and one of the presenting problems, it later emerged, was that he was not coping academically. Shahid was one of three children in an Asian Muslim family. He had professional middle-class parents with high aspirations for their children. In the family interviews, it emerged that Shahid's ideas about his future were at odds with those of his parents. His father wanted Shahid to follow his own profession so that he could eventually join him in his practice. He could not accept that Shahid was not sufficiently motivated or did not have the ability to do so. He kept arranging for him to attend further courses to encourage him and prepare him to resit the A level examinations. During the discussion, the father stated that it was his responsibility to ensure that his son achieved his full potential and that he has a respectable profession. The parents did debate and argue at length about the financial and emotional demands facing them. It emerged that they believed and expected that they would not only have to support their children to go on to higher education, but that they would have to provide them with suitable accommodation – buying each of them a flat, and eventually helping them find a suitable partner. A contentious issue between the couple was that the father had been financially helping his own mother and sister who had recently arrived in Britain – he had bought them a house. The mother objected that he was putting his own family before their children. The father felt it was his duty to his own mother as her only son. The father could not accept that Shahid wanted to take time off from studying, drop out and travel. Shahid's dilemma was that he wanted to enjoy the privileges and comforts his parents offered him but he felt trapped by their expectations of him. So while complaining about their unrealistic expectations, he still asked them to pay for his expensive holidays with his friends and his mobile phone. In fact he did get into a lot of debt, and expected them to rescue him financially.

The Western-trained professional or therapist might find the parents' expectation of their roles – and their beliefs about young people conforming and complying with parental wishes – difficult to deal with. Early on in his work with Shahid and his parents, the therapist in this case had to recognize the dangers of allying himself with Shahid's position in his efforts to gain some autonomy and independence, and the dangers of pathologizing the parents' behaviour. Instead he had to maintain a position of curiosity and interest towards both positions and help them explore their dilemma. Eventually, both sides realized that they had to compromise in order to find a way out of the impasse. The parents needed to recognize that their beliefs about parenting and their expectations of their relationships with their son, although consistent with their own family experience and upbringing, were from a different cultural context. Their son had grown up in a different cultural context with different expectations, and that an 18-year-old is entitled to have the freedom to choose and make decisions about his life.

It is important here to bear in mind that, in Muslim countries, economic and social factors rather than religious or spiritual factors are responsible for such differences. Most Muslim societies are still less industrial and less urban than Western ones. The large Muslim communities in Britain such as the Bangladeshis in east London or the Pakistanis in Bradford have rural origins in both Sylhet in Bangladesh and Kashmir in Pakistan. Al Azmeh notes that their culture is, above all, rural, with a Muslim religious element of mystical and magical character. This, he believes, explains their attitudes towards such things as girls' education. He compares them with Indian Muslims who belong to a more urban culture, are more economically affluent, and attach great value to education (Al Azmeh, 1993).

The family

The family is the only group recognized in law. Nearly a third of the Quran is devoted to family matters and relationships. The only other group Islam recognizes is the brotherhood of believers. Other social or political groups are discouraged or forbidden.

In the traditional Muslim family the hierarchy is organized according to age and gender. The hierarchy crosses generations with the extended family system. Men and older members of the grandparental generation hold greater bargaining power. So fathers assume the role of the head of the family with their duty to provide. Marriage is a contract in which both parties have duties and rights. The practice of arranged marriage is meant to prevent conflict as a result of disparities over wealth and to ensure compatibility in social class. The duties of the woman or mother are to look after the family, the husband and the children. The education of the children is a joint responsibility, with the mother taking a leading role.

The Prophet calls on men to treat their women well – 'That is the most perfect Muslim whose disposition is best and best of you is he who behaves best to his wife.'

Case example 2

Zaitoun, a 14-year-old girl, was referred by her school because of a range of difficult and rebellious behaviour. Zaitoun was playing truant from school and getting into fights and her teacher was concerned that she might be using, and dealing in, illicit drugs. She was one of six children in an Asian Muslim family, four older siblings and one younger. During the first family interview the eldest daughter spoke for the parents, who took more of a back seat. The father was retired due to ill health and seemed preoccupied with his own health. His English was very limited. The mother was also physically unwell and she had spent long periods in Bangladesh looking after her own elderly frail mother. Neither seemed concerned about Zaitoun's behaviour – they were only worried about the fact that she was not eating enough and was quite thin. Zaitoun was angry about having to come to the interview and spent the interview arguing with her sister and dismissing any concern about her behaviour. The older sister believed that Zaitoun had an eating disorder and needed professional help. What became clear during the course of the family interviews – as Zaitoun had to be admitted to a specialist unit – was that her family was one where the traditional hierarchy has become distorted. The parents seemed, for different reasons, to have abdicated their authority and responsibility, leaving their older children, two daughters, to act as parents in relation to the youngest two children. The four older children all had a relatively trouble-free passage through adolescence into young adulthood. It appeared that, as Zaitoun reached adolescence, the parents became emotionally and physically less available and less able to set clear boundaries and rules, which they had perhaps been able to do reasonably successfully with the older four children. Zaitoun was left confused by her parents' inability to meet her challenges to their authority and was resentful towards her older sister, whom she felt had no right to tell her what to do. The older siblings resented the burden being placed on them to act as parents to their younger siblings. Zaitoun's problems added to the family's social isolation and the shame in their community attached to the father, the head of the family, being unable to protect and control the teenage daughter. Zaitoun's behaviour and manner of dress was totally in conflict with her parental and family expectations and she spoke negatively and critically about Bengali culture and Islam. She had only white English friends. She seemed hell bent on a collision course with her family, which was quite divided and confused about how to respond to her out-of-control behaviour. She and the family withdrew from therapeutic work when she discharged herself from the specialist unit.

The hierarchical nature of the traditional family is often experienced as quite oppressive by young mothers who are brought into the family, as they have to submit to the authority of male figures and their mother-in-law.

There are no direct references in the Quran to rituals in relation to birth or training of children. The subject is, however, frequently referred to in the *hadith*. There are certain rituals attached to birth; after the child is born it is washed and then carried to the male relatives. Someone then recites the *azan* (call to prayer) in the infant's right ear and the *iqamah*, a Sura from the Quran in the left ear. Alms are given and distributed and prayers are recited for the child's health and prosperity. The amount of alms, according to tradition, should be the same weight as the child's hair, which is shaved for this purpose. Friends and neighbours are invited to the house for celebrations and to offer congratulations. The child is named on the seventh day. Following the Prophet's example a ceremony of sacrifice to God is made on the seventh day: two goats for a boy and one for a girl. When the child's speech and language are well developed, around the age of 4, he is taught the first words of the Quran : *Bismellah al Rahman al Raheem* ('in the name of God the merciful, the compassionate'). Children, particularly sons, are considered a blessing. Circumcision of boys is a common and a standard practice in all Muslim communities. In the case of girls the situation is more controversial as the practice existed in the Middle Eastern region before the advent of Islam. There is no mention of it in the Quran, neither is it recommended anywhere in the text. The *hadith* describe it as a customary tradition. Female circumcision is in fact outlawed in some Muslim countries like Egypt and Saudi Arabia. The practice is widespread in African countries such as Sudan, Ethiopia and Somalia. Nevertheless, it is still common in some countries where it is outlawed, for example in Egypt, where it is performed by *dayah*, elderly women who operate as the barber used to in Western societies (Al-Saadawi, 1980). Interestingly, female circumcision is almost unknown and is strictly forbidden in Saudi Arabia and all the Gulf states – the most orthodox and traditional of Islamic societies. This, commentators believe, is further indication that the origin of the practice is African rather than Islamic. In the case of boys, the age at which circumcision takes place varies according to local customs – it is usually between the ages of 2 and 7 years. According to Hadith, Abraham was 80 when he was circumcized. The practice among British Muslims is for the operation to be carried out by a doctor in hospital or by a GP.

In some Muslim countries where it is usually performed on groups of boys, there is a formal procession led by a boy who is dressed as a girl. There are no specific rituals attached to the practice among European Muslims. Although the practice is given little prominence in Islamic law, it is given value and prominence in popular opinion. There is no medical evidence, to date, to support the value of routine circumcision. However the argument regarding its merits and de-merits continues. Some consider it barbaric; others a hygienic opera-tion. Some believes it heightens sexual gratification in the case of men and others believe the opposite to be the case.

Strictly speaking, there is no special privilege attached to the eldest born, no special treatment in inheritance. But in practice there is a hier-archy of birth. The eldest son enjoys a special position in the family, and according to custom takes on a parental and an authority role in relation to younger siblings, especially girls, and in relation to the mother follow-ing the father's death. In general, older children are expected to set an example and to teach younger ones such things as the ritual prayer. In keeping with the hierarchical organization of the family, children are taught what is expected of them – for example, to respect older people.

Conformity and compliance are valued, whereas dissent and open con-frontation are discouraged. Usually, children are not expected to observe religious rituals such as praying and fasting in Ramadan until they reach puberty.

In the case of parental separation, the mother will usually have cus-tody of the children during their infancy. The period of custody is not specific. According to some interpretations of *hadith,* it is two years in the case of boys and seven in the case of girls. As a general rule the deci-sion is made at an age at which the child is considered to be able to dis-criminate and choose. However, it is stipulated that the mother must be respectable, stable, unmarred.

It is important to emphasize again that, unlike Christianity and Judaism, Islam does not prescribe any religious ceremony for birth or marriage, death, circumcision or the attainment of adulthood. Custom, rather than religion, prescribes ceremonies or rituals. So on such occa-sions like marriage and death, prayers would be conducted by an Imam, who will take part in the ceremony. This usually takes place both at home and in the mosque.

This explains the wide variations in practices and rituals marking such events in different Islamic communities. It is interesting to note the extent to which Muslims living in the West have adapted such practices, and in some instances have invented new ones to fit their new context.

Examples are the marriage ceremony and the rituals associated with arranged marriage.

In general, adolescence among Muslims is different from that of indigenous Western populations. So instead of it being a stage towards independence and autonomy, the degree of independence is quite limited and adolescence relates to a degree of maturation. Gilligan (1982) and Amar (1973), writing about Arab rural societies, noted that adolescence has assumed little importance in an individual's life. Writing about the problems facing adolescents living in Britain, Timimi notes that the adolescent and the young adult need to recognize and reorganize their emotional needs and aspirations so as not to conflict with their parents' expectations. In return their parents would be expected to actively help them find work and a suitable marriage partner. In resolving the resulting tension and conflict between the individual needs and family interests, the latter are given priority. Clearly such issues are more acute for Muslim families living in the West, where family and parental expectations could be constantly felt to be at odds or in conflict with those of the wider society and peer group. The task of trying to negotiate between two often divergent pathways is often fraught with difficulties

Gender issues:

Islam is regularly singled out as the religion that subordinates women (Kabbani, 1984). The prevailing belief in Western societies is that the problems of women in Muslim societies stem from the values of Islam. Al-Saadawi (1980) rejects the notion that problems facing women are linked to Islamic teaching and Islam's view of women. She believes that in reality the three main monotheistic religions – Judaism, Christianity as well as Islam – are all patriarchal and equally dominated by male establishments. For Al-Saadawi the plight of women in some Muslim societies in the developing world has more to do with economic and political factors than religious and cultural factors. Kabani, as a feminist, acknowledges that certain aspects of Islam are oppressive to women – for example, rules of custody and rules of inheritance, but Kabani adds that these issues are the subject of debate within Muslim communities and among Muslim women who are just as divided as their Western sisters. She points to the variation in practices across different communities. Like Al-Saadawi, she attributes such differences and variations to political rather than religious factors, and emphasizes the role played by economic factors, such as the lack of opportunity in education.

For Ahmed, ever since the rise of Islam, there has been a tension between the ethical vision of Islam, which is egalitarian in its conception of gender, and the hierarchical relations between the sexes in the marriage structure instituted by Islam. The egalitarian vision is consistent with the Quran, which explicitly addressed women. She also believes that

that social practices in relation to gender observed in Islam are the product of androarchy and the androcentric interpretation of the Quran and *hadith* (Ahmed, 1992).

During the Prophet's lifetime women fought alongside men in battles. Some, like his wife Aisha, led an army of men into battle. During the first Muslim community in Medina 622 AD women gained access to the position of Sahaba (companion of the Prophet), debated with men, and were involved in the management of political and military affairs (Ahmed, 1992).

One practice that has been the subject of much debate and controversy is the question of women's dress. According to Ahmed, Islam did not introduce veiling to Arabia. It is not prescribed in the Quran. The veil had already existed and was worn by women from certain classes in towns in countries and territories conquered by Muslims in parts of the Middle East, for example Syria and Palestine. There was a marked change in social attitudes towards women during the Abbsside dynasty in 1111 AD. In countries like Iraq and others in the Middle East attitudes became more misogynist and socially restricting of women. Such attitudes became articulated in laws and customs (Ahmed, 1992).

Western observers and feminist writers fail to see the veil or *chaddor* as anything but a sign of women's oppression. They ignore the fact that in Muslim communities both in Europe and in Muslim countries, women of all classes and backgrounds are choosing to wear such a dress. In talking to these women a variety of reasons for their choice of such mode of dress emerge. Some see it as to do with piety; others, especially older women, view it as modesty. It is now a familiar sight around university campuses and schools to see younger women wearing different permutations of dress and head cover. For such women it has become a sign of being radical or a means of protest at what they perceive as Western culture's devaluation and subjection of their own cultural and religious values. It is more a refusal to adopt Western modes of dress and social behaviour. During the Algerian war of independence in the 1950s, the veil became a symbol of resistance by women who resisted the colonizer's attempt to unveil them. It also became a technique of camouflage – a means of struggle – as the veil could conceal bombs.

Sexuality

Islam views sexuality positively, believing sexual union within marriage to be the highest good in the eyes of God. It is regarded as a duty and pleasure within marriage (Bullough, 1976). Islam's attitude can be described as naturalistic, unlike Christianity which views sex as a sin. Sex is not only a pleasure in life – it is also one of the delights awaiting those who go to paradise in the afterlife. However, parallel to this there is the idea common in Islamic teaching and philosophy that to succumb to sex can cause *fitna,* a crisis, disruption and anarchy in society (Al-Saadawi, 1980).

A way out of this dilemma is to lay down a system or a framework where sex can be enjoyed, within prescribed limits, allowing for abundant reproduction and avoiding *fitna*. Central to such a framework is the institution of marriage and certain social practices such as the segregation of the sexes and certain dress codes for women. However, such practices have developed as part of conservative patriarchal societies and have no religious or theological basis. They are similar to the practices advocated by Judaism and Christianity

In keeping with such a framework Islamic teaching views marriage as the only context for satisfying sexual desire. Masturbation is viewed as an evil, and adultery is an even greater evil. In the words of the Prophet Muslims are exhorted to 'marry and multiply'. The Islamic theologian and philosopher Al-Ghazali goes a step further in stating that refusing to marry is akin to disobeying God. He states that 'Since Allah has revealed his secret to us, and has instructed us clearly what to do, refraining from marriage is like refusing to plough the earth, and wasting the seed'. He continues: 'It means leaving the tools God created for us idle, and is a crime against the self-evident reasons and aims of the phenomenon of creation, aims written on the sexual organs in divine handwriting.' For Al-Ghazali, marriage aims to protect the community from the dangers of unsatisfied sexual desire. In the words of the Prophet 'he who marries has ensured for himself the fulfilment of half of his religion.'

This is linked to Islam's view of the power of sexual desire and passion of both men and women. For one theologian, Fayed Ibn Nageeh, 'if the sexual organ of the man rises up, a third of his religion is lost' and for another Ibn Abbas, 'he who enters a woman is lost in twilight'.

The sexual organs are thus imbued with special powers and compared to instruments used by Satan against man. This explains further the need to segregate the sexes and the prohibition on men entering a house of a woman whose husband is away: 'For Satan will run out from one of you, like hot blood.' A well-known Arabic saying is that 'Whenever a man and a women meet together, their third is always Satan.'

Islamic teaching views women's sexuality as potentially more dangerous and threatening to social order and stability. According to Ali Abu Talib, the Prophet's cousin, and the last of the Four Caliphs, 'God created sexual desire in ten parts then gave nine parts to women and one to men'. This is the reverse of Catholic teaching, where women are viewed as the less sexually active gender, who need to guard themselves against men, who are driven by lust. Al-Saadawi traces these ideas about women's sexuality and passion to attitudes towards Eve as the sinful woman who disobeyed God. She believes that Islam has inherited this from Judaism.

So sexual desire is primarily located with women who tempt and seduce men, who are portrayed as submitting, being incited to commit sin by the seductiveness of women. The term *fitna* in Arabic is an adjective to describe a woman's seductiveness or sexual powers. It is also used to describe an uprising or rebellion in society. Thus it is important and incumbent on men to satisfy the sexual needs of their women, to protect society's order and prevent *fitna*. In the *Perfumed Garden* by Sheik Nifzawi, a ninth-century erotic text in Arabic, female sexuality is depicted as being insatiable, so that a woman may go to any length to satisfy her desires. Timimi believes that the idea of the omnisexual women is central to understanding sexual politics.

In popular mythology the woman is portrayed as holding the key to interpersonal power whereas the man pales into a puny inert subject unable to satisfy her. For men, satisfying sexual desire is essential in order to clear the mind and the heart to concentrate on religious activities, worship of Allah, the search for knowledge, and service to society (Al-Saadawi, 1980). Despite the recognition of the importance of satisfying sexual passion for both women and men, social practices in Islamic societies place most of the constraints on women. On the other hand, men are allowed the satisfaction of sexual desire through various practices, such as polygamy. For Al-Ghazali 'some natures are overwhelmed by passion and cannot be protected by one woman. Such men should preferably marry more than one woman and maybe go up to four.'

Again, such notions or ideas are more the product of patriarchy and are without basis in the Quran or the Prophet's teaching. Polygamy is still common in some Muslim societies – mostly countries in the Arabian peninsula. There is an ongoing debate among Muslim thinkers and writers regarding the origin of such a practice and whether it can ever form the basis for a marriage based on equal justice and equal rights for both men and women.

Timimi suggests that segregation, combined with the emphasis on the importance of sexual satisfaction, could lead to tension and eroticization of relationships between the sexes in other spheres. For example, economic failures may be experienced by men as a threat to their virility and could lead to sexual impotence. Anxieties about premature ejaculation and the size of the penis are widespread in some Islamic societies.

Islam and mental health

Fundamentally, Islam's view of mental health is metaphysical, with emphasis on the psychological and the social rather than the biomedical, or nurture rather than nature. Nagatti (1993) sees the concept of balance between the demands of the body and those of the spirit as central to the Islamic view of mental health. He notes that Western psychologists, with the exception of Jung, have ignored the importance of spirituality in relation to mental health.

Early Muslim philosophical and scholarly writings cover a whole range of topics ranging from psychology and mental health, romantic love, the psychology of aggression to childbearing practices (Nagatti, 1993). The philosopher Ibn-Sina (Avicenna) described classical conditioning and the physiological changes in Galvanic skin responses associated with emotional changes. Al-Farabi (Averroes, 1126–98) wrote treatises on the interpretation of dreams, identifying the psychological function of dreams as fulfilling wishes and impulses that cannot be fulfilled during waking hours. Others, Al-Kindy, Al-Razy, Al Ghazali, described techniques similar to behavioural or cognitive methods of treatment. The first mental hospital in the world was built in Baghdad, Iraq, in 705 AD. This was followed by hospitals in Cairo in 800 and Damascus 1270. At the same time, psychiatric patients were being burnt and condemned in Europe (Oakasha, 1993).

In popular Muslim culture, there is a belief that mental illness is caused by possession by demons and spirits. Historically this belief is shared by others – for example, the Greeks, Hebrews and Chinese. In Arabic the word often used to describe madness is *jinoon,* which derives from the word *jinn* meaning 'evil spirit'. The word *wisas* refers to both the devil and worrying thoughts.

Case example 3

Assad, a 16-year-old boy was referred by his GP because of episodes of disturbed behaviour when he became aggressive and had to be physically restrained by his father. At the initial interview with the family they described a range of disturbed and odd behaviours. There were episodes when Assad would bark like a dog, go down on his hands and knees and raise his leg at furniture legs like a dog. He would put his plate of food on the floor and eat with his mouth like a dog. There were other episodes when he became very agitated, excited and physically threatening to his parents and siblings and had to be physically restrained.

Assad was the eldest of five children of a Muslim Pakistani family. The parents were settled in Britain and all the children were born in London. Five years ago when Assad was 11 they decided to send him to live with his maternal grandmother in a provincial city in Pakistan. The parents said the reason for this was that the grandmother has recently lost her husband and they thought Assad would be company for her. They also wanted him to have a first-hand experience of their own culture and have more comprehensive Islamic instructions. Assad was fine in Pakistan living with his grandmother and having a lot of contact with the wider extended family network. He related the onset of his current problems to an experience about 18 months prior to this. He was out playing cricket with his friends when suddenly he saw woman with long black hair in one corner of the field. This was a fleeting and brief experience. Nobody else saw her. It left him very frightened. He and his friend ran away. He believed that what he saw was the ghost of a dead woman, which he was told later haunted the area. He said it was bad ghost.

He recalled feeling that the woman ghost had got inside him, and feeling possessed by her. He attributed all his bad behaviour to the influence of the ghost inside him. This made him do bad things such as, on one occasion, attacking his father with a pair of scissors. He had been taken by his family in Pakistan to different *pirs* who performed rituals to free him from the *bala* or *jinn*. He and his parents believed that his behaviour had improved as a result of this. On the advice of the *Pir* they had been reading certain Qu'ranic Suras to Assad to calm him down when he became agitated. The parents were happy to accept the GP's advice, and he prescribed a tranquillizer for Assad, but they were quite sceptical about the idea that he might be suffering from some form of mental illness. They decided after the second interview that Assad's behaviour had improved and that they no longer needed further help

The Muslim traditional healing system is called *ilm ruhani* ('the spiritual science'). This encompasses a wide range of ideas and practices, from the mystical experiences and practices of Sufis to spiritualism, which has two branches – the *ruhani* and *shitani* (satanic) arts. Demonic possession is mentioned in the Quran and is condemned as a magic art. Seeking help for both physical and mental health problems from traditional and religious healers is a common practice in Muslim communities. In one study 60% of patients attending a psychiatric outpatient clinic had been to a traditional healer before consulting the psychiatrist. In some Muslim societies, religious healers deal with most minor mental health problems using suggestion and devices such as amulets and incantations.

Case example 4

Zainab was a 16-year-old British Muslim girl. Her parents came to Britain from the Middle East. She and her five siblings were born in London. She presented with a range of disturbed behaviours. She repeatedly harmed herself, for example by taking overdoses. She frequently presented to the accident and emergency department with somatic and physical complaints and was hospitalized on numerous occasions. Medical investigations did not reveal any underlying organic cause. During the psychiatric assessment of Zainab and family the following picture emerged. The parents presented as traditional and reserved. All their children were quite religious and strictly observant of Islamic codes regarding dress and social behaviour. The parents spoke little English and the interviews were conducted in Arabic. The parents were both distressed and puzzled by Zainab's problems. They believed that there must be something medically wrong with her. As the doctors and other professionals did not have a ready explanation for their daughter's condition they consulted the Imam at their local mosque, who concluded that Zainab might be under the influence of bad or evil spirits. He made a special amulet for her to wear around her wrist.

Apparently, according to Zainab, when she turned up at school wearing it her teacher was critical of her, suggesting that she should not believe in 'witchcraft'. The parents were disappointed and complained about the teacher's remarks. The parents also through their relatives in the Middle East consulted a local religious healer, who made up special *ta'a wiz* – a sacred potion. This was made up of Qu'ranic verses written on special paper to be added to a drink. The parents gave this to Zainab to take regularly while she was in hospital. However, they later discovered, to their disappointment, that the staff had discouraged their daughter from taking the *ta'awiz* and had, in fact, thrown it away.

The traditional healer *sayanas,* or sorcerer, caters for a whole range of clients regardless of class and social status. In South Asian cultures the healer is known as *pir,* and the word *bala* is used for *jinn. Jinns* or *balas* are all around on the ground, flying in the air. They are invisible to everyone except the men of knowledge – the *pir* or *sayans.* According to such beliefs, *jinns* and *balas* are responsible for a whole range of physical and mental disorders, from states of altered consciousness to trance states. The belief in the supernatural cause of emotional and behavioral problems underlies the belief in the evil eye, which is thought to operate directly through the agency of a wish. Those who envy the prosperity, health or beauty of others are believed to be able to harm them by just their gaze.

The function of the healer is to use healing practices to cast out the *jinn* or *bala.* The healer could also command the *jinn* to cause anything to take place – for example, to establish friendship between people or cause enmity between them. The rites and rituals used can be found in Islamic literature and in the *tafsir.* The healer's work aims to invoke Allah to get rid of a *jinn* if the client is possessed by one, or threatened by one. So the healer is seen as Allah's conduit, a channel for the divine force that does the actual work of healing.

Muslim cultures are quite tolerant of emotional suffering and behavioural disturbance. This, coupled with the feeling of shame and stigma attached to any kind of mental illness (Oakasha, 1968), might explain the fact that, in Britain and probably the Western world, Muslim clients of all ages and backgrounds are under-represented in referrals to mental health services. When they are referred they are less likely to engage with professionals. This is quite a complex process to elaborate here – one that is still not fully understood. Another relevant issue here is the fact that emotional or psychological problems are seen as private or personal – something to be discussed with people who are close, such as relatives or family, and not with perfect strangers such as professionals.

The issue of the tendency for clients from Muslim cultures to present their emotional and psychological distress in somatic forms has been well documented and debated in the literature. Somatic symptoms and conversion hysteria can be seen as a culturally sanctioned method of eliciting care. In some Muslim societies, in the Middle East, the more intrusive the treatment – for example, injections rather than pills – the more effective it is. So, in this respect, Western medicine is viewed as a form of Eastern magic.

Various explanations have been put forward for this phenomenon. One is linked to the view that the individual experiences distress in a holistic manner – one that does not make a distinction between the mind and the body. This may derive from the fact that Islamic cultures, like other Eastern cultures, have not been influenced by Cartesian thinking and ideas, which separate mind from matter. There is no hard evidence, to date, regarding the prevalence of somatic presentations among British second-generation Muslims, the only evidence being anecdotal. I think it is also important to note that somatic presentations of emotional and psychological distress are also common among British and Western clients from certain social and cultural backgrounds. In this case it is seen as linked to education and psychological sophistication.

Case example 5:

Ibrahim was a middle-aged man from a Middle Eastern country that has been torn by civil and sectarian war. He fled to Britain with his family and was seeking political asylum. He had been imprisoned and tortured as a member of a minority group that was fighting for social equality. He was referred to the author by the psychologist who saw him initially and realized that Ibrahim spoke only Arabic. His had a range of physical and somatic symptoms, but medical investigation had revealed no abnormality. His GP thought that he must be depressed and prescribed anti-depressant medication, which helped. He came to see me and, interestingly, was escorted to the interview by his wife. She waited in the waiting room. As his story unfolded, it emerged that he was quite incapacitated by various fears about his physical health. He was convinced that there was something physically wrong with him. He was afraid of travelling on his own and had suffered what sounded like panic attacks in public places, during which he thought he was suffering from a heart attack and was going to die. (This is why he had to be escorted to the interview by his wife.) He lived with his wife and four children in a council flat and was not able to work because of the above complaints. He also was not allowed legally to work while awaiting the outcome of his application for asylum. He and his family were living on State benefits. Before coming to Britain Ibrahim was a successful businessman who owned a small factory and they lived in an affluent suburb, owned several cars and had servants. He came from a large family. His siblings and their families all lived in the same city and were in regular – sometimes daily – contact. He spent most of the time in our sessions talking about his physical symptoms and fears about his health. He repeatedly asked for reassurance from me, as 'the doctor', and sometimes would ask for a different or new medication. He would also talk at length about the political situation in his home country and the Middle East. So our sessions at times were dominated by heated political debates. If I inquired about his life and family in London, he gave mono-syllabic and evasive answers. He seemed reluctant to see any link between his current situation, his recent life experiences, and his symptoms, or that his somatic complaints had another meaning.

Gradually we were able to explore the difficult dilemmas and conflicts in his life. A central theme was losing his main role as a provider for his family and consequent feelings of impotence and shame. I gradually real-ized that Ibrahim did not experience his distress as located in 'the mind' as separate from his body. This means the experience was affecting the whole person and was not compartmentalized. It did not make sense to view his symptoms as just an attempt to adopt the 'sick role' in response to the loss of expected role and status. They were more an attempt to restore lost meaning to expected roles. We gradually and slowly explored the painful feelings and memories about the way he left his home and country. The irony of his current situation became apparent. There he was seeking asylum in Britain, which he believed was historically responsible as a colonial power for sowing the seeds of the current troubles in his country. At times there were no words to describe what happened to him and no way to make sense of it. Ibrahim found his religious beliefs com-forting at such times. They provided him with a frame of reference and a way of giving some meaning to at times senseless sufferings.

References

Ahmed A (1988) Discovering Islam. Routledge: London, New York.

Ahmed L (1992) Women and Gender in Islam. London, New Haven: Yale University Press.

Al-Azmeh A (1993) Islams and Modernities. London, New York: Verso.

Al-Islam F, Ahmed SA (1971) Traditional intepretation and treatment of mental ill-ness. Journal of Cross-Cultural Psychology 2: 310–19.

Al-Saadawi (1980) The Hidden Face of Eve: Zed Books Ltd.

Amar H (1973) Growing Up in an Egyptian Village. New York: Octagon.

Bullough UL (1976) Sexual Variance in Society and History. Chicago: University of Chicago Press.

Gilligan C (1982) In a Differennt Voice. Cambridge MA: Harvard University Press.

Kabbani R (1989) Letter to Christiandom. Reading: Cox & Wyman.

McDermott MY, Ahsan M (1986) The Muslim Guide. Leicester: The Islamic Foundation.

Nagatti MO (1993) Studies in Psychology by Islamic Scholars. Cairo: Dar El-Sheronk.

Oakasha A (1993) Psychiatry in Egypt. Psychiatric Bulletin 17: 548–51.

Oakasha A., Kamel M., Hassan A. (1968) Preliminary observation in Egypt. British Journal of Psychiatry:114, 494.

Said E (1993) Representations of the Intellectual. 1993 Reith Lecture. Vintage.

Chapter 6
Religious beliefs and practices among Sikh families in Britain

RAMINDAR SINGH

This chapter focuses on some of the religious beliefs and practices among British Sikh families. Although Sikh theology is the prime source of most of these beliefs and practices, they may not be strictly consistent with orthodox theoretical positions because of the contemporary social and cultural contexts in which individuals practise their religions. Differences of opinion and interpretation of religious beliefs have therefore naturally arisen. The chapter is primarily aimed at professionals dealing with young people in Sikh families, in the context of the services they provide. It is not written for the student of religious studies and, therefore, the chapter does not attempt to cover religious aspects comprehensively. The discussion is limited to some of the practical aspects of the faith and social and cultural norms among Sikh families in Britain.[1] It is not intended to make any judgement on the rights and wrongs of current beliefs and practices of individuals or in the community.

A general profile of the British Sikh community

According to the 1991 census, Indians constitute the biggest single group amongst the South Asian immigrant communities in Britain (840 300 Indians; 476 600 Pakistanis; 62 300 Bangladeshis). The Indian population of Britain comprises two chief religious groups: Hindus and Sikhs. The Sikhs form nearly half of the Indian population – that is, 420 000. The Sikhs migrated to Britain starting in the mid-1950s, either directly from a very small area, the Jalandhar and Hoshiarpur districts of the Punjab, or from the East African countries of Kenya, Uganda and Tanzania. Ninety per cent of South Asians in Britain believe that religion has an important impact in their lives.[2]

The majority of Sikhs in Britain are settled in the south-east and in the west Midlands. Initially they were heavily concentrated in inner-city districts but over the years they have dispersed more widely and have moved

into better housing in the outer suburbs. Almost the entire Sikh population lives in owner-occupied properties. In the case of Sikhs, the 'all male
household' phase was over by the mid-1970s. Over two-thirds of Sikh
households are nuclear families. The remainder are horizontally extended
families comprising parents, married and unmarried siblings and some
other relatives. Three-generational families are less common.[3]

The textile and engineering industries employed two-thirds of the Sikh
male workers in the 1970s (almost in equal proportions) and the remaining third was fairly equally distributed between transport, construction
and small trades. During the last decade or so the employment pattern of
Sikhs has changed. A substantial number of them have left public transport and textiles and have gone into self-employment, largely into retail-
ing and service industries. More than half of the adult Sikh women go out
to work. They are mainly in jobs requiring lower skills and little knowledge of English, in textiles, garment making, making electronic components, service industries and so on. It appears that Sikh children have done
very well in education and a substantial number of them are moving into
professional occupations such as pharmacy, medicine, law and accountancy.

The development of Sikhism

There are about 15 million Sikhs in India. Thirteen million of them live in
the Punjab and the remaining two million in other parts of India. It is estimated that at least another million live overseas, including about 420 000
Sikhs in Britain today.

Sikhism emerged in the sixteenth century as a protestant movement
led by Guru Nanak (1469–1539 AD). It is therefore the youngest of the
major world religions. Even in India, Sikhs are one of the smallest religious groups, constituting just over 2% of the total Indian population.

The founder of Sikhism, Guru Nanak, was followed by nine gurus. The
last guru, Gobind Singh, died in 1708 AD. Over this period of nearly two
centuries the size of the Sikh community grew, particularly in the Punjab
and its surrounding areas. In April 1699, Guru Gobind Singh formally
transformed the character of the Sikhs from a purely religious group to a
community of 'saint soldiers', and created *khalsa* (the pure). He instituted
the practice of *khande-de-pahul* (baptism). He baptized his followers and
called them *khalsa panth* (the community of pure). The growing influence of the religious teaching of the Sikh gurus, and particularly the emergence of *khalsa* in the form of an organized army, became a threat to the
prevailing dominant state religion, Islam, and to the position of Mughal
rule and the Hindu rajahs of some small states in northern India. The
increasing interest of Sikhs in social and political issues of that time began
to worry the Muslim rulers. They made concerted efforts to check this
emerging force. Many ordinary Sikhs and the fifth and the ninth gurus

were tortured and sentenced to death by the authorities. Guru Gobind Singh fought many battles against the Hindu rajahs and the Mogul rulers around Punjab. After his death, the Sikhs continued their struggle to gain power and they eventually established their own kingdom in the Punjab and north-western parts of India. Maharaja Ranjit Singh ruled from 1799 AD to 1839 AD. After fierce battles with the British forces the Sikhs lost their kingdom to the British in 1849 AD.

Sikh identity

To be a member of the *khalsa panth,* a Sikh is expected to be baptized (*amrit paan*) and to follow the prescribed code of conduct (*rehat murya-da*). *Amritdhari* Sikhs (baptized Sikhs) are required to wear the 'five Ks': *kes* (uncut hair), *kangha* (comb), *kachha* (specially designed shorts), *kara* (a steel bracelet) and *kirpan* (a sword).

A male Sikh is required to wear a turban to cover his unshorn hair and adopt the name Singh. A Sikh woman is required to cover her head with a dupatta (scarf) or a turban and adopt the name Kaur. Traditionally, Singh and Kaur were surnames, but in practice, with most Sikhs, these have become middle names, followed by family names as surnames. Singh and Kaur seem to be gradually disappearing altogether from the names of most children. The prescription of a common surname, designed to hide the caste membership of an individual with a view to abolishing the social distinction and inequalities based on the Hindu caste system, is almost ignored these days. Many Sikhs in Britain have dispensed with turbans and beards. *Karah* is the most commonly preserved symbol of Sikh identity, even by the younger generation of males and females in Britain.

The right to wear Sikh symbols has been one of the serious concerns for Sikhs in the Western diaspora. Sikhs had to mount long campaigns to seek exemption from requirements concerning the wearing of hard hats as protective headgear when riding a motorcycle (Motor Cycle Crash Helmets (Religious Exemption) Act 1976) and at construction sites (Employment Act 1989). Currently, a similar campaign is in progress to seek exemption from wearing protective headgear as a requirement under a European Union Health and Safety Directive. They fought a long battle against the denial of schools (a 1983 House of Lords ruling, *Mandla v Dowell Lee*) and transport services and to allow Sikhs to wear turbans as a part of school uniforms where such uniforms are prescribed. Wearing of a *kirpan* (sword) and a *kara* (bracelet) had also caused concerns in schools and other public places (as they are seen as weapons and safety hazards in many situations). Recent legislation prohibiting the carrying of knives (the Offensive Weapons Act 1996) has acknowledged the right of Sikh children to wear a *kirpan* on religious grounds. The wearing of Sikh symbols causes serious harassment to Sikh children in schools. The tragedy of 13-year-old Vijay Singh, a Sikh child who wore a turban, from Stretford High School in

Manchester, who committed suicide as a consequence of bullying and racial harassment from pupils in his school, highlights the seriousness of the problem (*Guardian,* 17 October 1996).

The principal prohibitions or taboos for an Amritdhari Sikh include: eating of meat prepared in a ritual manner (*halal*), adultery, using tobacco in any form, and removal of hair. Sikhs do not normally eat beef, but Drury (1991) found that most Sikh girls in her survey ignored this traditional prohibition. Drinking alcohol is strongly discouraged, but it is also common a feature at all Sikh social functions.

Sikh beliefs and way of life

Sikhs believe in *one* God. The God is: eternal truth, without hatred, creator of all things, fearless, timeless, formless, self-enlightened and outside the cycle of birth and death.

Sikhism rejects the view that the God ever assumes any physical form, human or otherwise. The ten Sikh gurus are not regarded as sons of God but as the spiritual leaders whose holy words and thoughts (*gurbani*) are the foundations of Sikhism as a distinct religion, and provide its followers with the unique Khalsa identity. Sikhs have no living Guru. They were mandated by Guru Gobind Singh, the last human Guru, to treat the Guru Granth Sahib (the Sikh holy book in Punjabi language, written in the Gurmukhi script) as a living Guru when seeking guidance on spiritual and other matters. The Guru Granth Sahib contains the writings of the first nine Sikh Gurus and some Hindu and Muslim saints.

Despite a clear mandate from the last Guru, the need for a living guru or a spiritual leader has been a continuing issue of debate among Sikhs. Therefore, from time to time various spiritual leaders or saints have emerged (and keep on emerging) who claimed to preach the Sikh way of life and establish a following of disciples who virtually treated these leaders as their living gurus.

Guru Nanak preached a distinct but simple way of life for an individual Sikh: *nam japna,* to remember the Name of God ; *kirat karna,* to earn one's living through honest labour; and to *wand shakna,* to share the rewards of one's labour with others. He argued that this truthful living is the only way to merge with the eternal truth, that is, God.

Sikhism advocates the importance of a married and working life. It also stresses that self-mortification and withdrawal from society is not the way to attain salvation. *Sewa,* to serve humanity physically, mentally and materially is considered to be a moral and religious duty. The impact of these ideals is reflected in the general attitude of Sikhs to their life in Britain and explains, to some extent, the relative ease with which they have adapted and progressed.

At a personal level, Sikhs are advised to control five vices: *kam* (lust), *karodh* (anger), *lobh* (greed), *moh* (worldly love) and *ahankar* (pride).

Pilgrimages, fasts and self-inflicted harm find no place in the Sikh way of life. Sikhism opposes idol worship. The Gurus were highly critical of complex rituals and ceremonies associated with the Hindu way of worship. Sikh *rehat muryada* (code of conduct) includes advice to the Sikhs not to bow before monuments, pictures or figures of any human beings, and to avoid the lighting of lamps and the use of fragrances for prayer (*arti*). Despite the existence of such clear and firm guidance on a number of 'do nots' a lot of prohibited rituals are observed during the communal services in *gurdwaras* and personal prayers at home, which makes it difficult for Sikh children and other observers to rationalize the differences between prescription and practice.

A simple daily routine is suggested for individual worship. Getting up early, having a bath, and saying the prescribed prayers in the morning, evening and at bedtime. The prayers can be said whilst doing routine jobs. Visiting a *gurdwara* (Sikh temple) is essential for communal worship.

Gurdwaras and community life

Gurdwara is the religious place of Sikh worship. It is open to all, irrespective of their own religious beliefs. At present, in most cities with a significant Sikh concentration in Britain, namely, Greater London, Birmingham, Coventry, Leeds, Bradford, Nottingham, Huddersfield, Leicester and Derby, a large number of *gurdwaras* have been established. Before entering a *gurdwara* all visitors are required to cover their heads and take off their shoes. The Guru Granth Sahib is installed on an elaborately decorated raised platform. No other form of worship, except the reading and singing of hymns from the Guru Granth Sahib is permitted.

In Sikhism there is no institution of priesthood as such. In a *gurdwara* a service may be conducted by any Sikh man or woman. There is no single national organization that co-ordinates, controls and guides the functioning of *gurdwaras* in Britain. Each *gurdwara* has its own elected management committee, which runs the affairs of the *gurdwara* and appoints a *granthi* to conduct religious ceremonies. Most of the *granthis* are recruited from India. Only a few are formally trained for the functions they perform. An overwhelming majority are those who can read *gurbani*, do *shabad kirtan* (sing hymns from Guru Granth Sahib with musical instruments) and can perform religious rites at social events. Very few of them possess an adequate grasp of the English language to preach to the younger generation in English, and the younger generation generally has a limited understanding of the Punjabi language, even when it is spoken in most Sikh homes and in community gatherings.

Drury (1991) in her study of 102 Sikh 16–20-year-olds in Nottingham in the early 1980s discovered that 79% could not read and write Punjabi, and yet 72% would have liked to have studied it at school and 95% intended to pass it on to their children. Similarly, Ghuman (1994: 51) in his sample of 50 South Asian teenagers (including Sikhs) in Birmingham found that, although most of them preferred to speak English most of the time, 90% wished to learn to read and write their mother tongue.

All *gurdwaras* organize Punjabi classes for children. In some *gurdwaras* these classes are effectively organized and taught by trained teachers. More often, however, children are taught by volunteers who have no formal training in language teaching. A common complaint of teachers in these language schools concerns the lack of suitable teaching books and other materials. Most of the teaching materials are imported from India and are inappropriate in content and style for British-born Punjabi children. Some teachers have developed their own materials but such materials are not widely available. These schools do not seem to be very effective in teaching Punjabi and the Sikh religion. It is partly due to the fact that this is not a major priority for their management committees. Teachers also lay the blame on parents for their lack of enthusiasm in inspiring their children to attend classes.

The social and political life of the British Sikh community centres around *gurdwaras*. Strictly speaking, a *gurdwara* is a religious place of worship but, in practice, *gurdwaras* in Britain (and to a large extent in India too) also function as sociopolitical institutions. On Sundays the members of the Sikh community meet in local *gurdwaras* to take part in the religious service, meet people socially and to exchange views on various issues affecting the community. The *gurdwaras* provide facilities for the solemnization of social ceremonies such as weddings, births and deaths. The members of the local white community and mainstream organizations and institutions have used *gurdwaras* as their first contact with the local Sikh community.

Gurdwaras in a city may carry different names. However, different names do not mean that each represents a different section or a sect of the Sikh faith. Most *gurdwaras* provide very similar facilities for the community as a whole, even when the congregation in a particular *gurdwara* may draw more people from a particular caste group. The politics and the management of *gurdwaras* are male dominated but women play a significant part in the organization of different activities, particularly in the *langar* (kitchen).

Young people's lack of interest in attending *gurdwaras* is a serious concern among Sikhs in Britain. The children are happy to join their families on special social functions such as weddings and *akhand paths* (uninterrupted reading of the Guru Granth Sahib over 48 hours) but show little enthusiasm to attend *gurdwaras* for routine weekly religious worship. Their reluctance can be partly explained by the fact that the entire service in the *gurdwaras* is in the Punjabi language, much of which they do not properly understand. Although the younger children enjoy the informal environment in most *gurdwaras,* as they advance in years they put it down to chaos and lack of organization. The young people also fail to understand the fairly regular fights between rival factions in the management committees (almost a universal phenomenon in *gurdwaras* in most British cities). Many leaders are not seen to be suitable role models who can motivate and inspire the young Sikh children to participate actively in community affairs.

Ghuman (1994: 53) concluded that Sikh youngsters did not accord the same importance to their religion as their Muslim peers. They would have liked to know more about their religion but as the ethos of the *gurdwaras* is very archaic and traditional, it was virtually impossible for them to learn anything substantial. Sikh young people interviewed in Birmingham were woefully ignorant of their religion. He also commented that the Sikh community is far too lax and liberal on the issue of religious instruction.

The internal politics of the Sikh community can be understood only in the context of the *gurdwaras* despite the existence of other community organizations. The leadership of most *gurdwaras* in Britain was in the hands of conservative, relatively less-educated older members of the community until 1984. Since 1984 there have been a number of significant events in India. This has included the Indian Army's attack on the Golden Temple in Amritsar (Punjab) and the assassination of an Indian Prime Minister (Mrs Indira Gandhi) by her two Sikh bodyguards that followed the massacre of Sikhs in Delhi and other cities in India. These events had a serious effect on the politics of Sikhs in Western countries, including Britain, and significantly enhanced the Sikh identity in India as well as the West. In Britain, pro-Khalistan (a movement for an independent state for Sikhs in India) groups made vigorous attempts to control *gurdwaras*. In fact, younger and more militant Sikhs did take control of the management of many *gurdwaras* for a few years. Overall, Sikh politics in Britain are still very much dominated by the political issues in the Punjab.

The activities of the Indian workers' associations and other community organizations, which recruit extensively from the Sikh population, are directed and dominated by a very small number of relatively educated members of the community with a commitment to deal with issues of local concern. The Sikh community has made deliberate efforts to involve influential members of the local white population in their social and religious functions. For example, local lord mayors and members of Parliament have been the chief guests at *gurdwaras* and other community meetings or social celebrations. The Sikh community is fairly active and well represented in the activities of the local political parties.

Caste and sects

Sikhs believe in the oneness of the human race. During the Amrit ceremony, those receiving Amrit are reminded that distinctions based on factors such as social status, caste and occupation are irrelevant. A simple set of traditionally established rules and practical measures were introduced to emphasize equality among individuals, and these practices are followed in all *gurdwaras*. For example, during the service in a *gurdwara (sangat)* everybody sits on the floor. At the end of the service *karah parshad* (blessed sweet food) is distributed to all from the same bowl and a proper meal is served to all those present in the *langar (gurdwara* dining hall) sitting together in *pangat* (in rows at the same level). The adoption of a common name 'Singh' by all male and 'Kaur' by all females was another indication of belonging to a common family. *Gurdwaras* are open to all who are interested in taking part in the service irrespective of their religious, ethnic or caste background. Many of the historic *gurdwaras* have four doors, which also symbolizes their openness to all.

Sikhism rejects the vertical hierarchy of the Hindu caste system. Despite this religious principle and the prescribed practices designed to achieve social equality in reality, caste division still exists among Sikhs. For example, the British Sikh community is divided into three main caste groups: Jats (members of the peasantry and the farming community in the Punjab), Ramgarhias (village artisans, carpenters, blacksmiths) and Ad-dharmis (Ravidasias) (members of landless agricultural working classes). At a personal level, caste affiliation becomes evident and significant in the choice of marriage partners and at social functions involving the *biradari* (a wide network of relatives). At the community level, caste divisions have resulted in the establishment of separate caste-based organizations and *gurdwaras* by Bhatras, Ravidasias and Ramgharias. It appears to be voluntary exclusion by individual groups for religious worship. This social division may have little impact on individuals in their normal day-to-day relations but it has fragmented the Sikh community's unity on caste lines.

The relevance of the caste system in Britain is one of the most difficult social phenomena for Sikh children to appreciate. This is one of the areas in their lives where a contradiction between social practice and religious beliefs has the most impact. Parents' reluctance to lower the caste barriers in arranging marriages of their children is one of the serious concerns of young people growing up in a relatively secular and socially egalitarian Western society. Inter-caste marriages still cause a good deal of tension and conflict within families, as do inter-faith marriages. The more liberal views of British-born young people about inter-caste marriages seem to be making a very slow impact on the older generation's attitude towards change. However, inter-faith love affairs and marriages, particularly between Sikh girls and Muslim boys, are totally unacceptable. During the last few years, such friendships or partnerships have been a serious source of tensions between Sikh and Muslim students in many of the educational institutions in the Midlands and the London area.

There are also some well-established religious sects within the British Punjabi community. They claim to be Sikhs and use Sikh scriptures but interpret basic Sikh beliefs in their own particular ways. They have established their own distinctive worship practices, religious rituals and temples. The main groups among these in Britain are Namdharis, Nirankaris, Radhaswamis and Ravidasias.

Status of women

Sikhism advocates equality between men and women. In Guru Nanak's times equality for women was denied in practice. Polygamy and child marriages were a common practice. *Sati,* the burning of a woman on the funeral pyre of her husband, was prevalent. The remarriage of a widow was not allowed. A woman was considered temptation incarnate. Sikh Gurus rejected all these practices and preached for women's liberation. They encouraged women not to veil their faces in public and to participate actively in all aspects of life at home and outside.

Unlike Muslim women, Sikh women face no religious or cultural restriction on them with regard to doing paid employment. A significant majority of them do work outside their home. In most British Sikh families, women are encouraged to take full advantage of educational and training opportunities available to them. Therefore, girls going away from home for higher education or to pursue a career face less resistance from parents than a decade or so ago. Work has given many Sikh women greater economic freedom. It has enhanced their status in the family and allows them a significant say in family financial decisions. As a result of their hard labour, most Sikh families have achieved a good standard of living since their arrival as immigrants some three to four decades ago with hardly any financial capital.

The growing economic freedom of Sikh married women has also brought about a change in the nature of the relationships they have traditionally been expected to have with their 'parental family' after marriage. Many of them sponsored their parents to join them in Britain. Some of them have contributed (and continue to do so) more generously towards social functions and helped generally in raising the economic standard of their parents' family.

Modood, Beishon and Virdee (1994, Chapter 5) conclude from their research that the most important constraints on the choice of marriage partner for the second generation of South Asians were parental wishes and parental authority. In this context, economic freedom combined with better education and growing up in a Western cultural environment has enhanced the influence of Sikh girls in their choice of marriage partners. Media stories of 'Asian' girls leaving home from fear of an arranged marriage concern Sikh girls less frequently. Only an insignificant minority of Sikh parents may wish to find marriage partners for their children from India. Most marriages take place between young people born in this country and more often with decisions jointly involving parents and young people. This, of course, does not mean that all marriages are successful and cause no tensions in the family. However, traditional social blackmail and pressures from family and relatives are becoming blunt instruments in keeping unhappy marriages intact. There is a slow increase in broken marriages and divorces in the Sikh families. The Sikh community's attitude towards the marriage of widows is quite positive now and divorcee marriages no longer carry a social stigma.

Sikh women play an important role in the activities of various community organizations, particularly in *gurdwaras*. However, not many are seen in leadership roles. In spite of the liberal cultural and religious Sikh traditions women find little encouragement from men in raising their expectations for positions of status and power in community organizations or in public life in general. Sadly, very few seem to be sufficiently assertive to find a place for themselves.

Sikh ceremonies and festivals

Birth and naming ceremony

There is no specific ceremony connected with birth. However, the common practice is for the mother and the new-born child accompanied by the rest of the family to visit a local *gurdwara* five weeks after the birth. This is to offer thanks to God and to seek the blessings of *sangat* (the congregation). Some parents also use this visit to seek guidance for a name for the baby. To receive such guidance the Guru Granth Sahib is opened at random and a hymn is read out. The parents can choose a name beginning with the first or the second letter of the first word of the hymn. The birth of a son is generally celebrated in a high-profile way by distribution of *ladoos* (sweets) to friends and relatives, followed by a social party or an *akhand path* (reading of Guru Granth Sahib). Most baby girls miss out on such an elaborate welcome in the family. However, this cultural practice of preferential treatment of boys is being questioned and attitudes are gradually changing.

Marriage ceremony

In the arrangement of marriages, families of the couple play a central role. In most cases the search for suitable partners for their marriageable children is still initiated by parents. The final decision is made or endorsed and wedding expenses are also paid for by the respective parents. Marriages normally takes place in a local *gurdwara*. The religious ceremony is followed by a social function, generally in a hired community hall or a hotel. These functions are becoming big, elaborate and expensive. Activities such as the *bhangra* dance, generous provision of alcoholic drinks, and cake cutting have become common features of most Sikh weddings. A number of traditional marriage-related cultural and social rituals are performed during the days prior to the actual wedding day. These occasions, with the rituals, are carefully videoed and watched with great interest, particularly by the womenfolk. Irrespective of whether young people fully understand and appreciate the significance of marriage rituals, most of them seem to show an enormous interest in them and take maximum pleasure from their participation. For them it is a vital experience in their socialization process.

A Sikh marriage is seen as the bringing together of two families and, for the spouses, equality in partnership. It is believed that 'only they are truly wedded who have one spirit in two bodies'. However, it appears that marriage is becoming more contractual and more of a partnership between individuals, even among Sikhs in Britain. Unworkable and unhappy unions tend to dissolve more easily and quickly in Britain, as social pressure is less intense, social sanctions are less severe and access to the courts is easier.

Death ceremony

Sikhs cremate their dead. The ashes and remains are normally put into moving water. Most families still take or send the ashes back to the Punjab, where they are scattered in the River Satluj at Kiratpur. The mourning period is generally long and it is more of a public affair. It is ended by a *sadharan path* (complete reading of the Guru Granth Sahib at home or in a *gurdwara*) or an *akhand path* (non-stop reading of the full Guru Granth Sahib over 48 hours). In Britain *bhog* (end of the *path,* the reading) generally coincides with the day of the funeral. Children born in this country, find it difficult to cope with the lengthy and public nature of the whole event. The rituals connected with death do not seem to have changed much.

Other ceremonies

The most commonly observed Sikh religious functions include: Vaisakhi, birthday of the Khalsa; Guru Nanak and Guru Gobind Singh's birth anniversaries; martyrdom days of Guru Arjan Dev and Guru Tegh Bahadur; and the day Guru Granth Sahib was installed as the Guru. Akhand Paths are carried out in *gurdwaras* on all these occasions. More recently, on these occasions, and particularly on Vaisakhi, public parades are arranged in most cities in Britain with a concentration of Sikhs. The public parades have taken a much higher profile in the community since the mid-1980s due to the events in the Punjab. Sikhs in Britain, like the members of every other ethnic minority group, have started to assert and stress their visible identity publicly. The actual dates of festivals vary each year. In most *gurdwaras,* each festival is celebrated at least in a symbolic form on the actual day but full community-level celebrations takes place normally on the first Sunday after the festival.

Some of the traditional cultural events which Sikhs celebrate include: Lohri, an occasion in the middle of January, associated with the new marriages and birth of children in the family; Diwali, function of lights, celebrated by both Hindus and Sikhs, which normally falls in the month of November. Most of these traditional festivals are celebrated by individuals as well as at community level.

Changing value system and identity

Gradual changes are taking place in the social value system of the Sikh community. The older generation feels that the practice of mutual help, so common in the earlier years of their immigration, is disappearing. Individualism and competition is supplanting mutual co-operation, within both the family and the community.

The consumption patterns of Sikhs are undergoing a rapid change. As the children born in Britain grow up, the pattern of family expenditure is moving in the same direction as that of the local population – expenditure on items such as cars, telephones, hi-fi equipment, and other items of conspicuous consumption is growing. In addition to that, they spend generously on social occasions such as weddings.

Sikh woman have become more varied, sophisticated and elegant in the choice of clothes and in their lifestyle in general. They may wear a trouser suit at work, traditional *shalwar, kameez,* and *dupatta* at home and may prefer to wear colourful embroidered sari on a social occasion like a wedding. Young unmarried girls have started wearing make-up and jewellery. The changes in these values, traditionally a source of serious tension between parents and young people, have minimized open generational conflict. Most young people and their parents are learning to make compromises on a whole range of cultural, social and educational matters.

Sikh women feel free to obtain contraceptives; they are having more say in the financial affairs of the family; and men are gradually learning to share domestic tasks with women, although they may still be reluctant to hold their wife's hand in public. Abortion and the use of contraceptives for family planning have not developed as major issues in the British Sikh community. There does not seem to be a specific religious position on these matters. The general impression is that contraception is widely practised by Sikh women.

The English pub, which provided entertainment to most Sikh male immigrants at weekends, seems to have become less important than visits to the *gurdwara* since the 1980s. It is not suggested that drinking has gone down among Sikhs but, rather, it has been replaced to some extent by family entertainment. For many Sikh women, visits to the *gurdwara* provide an important opportunity for entertainment, social mixing and religious worship. The use of drugs, tobacco and alcohol are generally accepted to be prohibited for Sikhs but drinking seems to attract the least criticism.

In the 1950s and 1960s the majority of Sikhs in Britain dispensed with visible symbols of Sikh identity for many practical reasons. However, as single males were joined by their families in the 1970s, and with the development of a stronger social and religious infrastructure, an interest in traditional values was revived. External factors such as racism, racial discrimination, anti-black/South Asian political rhetoric in Britain and political developments in the Punjab since 1984 have increased interest in, and commitment to, the traditional Sikh religious values and Khalsa identity even further. The present position appears to be that Sikhs in Britain have maintained many of the distinctive features of their religion and culture.

Ghuman (1994: 68) found that the identity of Sikh youngsters is tied to their religion rather than to their parents' original nationalities. His conclusion appears to be more consistent with Drury's (1991) than with that of Modood et al. (1994: 50, 58), who state that none of their respondents gave the spontaneous answer 'Sikh' as their identity but rather 'Indian'. Furthermore, the respondents in Modood's survey believed that religion was largely unimportant in the way they led their own lives. The authors, however, accept the anomalous nature of their findings given the situation of political alienation of Sikhs from the Republic of India following the events in 1984 onwards, and advise caution in the interpretation of results.

Sikh parents are concerned about the lack of facilities for their children to learn Punjabi, Sikh religious and cultural values; and the history of their faith and country of origin. Many of them are aware and concerned about their own conformist attitudes, and weak allegiance and commitment to the traditional Punjabi Sikh values of life. However, it appears from general observation of attitudes and behaviour of most Sikhs in Britain that they have adopted a pragmatic approach to their new life in Britain.

Notes

1. Those interested in more detailed information on particular aspects of Sikh beliefs, religious practices, development of British Sikh community and changes in the social and cultural norms of life among British Sikhs may find the sources listed in the bibliography useful.
2. 1991 Census population figures quoted in Office For National Statistics (1996) Social Focus On Ethnic Minorities. London: Government Statistical Service. See Table 1.2, p. 2 and Table 1.8, p. 17.
3. There is little information officially collected using religious categories. For details of sources for the information used here, see Singh (1992).

References and Bibliography

Ballard R (1994) Differentiation and Disjunction Among the Sikhs. In Ballard R (ed.) Desh Pardesh, The South Asian Presence in Britain. London: Hurst & Company.

Bhachu P (1985) Twice Migrants: East African Sikh Settlers in Britain. London: Tavistock.

Cole WO, Sambhi PS (1978) The Sikhs: their Religious Beliefs and Practices. London: Routledge & Kegan Paul.

Drury B (1991) Sikh girls and the maintenance of an ethnic culture. New Community 17(3): 387–99.

Ghuman PAS (1994) Coping With Two Cultures: British Asian and Indo-Canadian Adolescents. Clevendon: Multilingual Matters Ltd.

Kalsi SS (1992) The Evolution of a Sikh Community in Britain, Department of Theology and Religious Studies, Leeds, University of Leeds.

Kohli SS (1975) Sikh Ethics. New Delhi: Munshiram Manoharlal Publishers.

Modood T, Beishon S, Virdee S (1994) Changing Ethnic Identities. London: Policy Studies Institute.

Office for National Statistics (1996) Social Focus on Ethnic Minorities. London: Office for National Statistics.

Singh Ramindar (1992) Immigrants to Citizens: the Sikh Community in Bradford. Bradford: Race Relations Research Unit, Bradford and Ilkley Community College.

Weller P (ed.) (1993) Religions in the UK: a Multi-Faith Directory. Derby: University of Derby.

Chapter 7
Jews, Christians and Parsis

FARROKH VAJIFDAR

Particular challenges confront the Jewish, Christian and Parsi minority communities living today in Great Britain amidst its populations. The English, Welsh, Scots and Irish represent these historically longest established majority ethnicities of the British Isles, followed by the sizeable later immigrant sectors of Hindus, Sikhs and Muslims from the Indian subcontinent, and the Afro-Caribbean groups. Whilst generally welcomed, tolerated and to limited extents integrated, these minorities – either as individuals or groups – have traversed with difficulty the uncertain patterns of new immigration, overcoming initial hostility, seeking assimilation, gaining acceptance, and eventually acculturating in various ways. These stages have never been easy to attain for reasons which are complex but capable of analysis here from a *religio-social* culture perspective, skincolour discrimination through Eurocentrism being prominent. They may be explained through empirical findings based on factors of religion, culture, race and identity. The perspectives are therefore necessarily drawn from the viewpoint of the groups discussed under this chapter title.

The frame of reference demanded by the term *Asian* needs clarification. In terms of commonly understood geography, Asia would embrace all lands from east of the Bosporus to the western Pacific seaboard, from the Arctic to the Indian Oceans and the Indonesian archipelagos. This article, however, is restricted to the South Asian, in particular to the Indian subcontinental countries. Most entries into Britain occurred from there in the 1950s and 1960s, the latter decade accounting also for the sizeable immigrations of Indians from various religious denominations settled in the newly re-Africanized former British colonies of Kenya, Tanganyika, Zanzibar and Uganda. Others, though fewer, came from various central and southern African states, and some from Trinidad and the former British Guiana in the wake of their independence from British sovereignty. Their earlier allegiance to the Crown, their common lingua franca of English, and continued membership of the Commonwealth naturally made the United Kingdom a favoured destination for these immigrant groups.

Historical Background

Early settlers

It is important to distinguish the status of religious refugees with a superior culture from that of the dispossessed refugees whose fate it was to be driven regardless before waves of the periodic invasions of India. The law of absorption did not apply to the former for they had the background of a social and ideological foundation which withstood the all-assimilating embrace of Hinduism. The other kind found asylum within the less accessible areas of the vast Indian terrain, becoming submerged within the majority culture. Within the diversities that are India and Pakistan, the communities under discussion contributed a well-defined presence and often played a significant role in national life.

The Jews and Christians of Cochin on the Malabar Coast had settled there since the earliest days of the Common Era (CE), the former to escape persecution under Roman occupation of Syria and Palestine, the latter being native converts to Christianity since the apostolic mission of St. Thomas, followed by Nestorian and Syrian Christian latecomers from Persia and the Levant. The Syrian Christian church is believed to have existed since the third century CE in India where today it numbers over two million. As regards the Parsis, or Indian Zoroastrians, never very numerous, it is known that the very first arrivals had settled on the subcontinent *before* the downfall of the Sasanian Persian Empire to found trade and business concerns. Thereafter, groups of Iranians had continued to make their way to north-western India where they spread out and intermingled with the local populations. The Arab conquest of Iran in the midseventh century finally decided the fate of the state religion in its original homeland. Groups of disaffected Zoroastrians fled beyond the reach of a fiercely proselytizing Islam, some to Turkestan and on to China itself, others to the safe havens of Gujarat in western India from the eighth to the twelfth centuries.

The Jews in India

The Jews having fled an Israel under harsh Roman domination, some finding refuge in the coastal areas of the Arabian peninsula and inland Mesopotamia where they lived alongside Exilic Jews ruled by the eclectically tolerant Parthians, once more departed before the uncertain religious conditions prevalent under the Sassanian pan-Iranianism of third-century Persia. Some travelled through to Central Asia and then further east into China; others left for the west coast of India where they finally settled in the Malabar region of Cochin, becoming organized as two castes. When in 1948 the State of Israel was founded after some 1900 years of Diaspora, many young Cochin Jews, caught up with Zionist fervour, were tempted to emigrate; a fast-dwindling remnant stayed behind after Indian Independence and beyond the establishment of the Republic in 1950. The upheavals of the First World War (1914–18) in Armenia and Mesopotamia saw groups of Jews migrating eastwards towards the major port cities of Bombay, Calcutta and Madras, where they established highly successful trading concerns. Once again, with Eretz Israel beckoning, many pulled up their temporary Indian roots, and with their renowned energy and drive successfully settled in their newly constituted ancestral homeland, some passing onwards into the Americas.

The Christians of India

With the Christians of India we enter a different world. The Apostle Thomas is supposed to have begun his missionary activity as early as 52 CE among the brahmins of South India where a freer caste system seems then to have prevailed. There he founded the Christian Churches in Malabar whose devotees became famed as the 'Christians of St. Thomas'. The evangelist was murdered soon after by a disgruntled brahmin, it is said, in Mylapore near Madras. But there were Christians, too, of East Syrian and Nestorian origins who came from Persia. In the fourth century the merchant Thomas Cana emigrated from Syria, leading out some 400 families to establish the Nestorian Church in Kerala. Of the partisans of this latter creed, some settled in Kalyan, to the north of Bombay, before 550. Their origins are highly interesting for they represented a surviving branch of the extensive Nestorian missions, which also had travelled into Turkestan and China. Thomas the Apostle was rumoured to have met the Gandharan ruler Gondophares, though nothing is known of any north-western Indian Christian missions founded by him. The Indian caste system, however, also affected and influenced Syrian Christianity which for many centuries lived on caste privileges, withholding its Gospel from those outside them.

The Portuguese navigator Vasco da Gama landed in India in 1498. The coastal ports with their rich hinterlands were rapidly colonized and expanded by the trade and mission-conscious Portuguese, and the Roman Catholic Church very soon gained footholds in Goa, Diu on the Kathiawar Peninsula, and Cochin. The great Jesuit missionary St. Francis Xavier came to India in 1542, preached among and proselytized many Indians, mainly around Goa at first, then south among the pearl fishers, where he is said to have converted thousands. Missionaries from the German Pietist movement, recruited and trained by August Francke of Halle University were sent to the Danish trading post at Tranquebar (today, Tarangambadi) by Frederick IV from 1705 onwards.

Still later, with the advent of the British in the mid-1600s, Anglicanism also founded its own churches towards the end of the following century. The Baptist Missionary Society sent William Carey and John Thomas to India in 1793 as its first agents. Ignorance, illiteracy and physical suffering among the helpless natives were regarded as indications of the realm of Satan and therefore to be vigorously combated. William Carey, Joshua Marshman and William Ward set the robust pattern for mission work in India. Becoming reputed as the Serampore Trio, they placed emphasis upon Bible translation, the drafting and printing of Christian literature, founding schools, and the training of a native ministry. The classes most receptive to this kind of Christianizing were again those outside the Hindu caste system, or whom Hinduism regarded as degraded. Informal missionary fellowships, of which the earliest was the Bombay Missionary Fellowship of 1825, soon became regional and national organizations. India was to set the example for other areas. In 1947 the Church of South India was formed by a union of Anglicans, Methodists, Presbyterians and Congregationalists. Today it is Kerala State which accounts for the largest Christian population in India. Representatives of all three major churches number amongst the far larger communities of Hindus, Sikhs and Indian Muslims settled in Britain since the formation of the Republic and after the 1962 Immigration Act.

The Parsis

The Gujarati-speaking Parsis of western India are said today to number several tens of thousands in the land which offered them asylum some 1300 years ago. Again after Independence, many emigrated to the West in the wake of much uncertainty as to their economic prospects and material advancement. There are reckoned to be upward of 5000 Parsis in Great Britain, having been among the first visitors from India to these shores since the early eighteenth century. Originally temporarily resident for study and commercial purposes, the first few actual settlers came in the mid-1800s and, having a particular fondness for British ways and institutions, quickly acculturated. Others followed before Indian Independence. Some were engaged in trade, most took up professions, and as lawyers, doctors, accountants, bankers and engineers, soon made their mark amidst the society into which they easily integrated. With growing demands for Indian independence from British colonial rule in the late nineteenth and early twentieth centuries, some having aligned themselves to the Freedom movement, Parsi loyalties became divided, though community cohesion remained relatively unaffected. Parsis are adherents of Zoroastrianism, named after their spiritual preceptor Zoroaster – properly, Zarathustra – who preached his monotheistic religion with its strongly ethical message in Eastern Iran some three thousand years ago. From Iran itself many Persian Zoroastrian families emigrated after the deposition of the last Shah in 1979, most opting for North America, some for Great Britain, and a comparative few for western Europe and Australia.

Religious Precepts

Judaism

The ancient faith of the Jews of India was allowed the same open-handed freedom accorded by the majority Hindus to the other religious systems which, generally amicably, coexisted in the tolerant Indian climate. Synagogues were established first in Cochin, Madras, Calcutta and Bombay. Worship there historically must have followed the patterns of the beliefs and practices of the various settlement waves indicated above. Judaism, if not the first, is certainly among the earliest of the monotheistic faiths to which Zoroastrianism since 1000 BCE and Christianity, now some 2000 years old, also lay claim. It is necessary to distinguish the two major Abrahamic religions along Biblical lines. Judaism is an anthology of religious teachings and commentarial reflections to grasp the setting, function and purpose of the Divine will which is the Law of Israel. This Law or rule of practice is called *Halakha*, or the 'oral' religious law embodied in the *Talmud*; its inner facet being the illustrative stories of the *Haggadah*. Although held in great esteem, being composed by virtuous and revered teachers or Rabbis (lit. 'my master') it is not comparable with the Torah. The Biblical Jew would adhere to the teachings and beliefs which are contained in the inner part of Judaism, the *Tanakh*, an acronym embracing the *Torah* or Pentateuch (the Five Books of Moses), the *Nevi'im* or the Books of the Prophets (including the historical books, the major and the minor Prophets), and the *Kethuvim* or Writings; this collection constitutes the Jewish Scriptures. These *Nevi'im* and *Kethuvim* portions are historical rather than properly sacred. For the Jews it is their Bible possessing binding authority; for the Christians, it is the first part of theirs, and is referred to as their 'Old' Testament. There is no smooth and easy transition from the Old Testament to the New.

Jewish orthodoxy firmly believes that absolutely every part of the Mosaic Books is the received wisdom and commandments of *Yahweh*, the personal name of their one God which the truly pious would not pronounce, one who was unique in his transcendent unity. *Torah* properly means instruction, teaching, or guidance. For orthodoxy, modern critical Bible scholarship conflicts with its hallowed tradition. The Jewish national or group continuity is based on the belief that these holy books belong to them as a particular people: religion and nation can only be and are as one, Israel and its Mosaic Law being inseparable. As believer, the Jew serves this one God unquestioningly, as one creature among many, knowing his place in creation, and certain in the knowledge that he was destined to be holy: "You shall be holy, for I, the Lord your God, am holy"

(Leviticus, 19.2). He is fully human, but in imitation of the numinous traits of his God. If he would walk in the way of his Lord, he should hearken and obey His voice. It should be emphasized that in Judaism, as in Zoroastrianism, God has no bodily form or substance. Worship of *Yahweh* is inculcated through obedience and righteousness. He establishes his Covenant, reaffirming that of the patriarch Abraham, being both his solemn word and his social bond. The physical token of this sacred acceptance is the circumcision of the newborn male, its spiritual explanation being the permanence and increase of life – its very sanctification.

Judaism abounds in the minutiae of ritual and practice as well as in religious lore; it is the former only which is fixed, codified and treated as absolutely binding. Its framework was the Decalogue (Exodus 20), unchanging and ageless, which Moses brought down from Mount Sinai as the Tablets of the Law (Exodus, 34.28). The contents of these Ten Commandments – three inculcations and seven interdicts – are respected as the basis of belief and conduct for both Jewish and Judaeo-Christian communities.

Rabbinical Judaism counted 613 Biblical commandments including dietary laws, what was therein considered improper, kinship and sexual relations and improprieties, and most regulations which could properly govern the social and religious conduct and outlook of the pious Jew. Much of it was necessitated by cultural and religious differences with the Persian and the Hellenistic, and for Judaism to retain its particularisms, Rabbinical intervention was deemed imperative for the continuity of the essence of the faith. Here entered clear directions for belief in national restoration, a future saviour, redemption, individual destiny implicating reward and punishment through divine justice, and bodily resurrection. Some scholars have seen Zoroastrian beliefs as underpinning these Jewish articles of faith though Messianic anticipation and belief in resurrection were not fundamental to the Abrahamic system. Be that as it may, it should be happily remarked that there today exists an awareness and increasing acknowledgement of close ideological affinities born of old historical ties between Zoroastrian and Jew. Certainly Judaism and early Zoroastrianism have this in common – that both constitute a philosphy and a code of life. Their similarities are instructive and spiritually nourishing. For the Jews their sacred books and commentaries would sustain them throughout the Diaspora, just as for the Zoroastrians, in internal exile within Iran and voluntary settlement abroad, their Avestic literature and expository texts were to uphold their communal and devotional life.

Belief in Messianic deliverance is seen as common in the development of all the three religious systems discussed here. Among the Jews he was to be a king in the house of David, appointed by divine command, whose reign would confer eternal justice, security and peace. His coming inferred a divine intervention within history, bringing an end to suffering and injustice. The Indian Jews in their isolation were unaffected by the later philosophical trends on the European Middle Ages, having effectively little contact with rationalizing tendencies; for them early Rabbinical Judaism represented the culmination of religious belief and the core authority for religious practice.

Christianity

Indian Christianity, like the various denominations of the West, was based on the fulfilment of Messianic expectation. The fact that the divine and human natures of Jesus the Christ, or the Anointed One, were the subjects of much speculation, and resulting serious differences of opinion made little impact on the majority Hindu populace of India. Conversions to Christianity there being the result of missionary activity among the originally outcaste Indians shunned by Hinduism, the appeal of an egalitarian vision gained firm adherence to the salvationist doctrine of that imported faith. After St Thomas and Francis Xavier had come Lutheranism with German missionaries to South India. The Lutheran community they had established continues with Danish and Anglican support.

For the descendants of the Christian immigrants from Persia, Syriac, an Edessan dialect of Aramaic carried by Nestorian missionaries into China and India, has continued as the ecclesiastical language. The Malabar liturgy remained essentially a form of the Persian Nestorian rite, being sometimes called 'East Syrian', and the theology of the Christians of St. Thomas is of a Nestorian type. That liturgy was almost completely assimilated to the Roman rite by Portuguese Jesuits after 1599.

Before Christianity had reached Edessa, the more important parts of the Old Testament had been translated into Syriac by Jews, and it is this translation, since revised and supplemented, which is still used by Syriac-speaking churches in the *Peshitta*, or Simple, version. The Syriac version of the New Testament, however, does not officially acknowledge the last book of its canon. the *Apocalypse of John* or *Revelation*. Additionally, the Nestorians had never accepted the doctrine of the Virgin Mary as the mother or bearer of God.

Zoroastrianism

The Parsis are the descendants of Persian Zoroastrian immigrants into India around the eighth century CE and after. The story of a particular group of original asylum seekers, fleeing the harsh conditions imposed upon non-Muslims by the Arab invaders and Iranian converts to Islam, was first told in the *Qisse-ye Sanjan* ('The Sanjan Saga') some 800 years after its event by a Parsi priest who claimed to pass on the traditional lore imparted to him by a learned elder in 1600. It recounted the vicissitudes of a body of beleaguered refugees who arrived destitute in Western India to be conditionally welcomed by a local Hindu kinglet of Sanjan, Jadi/Jaydev Rana. Among the stipulations agreed with him for the Persians' stay and the preservation of their ancient religion was the discontinuance of their ancient mother tongue, the adoption of Hindu outward customs and dress, the setting aside of their arms and the taking up of peaceful occupations. The willingly compliant Parsis asked an additional favour: that they be granted land for the establishment of a separate place of worship and the right to follow their religion based on the age-old reverence of Fire, being the visible symbol of their sole deity Ahura Mazda. Thus was explained their arrival in India and the resumption of their lately disrupted ancient religious practices. The Parsis took every care that, whilst their cultural milieu remained Hindu, their allegiance as a law-abiding and long-settled community should be seen to be accorded to the successoral Muslim rulers of Gujarat. Later, it would be the British who would benefit in turn through a similar acknowledgement which to this day continues in Britain.

Parsi religious beliefs are centred around the symbolism of fire celebrating the oneness and omnipotence of Ahura Mazda, Lord Wisdom. The Revelation received from Ahura Mazda by his Prophet Zarathustra contains the core precepts of the Zoroastrian religion transmitted in a highly abstract yet accessible form. They are enshrined in the *Gathas* or Sacred Songs in a 3000-year-old language akin to Sanskrit called Gathic Avestan which, despite keenest philological attention, still presents formidable difficulties of interpretation, but nonetheless allows of clear discernment of the principal themes of the Prophet's teachings.

Here we see a highly ethical message emerging from an interactionist theology involving the aspects of Ahura Mazda. Its foundation is the universal Truth of an Ideal Order which may be grasped by good Mental perception – something realizable spiritually through the rigorous practice of Good Thought, Good Word and Good Deed. It is this ethical basis of Zoroastrianism which makes appeal to each individual worshipper through his free choice and personal responsibility for the adoption, or rejection, of the right way of conduct towards his fellows, to society as a whole, and indeed in his religious attitude. Armed with these discriminating faculties, the Zoroastrian could and should work towards his own salvation and that of this world. The Prophet explains Right and Wrong through the choice made by two Primordial Principles which manifest themselves as dynamisms in the mind of man. This psychological basis of such an ethical system gave rise to a unique concept of Heaven and Hell as earthly mental states. At a pragmatic level, the notion of Reward or Retribution, conferring Weal or Woe, settles the fate of the beneficent and the maleficent, each of whom is deemed to receive his/her just dues as a direct consequence of their respective actions. Later Zoroastrianism was to present this through the picturesque imagery of a weighing of the souls of men whose deeds, righteous or wicked, determine their ultimate fate in an other-worldly setting.

Zarathustra had inculcated goodness in man for his perfection towards the creation of a perfected world. He had fully hoped that this regeneration would be achieved in his own lifetime through a transfigured society; that it had not so happened exercised the ingenuity of subsequent theologians who arrived at the compromise solution of a millennial series of saviours who would purify the world of evil and usher in the Age of Righteousness. Each of the universal saviours are to be born from virgins impregnated by the miraculously preserved seed of Zarathustra – an idea current in Zoroastrian thinking five centuries before the Common Era. The advent of the final Saviour, *Saoshyant* (= 'he who shall save'), signals the final purging of residual evil from this world and the commencement of its renewal in spiritual purity. As God's co-worker, man enables this regenerative process to be achieved through proper ethical activity, being prepared by both physical and ritual purity.

The Zoroastrian ritual text par excellence is the *Vendidad* or Demon-repelling Law, often likened to the Old Testament's *Leviticus*, in which are contained purity laws and the minute regulations to enforce them. Herein also are to be found precautions against contagion from infectious dead matter, the means of circumventing it, and careful details of purification. The greatest danger is seen to be present from the pollution arising from human cadavers which are therefore to be disposed of through exposure within purpose-built funerary structures called *dakhmas*. Originally remote from human habitation and arable land, and open to the skies, the action of the elements and predatory birds ensured the safe, complete and hygienic disposal of the remains, only the skeletal residue being subsequently gathered up and destroyed. Noticeable throughout is the anxiety displayed against accidental or deliberate defilement of the sacred elements of earth, water and fire. Additionally, the *Vendidad* deals with contracts, outrages, the isolation of women in their courses, propriety in sexual relations, sexual taboos, ritual purification, methods of healing, and the care for domesticated animal life. This eclectic text has been described as a sanitary code, though its scope is obviously wider. That much of its prescriptive content has today fallen into desuetude, due to the progress over time of science as well as the urbanization of a formerly rural populace for whom these sagacious purity laws had been initially formulated, presents no bar to the frequent and futile debates which still centre around this ancient tract. The apparent disparity between original doctrine and later ritual has been exaggerated according to the viewpoints of traditionalists, vaguely termed orthodox, and the progressives who are erroneously considered to be anarchistic in their reforming zeal.

Later texts, mainly of a compendious nature and sometimes encyclopaedic in scope, contain commentarial material. These are composed in Middle Persian or *Pahlavi*, notoriously difficult to decipher, but present a comparative ease of interpretation. They are mostly datable to the post-Sasanian period, i.e. after the seventh-century conquest of Zoroastrian Iran by Arab hordes under the banner of a nascent Islam. The ninth and tenth centuries were, however, particularly favourable for the revision and compilation of these *Pahlavi* texts under the relatively relaxed rule of some enlightened Islamic caliphs. Orthodoxy today lays claim to the Zoroastrianism of the Sasanian era (226–652 CE) in substantiation of its modern-day beliefs and practices. In reality a good deal of Parsi Zoroastrian practices have been steadily influenced over the centuries of stay in India by surrounding Hindu customs and usages, and conditioned, both in India and in Iran, by the intervention of Muslim rule.

Religious practices in family life today

The first Parsi immigrants into Britain brought with them an assortment of beliefs and practices which differ in detail but are generally consistent over- all. They reflect an Indian religious milieu in which generations of Parsi Zoroastrians had been nurtured but whose more overtly Hindu traits were consciously suppressed under the Protestantizing influence of the British administrators. But the two generations which now separate the percep- tions and usages of the colonial Parsi from the republican meant a shift towards those of the majority populations in India. What culturally entered Britain depended therefore on the age differential of the Parsi heads of fam- ilies settled here and their post-colonial Indianized preferences.

Family traditions count for more than textual injunctions as there is no properly structured religious education to provide uniformly reliable guid- ance. True, there are various catechisms compiled in India by Parsi priests and educationists, but many of these are now unavailable or unrecognized. A recent trend towards the popularization of earlier works should be cau- tiously welcomed; most of these reworkings are, however. intended for use by children, and it is doubted whether parent participation in early reli- gious education has at all been enduringly effective or consistent. There are additionally childrens' stories culled from the tenth/eleventh century *Shah-Nameh* or Book of Kings by the epic poet Firdausi of Tus, a Muslim Persian who utilized earlier Zoroastrian sources to recount the history of Ancient Iran. These enjoy a certain vogue together with stories of the Prophet Zarathustra's life from the Pahlavi *Zartusht-Namag* (ninth century) and some neo-Persian compositions. The unfortunate Hinduizing trend towards theosophy has greatly marred the earlier, fresher, vision of the proper Iranian content of a Zoroastrian education among the Parsis. Sporadic efforts are being made to reverse this insidious trend, though with (sectarian) sharp conflicts of interest in the religious education field it is not known with what measure of success.

Commencing with the birth ceremonies of a Parsi Zoroastrian child and ending with the funerary customs as generally observed here, it is possible to offer a broad description of beliefs and practices.

It appears that the Indian custom of casting horoscopes for new-born Parsi male children has largely lapsed in Britain. Western educational influences affecting traditional modes of upbringing have steadily taken over from the indulgence of extended family milieux in which religious instruction often took the form of rote performance of simple prayers and ritual actions. There are now occasional religious teaching sessions for the very young, though an unfortunate apathy is all too often evident amongst parents for whom the urgency of 'Catch 'em little; teach 'em young' does not seem to have been communicated. All-important for the parents and elders is the child's *navjote* or initiation ceremony which is usually performed at any time between the ages of seven and eleven. Here the initiate is invested with the *sudreh*, a vest-like undershirt, and the *kushti* or sacred cord triple-wound over it at waist level. Thereafter the cord is solemnly tied around the *sudreh* at least twice each day, after rising and ablution, and before retiring for the night. This ritual tying and untying of the *kushti* usually suffices as religious observance, and apart from some desultory prayers, no more is expected from the modern-day British Parsi. It is doubtful whether the occasional bouts of curiosity to know more factually about their ancient culture has resulted in any sustained increase in basic knowledge and practice at all among the British Parsi youth for whom a soundly structured religious education is lacking.

There has never been communal worship, properly speaking. Numbers of Parsis attend *jashans* or commemorative prayers at certain times in the religious calendar, but here the officiating priests alone recite the prescribed prayers – always before a metal urn containing the ceremonial fire. Pious worshippers offer up token pieces of fragrant wood, usually sandalwood, to this sacramental flame with an inwardly intoned brief prayer. Traditional Parsi homes often have a little oil-lamp flame or *divo* alight within little containers; prayers are recited before its light. The most recited short prayers are the *Yatha ahu vairyo*, the Right Choice of Good Mind, whose 21 words have assumed their own sanctity with their profound significance being realized among but a few worshippers; likewise the brief *Ashem vohu* or Laudation of Truth. There are also affirmations of faith and praises of the Good Religion, as Zoroastrianism came to be known amongst its followers.

Public worship in the home countries was always within the confines of fire-temples where the sacred fire in the inner sanctum is constantly maintained by priests who feed it with sandal-wood and frankincense to the accompaniment of ancient sacred chants. In Britain, where there is no such permanent edifice, prayer services are restricted to occasional small gatherings within a room containing an enclosure where only priests may attend to the sacred fire, witnessed from outside it by the lay worshippers.

Parsi marriages are celebrated, much as in India today, before assemblies of invited guests, and witnesses from each of the families. For the ceremony the bridegroom frequently dons the customary Parsi white *jama-pichhori*, or knee-length coat bow-fastened up to the collar, and trousers to match. The bride usually wears an ornately bordered sari with the shoulder drape modestly covering her simple coiffure. The groom's headgear is the traditional *fehto* or flat-topped hard rimless hat, or, very rarely nowadays, the 'cow's-heel' tall-peaked shiny *paghri*. The man's forehead is marked with a vertical red ochre dash, the lady's with a dot – the sexual connotation of the original Hindu custom being discarded in favour of its bland explanation as a symbol of Good Fortune! Both are garlanded with floral chains. Marriage vows are solemnly exchanged before two turbaned and shawled white-clad priests who, after a series of benedictions and reminders of conjugal duties, then scatter some rice grains betokening prosperity over the affianced pair. In Britain the traditional wedding ceremony, performed just after sunset, is usually preceded by an official brief Registry marriage.

The last Parsi ceremony of note to be described has to be the funeral. The prescribed funerary enclosures and exact sanitary regulations for the exposure and disposal of the deceased's remains are impossible today even in places in India; here in Britain they would be entirely out of the question. Hence the disposal of the body is reluctantly permitted by cremation or by burial. The Zoroastrian Cemetery in the vast Brookwood complex in Surrey has been in use for inhumation since the late nineteenth century, initially arousing anxious protests among the orthodoxist party who pointed to the ancient interdicts against the wilful pollution of the elements. Today such methods of disposal, being the only alternatives available, are stoically countenanced. The actual last rites are pronounced by priests who make their appearance before the coffined body only after the pall-bearers have withdrawn. Being ritually purified beforehand, it is considered improper for the officiants to be in the vicinity of those who have transported the body to its final fate. After brief prayers, the family and friends pay their last respects, and the nearest of kin finally commit the remains either to the flames or to the earth.

Apart from family births and marriages, festivals celebrate the New Year's Day or *Now-ruz*, the birth anniversary of the Prophet Zarathustra (as also the solemn one of his death), and the conjunction of month- and day-names of certain worshipful beings. The *jashan*, or act of public worship, itself averages an hour's duration when white-robed priests chant the prescribed prayers – always before a fire-urn to the accompaniment of certain ritual gestures and the symbolic exchange of flowers. Fruit, nuts and yoghurt kept on a nearby tray are consecrated, and after the close of the ceremony are shared among the assembled worshippers who do not themselves participate in the prayers, though some frequently intone them *sotto voce*. After partaking of the contents of the consecrated tray, the *jashan* congregation often attends a communal meal. The *gahanbars*, or seasonal festive communal gatherings, continue to be attended by sizeable crowds in London's Zoroastrian House. Six in number, and spread through the religious year, these festivals have a long tradition and ancient history behind their observance.

The sixth *gahanbar* coincides with the last five days of the 360-day religious calendar to which are added five intercalary *Gatha* days. These ten days are solemnly dedicated to the souls of the departed who are believed by the pious to revisit the living during this period. This commemorative festival, known among the Parsis as *muktad*, has a solemn simplicity and quiet beauty. Flowers are placed in metal vases for remembrance prayers to be recited over them by priests requested so to do by the families of the deceased. The last day of the religious calendar – the New Year's eve, corresponding to the fifth Gatha, is given over to the *patet* or atonement prayers for transgressions unwittingly or knowingly committed during the past year. It could be regarded as the Zoroastrians' Day of Atonement. The Zoroastrian equivalent of All-Souls' Day, *Fravardegan*, is observed, with suitable solemnity, on the nineteenth day of the first month, both named *Fravardin* after the term for the tutelary souls of the living and the departed.

It should be noted that whilst every solemnity is observed during the above-mentioned festivals and ceremonies, among the Zoroastrians it is their *festive* nature in the fullest sense of the word which predominates; for them the gloom of excessive sobriety is something to be dispelled with all vigour and despatch.

Apart from the occasional attendances at such ceremonies, there is no further binding religious duty on the average lay British Parsi.

* * * * *

Despite the growing rift within British Jewry between the orthodox and liberal sections of their highly motivated communities, the enviable example of their religious education drive presents the Asian communities' parents with an exemplary model for their own children. It is not easy to account for the Jews' excellent lead in religious education, so closely associated has it hitherto been with their social and familial organizations.

We had briefly touched upon the obligation to have all Jewish male children circumcised when 8 days of age. This is in accordance with injunctions in the *Torah*. Thus the patriarch Abraham is commanded by *Yahweh* to initiate this custom in his immediate family as a token of His covenant (Genesis 17.12). The practice of male circumcision is not, however, restricted to the Jews, it having been prevalent among some Middle Eastern and African societies where the custom probably had as origin a rite of passage from juvenescence to adulthood.

The bar mitzvah of a Jewish boy at the age of 13 is a deeply significant social occasion betokening the assumption of his full religious obligations. The term means 'Son of the Law', the *mitzvah* being the Biblical precept or commandment. On such occasions the initiate is expected to show his religious knowledge and cultural affiliation by a reading of the weekly portion of the Torah and a carefully rehearsed speech on some edifying aspect of these. The female counterpart, the 'daughter of the commandment' or bat/bas mitzvah, confers a similar dignity upon a Jewish girl who has reached the age of religious majority at 12.

Marriage, however construed today, owes its characteristics to the Old Testament regulations. Thus among the Jews it is monogamous and mutual fidelity is religiously enjoined. This has remained the ideal. Marriage within the community was the norm; today it is admitted – to the consternation of the orthodox – that a very large proportion of marriages are exogamous. Among these conservatives this is unfavourably regarded as there is always the fear of apostasy. (A similar anxiety is frequently expressed by the Parsis, although there is no religious interdict against out-marriage.)

The role of the marriage broker, the *shadchan*, assumes a peculiar importance when the arrangement of a Jewish marriage – a *shidduch* – is contemplated. The right of the woman to choose her partner was attested since Genesis, and the status of women was accordingly respected. Marriage too was religiously viewed among these pious ancient people: it reflected the basis of the family, and ultimately the union of the people with their God. Seven Blessings, the *sheva brachoth*, are solemnly intoned during the marriage service and reiterated at the social celebration thereafter.

The closeness of Jewish family ties and the solicitude for children was expressed through their early religious education. From kindergarten age at the *yeshivas*, or orthodox schools, they are taught simple folklorico-religious texts with their meanings in Hebrew, and thus from early infancy a special regard and respect for the Jewish faith and culture is ingrained. The prayers, to the accompaniment of ritual gestures, are expressive of the communion felt by the worshipper with his God. Among these are petitionary prayers, praise formulas and hymnic compositions. Prayers for particular times and feasts are indicated. Perhaps best known is the credal *Shema* with its wonderful simplicity and unambiguity: 'Hear, O Israel: the Lord is your God; the Lord is One!' recited during the morning and evening prayers and on retiring for the night. It is also the deathbed prayer.

Strict dietary laws were promulgated in Leviticus 11 and Deuteronomy 14, where lists of clean and unclean animals for consumption or rejection are found. Food restrictions apply both to the priesthood and to the general body of believers. In the Torah these are presented under the highest authority. Suffice it to say that the flesh of swine is rigorously excluded, as is the flesh of swarming things, of any shell-fish, and of predatory birds. A significant interdict appears against the dietary mixing of meat and milk (Deuteronomy 14.21). The use of wine, a staple of life as reflected in the collocation 'grain, wine, and oil' (Deuteronomy 11.14), was permitted throughout and became a regular component of ritual. Neither overindulgence nor abstinence was ever condoned.

Jewish funerary customs too have their foundation in biblical teaching. The body is disposed of through burial in individual graves in cemeteries, the idea of a physical resurrection – very likely from a Zoroastrian source – prompting this method. The period of mourning lasts for seven days from the funeral, the mourners staying indoors for the duration when the bereaved are said to 'sit *shivah*'. Prayers are said on the anniversary of death.

The absolute day of rest is the *Sabbath* on the seventh day of the week, Saturday, devoted to worship and abstention from work. It was taught that one should not desecrate the *Sabbath* for things that can be done the day before or the day after. The main Jewish sacred feasts rigorously observed amongst the orthodox sections are the historical eight-day *Pesach* or Passover, also called the Feast of Unleavened Bread, which commemorates the passing over or sparing of the Israelite children during the Captivity. In Jewish homes the ceremonial meal with the reading of the *Haggadah Shelpesach* or narrative of the Exodus from Egypt is observed on the first night of the Passover festival. It is fun for children but with an underlying reminder of generations of persecution. Agriculture and religion being intimately connected in Old Testament times, two major festivals were linked with the agricultural year. *Shavuot*, the Feast of Weeks, is a mid-spring festival associated with the first fruits and the end of the grain harvest, commemorating also the giving of the Torah on Mount Sinai. The name refers to the period of seven weeks' deferment of the festival after the spring harvest.

Marking the New Year is the autumn festival of *Rosh Hashanah*, with penitential prayers and the sounding of the ram's horn or *shofar*. Shortly following is the most solemn festival of spiritual accounting through the expiation of sins – the Day of Atonement or *Yom Kippur*. The rabbinical view is 'Let the sinner repent, and he will find atonement'. It originally also served as the day for the purification of the sanctuary and the priesthood in preparation for the autumn pilgrimage festival. In ancient times the sins of the Israelites were symbolically laid upon a scapegoat which was then driven off into the desert. Today prayers of penitence are recited throughout the day in the synagogues, it being one of the most solemn days in the Jewish religious calendar.

Beginning five days later is the autumn harvest festival of *Sukkoth*. Lasting eight days, it commemorates the period when the Israelites dwelt in the wilderness. Also known as the Feast of Tabernacles or Booths, taking its name from the booths, *sukkah*, erected by the orthodox for eating and even sleeping in during its period. It is an occasion of joy at the completion of harvesting of fruits.

Chanukkah, the eight-day Festival of Lights, a more secular occaision takes place in the first winter month. It celebrates the rededication of the

Second Temple in Jerusalem, and is named after the kindling of lights, one light being added on each day of the festival on to the eight-branched candelabrum or *menorah*. The *Hallel*, or Psalms of Praise from the liturgy are recited.

Purim is the annual feast in memory of the deliverance of the Jews from their massacre planned by a wicked enemy – the deviously malevolent Haman (Esther 3.6,13; 9.20f., 24–26) during the fifth century BCE under Persian Achaemenid rule. On this occasion it is the custom to recite from the Esther Scroll and to exchange gifts in celebration of that deliverance. It is noteworthy that all the biblical feasts and festivals, the *yamim nora'im* and the *yamin tovim*, are celebrated throughout the world wherever the Jews are settled, ensuring a continuity of their ancient and hallowed traditions. As communal institutions, the synagogues serve both as buildings for religious services as well as for religious instruction. Rabbinical teachings from the various schools of Jewish thought are studied and respected.

*   *   *   *   *

Christian practices present difficulties owing to the variations observed by different denominations. What is attempted here is based on general observances by the Anglican and Roman Catholic Churches, being the chief representative sects, though the Eastern Churches show an increase in their following in Britain. The various Christologies would account for divergences in rites and practices.

Throughout is present the concept of atonement by the expiation of sins. The Christian sacraments establish the connection between the redemptive acts of Christ and their liturgical representation. For Protestants these are the baptism and the Lord's Supper or *Eucharist*; for the Roman and Eastern Churches the sacraments were baptism, penance, confirmation, the Eucharist, holy orders, matrimony and extreme unction.

Baptism for Christian infants was a purification ritual and became routine within the Church as the doctrine of original sin became widely accepted; for older converts it was the preaching of repentance for the forgiveness of sins. Disciples of all nations – Christianity is a strongly proselytizing religion – are to be baptized in the name of the Father and of the Son and of the Holy Spirit (Matthew 28.19) as a sign of incorporation into the Christian Church.

In Christianity circumcision is not recognized as a sign of the covenant with God. St Paul, the apostle to the gentiles, had held that the Old Testament rite was part of the old contract which had been superseded and was therefore no longer appropriate. That view ultimately became normative for Christians.

The other commonly accepted sacrament was the Lord's Supper or the *Eucharist*. From the earliest times, the communal meal brought together the Christians for the 'breaking of bread'. Bread and wine symbolically denoted the body and blood of Christ who through his crucifixion had transcended death. The meal was a powerful sign of unity within the congregations who partook of this thanksgiving sacrament. The elements of the Last Supper of Jesus were connected with the Jewish Passover, though here the distribution of bread suggests his sacrificing of himself for others, and the wine the symbolism of the New Covenant. In modern church ceremonial the wafer of unleavened bread and the sip of communion wine are symbolic of the *Eucharist*.

The most sacrosanct prayer for the Christians is the Lord's Prayer or *Paternoster*. Both the Matthean and Lucan gospels give its original shape which uses Jesus' form of address to his deity. It was thus taught to his followers as members of the large Christian family who thereby also shared in Jesus' own communion with God. Its main elements: God's name, His kingdom and His will are invoked before the petitioning for the spiritual and physical bread, and the forgiving of sins or transgressions. The prayer ends with an acknowledgement of spiritual frailty in the face of evil – may temptation be kept away from the worshipper.

Christian themes greatly inspired religious and scribal art and solemn music. Churches and cathedrals are richly endowed with choirs schooled in the solemn chants to accompany religious services. The High Mass celebrates the Eucharist or Thanksgiving whose musical settings are sung by the choir and the congregation. Hymns, motets, and anthems also figure in church music, most often accompanied by organ music. Bell-ringing and the lighting of candles are notable features.

Christian feasts and festivals include the *Epiphany* or Twelfth Night to commemorate the manifestation of the infant Jesus to the Magi (in the Eastern Church it is his baptism). The Lenten period of 40 weekdays is observed as a time of penance and fasting in commemoration of Jesus' fasting in the wilderness; it extends from *Ash Wednesday* (so called after the custom of the placing of ash on the forehead as a sign of penitence) to Holy Saturday. Eastertide commences with *Good Friday* when the crucifixion of Jesus is remembered.

Easter Sunday commemorates his resurrection. *Ascension Day*, the 40th day after Easter, celebrates Christ's ascension into heaven. The Christian *Pentecost* on Whit Sunday marks the descent of the Holy Spirit upon the apostles in fulfilment of Jesus' promise that his followers would receive spiritual power. It is also a promise to all nations of the coming of the gospel to the gentiles. The following Sunday, *Trinity*, marks the three-fold unity of Father, Son, and the Holy Spirit. The season of *Advent* precedes *Christmas*, the annual commemoration of the birth of Christ, a fixed festival in the Christian religious calendar. Saints' feasts are also observed, and the worship accorded the Virgin Mary.

Church weddings are still the preferred custom among British

Christians of most denominations. The exchange of marriage vows and of wedding rings takes place before the officiating priest and the congregation of families and invited wedding guests. Registry marriages tend to be more of a secular nature. Divorces and re-marriages, for whatever reasons, are unfortunately on the increase, and from the religious viewpoint can only reflect a loosening of spiritual bonds and a neglect of the marriage vows solemnly uttered during the church nuptials. The effect on families and children are only too distressingly visible to need further comment.

Death and disposal of the dead among the Christian communities, as indeed among the British Jews and Parsis, is again under the supervision of their respective priests, with bereaved families and other mourners attending the last rites. Both burial and cremation are the permitted methods among the Christians and the Parsis for the disposal of the remains. Memorial services are held to commemorate the passing of the communities' members who, in their lifetimes had professed divergent religious beliefs, but who in death had shared the common fate of the dissolution of the body and the release of the soul.

* * * * *

Whether the religious beliefs and practices of the Asian elders will be continued by their youth here in Britain, and if so, in what precise form, is something which only increased spiritual awareness, structured religious guidance and a sense of heritage can ensure. Traditions and customs as part of the cultural baggage of the first immigrants from each of the three religious groups discussed have acquired new significance for succeeding generations in their new social milieu. Inevitable as is the historicism of social encroachments within their religious observances, it remains to be seen how the Asian youth from these categories will accommodate themselves to change. Tribalisms struggle for survival in their outmoded forms – a persistence of cultural identity of which religious traditions form an enduring but not always wholesome aspect. Surrender of long-held ancestral values never comes easily when such identity is seen to be compromised. Compelling challenges await those who wish to preserve ancient beliefs and cherished traditions of which their youth cannot perceive the relevance or with which they can no longer identify in an increasingly secularized and wholly urbanized society.

The role of customs and practices, however, cannot be diluted; they are seen as fences for the protection of religious principles against their erosion. Maintenance of socio-religious distinctions is not a priority for South Asian youth here in a libertarian environment and family tensions frequently result. The various orthodoxies cannot reconcile themselves to latitudinarian or even reactionist elements now prevalent amongst the youth from all three religious backgrounds. Leaders with foresight and farsightedness from among this youth face the burden of achieving a lasting harmony between ancient beliefs and new observances. Social bonds are forged, strengthened and perpetuated through assimilation, not division. Religious exclusivities in the past have served their purpose of socio-religious cohesion; they are now increasingly seen to have contributed in minkind's recent history to the most oppressive acts of inhumanity. With the movements and mingling of peoples from the three religious systems, hope once again dawns for a true ecumenalism – one which rejects the factionalisms within these ancient faiths towards the rediscovery of the Hummanitarianism which lies at the heart of their original doctrines. In these times of rapid travel and instant global communication, cultural isolation becomes increasingly difficult – indeed, undesirable. Cultural identities, however, can still be maintained through merging of social ideals whilst preserving religious character.

The Asian heritage is an important step towards the fulfilment of humanity's true destiny – a united humanity to which the sacred trust of the perfection of this world has been divinely conferred. The Indian subcontinent has long shown the way towards the peaceful and amicable coexistence of these three systems within the conflicts of its majority religious groups; its example can provide a lead for the youth of Great Britain, and beyond to the rest of the civilized world. Religion itself rarely travels well from its original homeland to the lands of immigrant settlements; man's spiritual values, however, transcend both space and time and it is time alone which will truly determine their outcome.

Sources utilized and suggested further reading

General
Eliade M (1978, 1982, 1985) A History of Religious Ideas. 3 vols. Chicago: The University of Chicago Press.
Eliade M (1958) Patterns in Comparative Religion. London: Sheed & Ward.
Hastings Encyclopaedia of Religion and Ethics (1909–1921). Edinburgh: T & T Clark.
Zaehner RC (ed.) (1988) (4th ed) Hutchinson Encyclopaedia of Living Faiths. London: Hutchinson.

Judaism & Christianity
The Apocrypha and the New Testament (Revised English Bible) (1989). Oxford and Cambridge: Oxford University Press and Cambridge University Press.
Davis JD, Gehman H S (1944) Westminster Dictionary of the Bible. London & New York: Collins.
Dimont MI (1962) Jews, God and History. New York: Signet Books.
Metzger BM and Coogan MD (1993) The Oxford Companion to the Bible. Oxford: OUP.
The Tanakh: The New JPS Translation (1985). New York: The Jewish Publication Society.

Zoroastrianism

Boyce M (1979) Zoroastrians: Their Religious Beliefs and Practices. London: RKP.

Duchesne-Guillemin J (1952) The Hymns of Zarathustra (English translation Maria Henning). London: John Murray.

Karaka DF (1884) The Parsis (2 vols). London: Macmillan.

Reuben Levy (translator) (1967) The Epic of the Kings. London: RKP.

Modi JJ (1911) A Catechism of the Zoroastrian Religion. Bombay: J N Petit Parsi Orphanage.

Modi JJ (1937/1986) The Religious Ceremonies and Customs of the Parsees. Bombay: SPZRKE.

Moulton JH (1917) The Treasure of the Magi. Oxford: OUP.

Zaehner RC (1961) The Dawn and Twilight of Zoroastrianism. London: Weidenfeld & Nicholson.

Chapter 8
Health of children from Asian ethnic minorities

ANNA SHARMA

My clinical experience of dealing with children from ethnic minorities comes from over 15 years of paediatrics in inner-city London, an area where over 20% of children come from Asian ethnic minority groups.

The principles of maintaining good delivery of health care to ethnic minority children and their families are exactly the same as for the indigenous population. The differences are that the ethnic minority groups can be both more vulnerable and more isolated, due to social deprivation, increased mobility and unfamiliarity with English and English cultural norms. Thus there is a strong argument for targeting health resources, such as health visitors to this vulnerable group.

Use of interpreters

All health professionals working with non-English speakers should be strongly supported by interpreters for health promotion, health advice and health consultations. In this respect it should be remembered that a telephone interpreting service can be very useful. The good use of interpreters includes basic principles such as making sure that the interpreters and the patient's or patients' mother speak the same language and do not come from warring cultural groups. Another point is that it is not tactful to have a male interpreter for a female for a gynaecological or obstetric consultation or even sometimes for a pediatric consultation. It is common for males to take decisions where this involves the woman's body, so this needs to be recognized particularly in screening for antenatal fetal abnormality where it is probably best for the woman to be seen and counselled separately. There are many instances of women being ostracized if they give birth to an abnormal child. Another instance is a child with pyloric stenoses where the father blames the mother's breast milk for the problem. This is not only misconceived but harmful to the children's well-being. Female Asian workers can be invaluable and need to be left alone with the mother. On a ward round, a white male consultant paediatrician asked an Asian mother if she had any questions. She was silent, but the minute she walked out of the door, the female Asian senior house officer was bombarded!

Other important points are to maintain eye contact with the patient and not the interpreter, to give time for the patient to ask questions, and to provide written information in the patient's own language to take home when possible. Perhaps the most important principle is never to use children as interpreters as this reverses the normal roles of parental responsibility for children, effectively disempowers the adult and may unwittingly involve the child in something the parent wishes to keep confidential.

There are specific health problems that children of ethnic minority families have and that others do not have.

There is much published evidence to show quite clearly that there are inequalities in health between children and families from ethnic minorities and indigenous Caucasian groups throughout the Western world, but particularly in the United Kingdom.

Prematurity

Children from ethnic minorities are more likely to be born prematurely, are more likely to be born by forceps delivery attendant upon an epidural anaesthetic given in labour, and more likely to be born by Caesarean section. The children, when born, are of lower birth weight and have a higher perinatal and infant and neonatal mortality.

Some of the inequality is undoubtedly because of the association of social deprivation with some ethnic minorities and it is not known, for example, whether ethnic minorities of higher social classes would have as healthy children as indigenous Caucasians. We can surmise that the children may well be just as healthy because work on nutrition and birth weight of second-generation immigrant Punjabi children indicates clearly that they catch up and that these children are as tall and as heavy as the indigenous population.

The implications of premature birth are serious. It is associated with difficulty feeding, poor temperature control, a tendency to hypoglycaemia and respiratory distress syndrome as well as increased susceptibility to infection and an increased risk of side effects from hyperbilirubinemia, necessitating early phototherapy for jaundice.

Mothers of children born prematurely may feel disempowered and detached from the child in the incubator on the special care baby unit and may have difficulties with bonding. Complications of prematurity may include cerebral palsy or chronic lung disease, causing the family additional stress at the time of birth and after discharge from the neonatal unit. The other side is that in the home country, some of these children may not have survived or medical care would be expensive, so parents are often very appreciative of health service input.

Growth, nutrition and weaning

Nutrition of children from ethnic minorities begins in the womb, mothers from socially deprived groups may suffer from poor nutrition, resulting in intrauterine growth retardation and low birth weight (defined by the World Health Organization (WHO) as having a birth weight of less than 2.5 kg).

However, it is also true that low birth weight may be familial. Familial low birth weight can be distinguished from low birth weight due to intrauterine growth retardation mainly by examination of the placenta, which, in intrauterine growth retardation, will tend to be small and gritty. Interesting studies of birth weight in both the UK and internationally have indicated that this is not related primarily to ethnic group but to the nutritional status of the mother. Children of second-generation Punjabi immigrants in the UK tend on average to have the same birth weight as children of indigenous Caucasians of the same social class.

Children in Hong Kong in 1991 had the highest birth weight in the world and this was thought to be due to the high standard of antenatal care and maternal nutrition in the colony.

Thus low birth weight in children from ethnic minorities of second generation immigrants should be taken as a possible indicator of poor maternal nutrition. One should not simply assume that this is familial.

Some ethnic minority children with a low birth weight display 'catch-up growth' whereas others remain short all their lives. All paediatricians will have seen short but normal children whose weight and height may be below the 0.4 UK 1993 centile or the third Tanner centile, but who are growing at a normal speed and warrant no further investigation. Most short children are healthy but some may have chronic asthma or renal problems. Short Asian children should be monitored in the same way as Caucasian children until it has been demonstrated that they do indeed have a normal growth rate and normal weight gain.

The height of some newly arrived immigrant children may be an issue where there has been chronic malnutrition, which cannot always be totally reversed, or where the accurate date of birth is unknown. I am reluctant to request radiological estimations of bone age in children where the main concern about date of birth comes from the Home Office; but when clinically indicated – for example when investigating short stature or learning difficulty – bone age can be very useful.

Breastfeeding and weaning

Two extremes are sometimes found in newly immigrant mothers of children from ethnic minorities. Some mothers will breastfeed infants up to the age of 2 years and I have come across a 4-year-old, still being breastfed at night. As long as this is not the main source of nutrition beyond the age of 3 to 6 months, I see no reason why limited breast feeding should not continue if the child is receiving an otherwise balanced diet and there is no evidence of dietary deficiency.

Unfortunately, prolonged breastfeeding may be associated with poor intake of vegetables, leading to iron deficiency in particular, and leading to nutritional deficiency. The other risk is immaturity in the developing of feeding patterns. Chewing, and the intake of a varied diet at mealtimes may be hindered, leading to difficulties even when the child is ultimately weaned. The other significant side effect of prolonged breastfeeding (or is it a cause?) appears to be a lack of normal separation of the infant from the mother. I have found that the solution here is to avoid the polarization that often occurs among health professionals when an older child is breastfed and to enable the mother to think of breast milk as part of a balanced weaning diet rather than trying to discourage her completely.

At the other extreme, many mothers bottlefeed from day one, thinking that formula feed is somehow nutritionally better for the child due to the added vitamins and minerals. This misconception continues to be held worldwide and in UK immigrant communities. This is in spite of concerted health promotion efforts internationally and nationally and limitations on the support given by organizations such as the Royal College of Paediatricians and Child Heath to advertising by formula milk manufacturers.

In my experience, the very best educators come from within the minority community itself. No one is a better health advocate than an educated and articulate member of the same ethnic minority community. Children also make very good advocates. I have seen bright young primary school children eagerly absorb nutritional advice given to them by school nurses and grow to become health advocates in local clinics on leaving school as well as taking the ideas back home to their families.

Iron deficiency anaemia

Many studies have now shown that iron deficiency anaemia is more common in children from Asian ethnic minority groups. Studies show that up to 30% of 15-month-old children may suffer from nutritional iron deficiency anaemia.

Some health authorities and general practitioners in Britain adopt a screening approach on the basis of a sample of blood done at the health visitors' 18-month check. This has been shown to be acceptable to health professionals and parents alike. Unfortunately this test (currently marketed by Haemacue) cannot distinguish between iron deficiency and anaemia due to thalassaemia. Indeed both may co-exist, and frequently do. The diagnosis can be made clinically. Effects are mitigated to a certain extent because the oxygen disassociation curve in thalassaemia shifts to the right in children with thalassaemia. In addition, children with thalassaemia have mild anaemia. Laboratory tests should be used to confirm the diagnosis. Haemoglobin concentrations as low as 5–6 gm/dl may be found in iron deficiency. The diagnosis is confirmed by a low serum iron with high total iron binding capacity.

Iron deficiency should be treated with elemental iron and also dietary advice. In particular, advice should include recommending adequate intake of fruit as well as green vegetables. This is because vitamin C aids the absorption of iron. Phytates in *chapati* flour decrease absorption and so fruit is even more essential. Apricots are to be recommended as they are also high in iron. One important point is that iron deficiency can coexist in socially privileged groups as well. A recent report from the Department of Health showed that children from ethnic minority groups were eating fewer fruit and vegetables in the 1990s than in the 1980s.

Rickets

Rickets is the bony abnormality caused by vitamin D deficiency and phostphate deficiency resulting in decreased bone density and bowing of the legs with splayed epiphyses and the phenomenon known as the 'rickety rosary' at the interchondral junctions. Widened radial heads lead to splaying at the wrists and decreased bone density leads to a widened anterior fontanelle and sometimes indentation of the skull with a rather peculiar crackling sound on palpation. The reason for the increased prevalence of rickets in Asian children is twofold. Firstly, some children hardly see the daylight, particularly in the winter when their mothers, used to warmer climates, have an understandable reluctance to wander out of doors, not yet having adopted the English passion for fresh air. The lack of sunlight predisposes to rickets. Decreased intake of vitamin D is less of a problem nowadays than it used to be as infant formula feeds are all fortified with it. However, breastfed children should be started on a preparation containing vitamin D such as Abidec, which is available in the UK over the counter in 'well baby clinics' run by the health authorities. The diagnosis of rickets can be confirmed radiologically and by laboratory tests, which show raised plasma phosphate levels, low or normal plasma calcium, and highly raised alkaline phosphatase levels. The finding of raised plasma alkaline phosphatase in isolation should be treated with caution as children have raised plasma alkaline phosphatase anyway, especially during a growth spurt. Rickets is treated by administering calcium and vitamin D in the recommended dosages. A word of caution: it is important to ascertain that the mother is not already giving some other vitamin-containing preparation such as cod liver oil, since there is a danger of toxicity with excessive vitamin D intake.

Mothers should be advised to stop other preparations containing vitamin D when a child is prescribed treatment for rickets.

Vitamin B

Some vegan mothers may have low levels of folate and vitamin B_{12} and vitamin B_6. The current recommendation to prevent neural tube defects (spina bifida) is that folate supplementation should occur before conception, when the parents are thinking of having a baby. Folate is found in fresh green vegetables but vitamin B_6 may be deficient in the diet of Hindu vegans. Here we can recommend the yeast extract, Marmite, spread thinly on toast, as an ideal vegetarian source of all the B vitamins. This product is available over the counter at reduced prices in well baby clinics run by the health authority.

The older child

Asian mothers of two to seven-year-old children invariably complain that their children will not eat. Sometimes this is the result of unrecognized illness, commonly (in my experience) asthma. Sometimes the child's nutritional status is normal from a Western point of view but one needs to bear in mind that the ideal Eastern child is chubby.

Here the centile charts and three or four serial measurements of height, weight and head circumference not less than three months apart in conjunction with knowledge of parental height can be very useful, reassuring both the mother and the physician that her child is normal.

Often, however, eating is a real problem. The immigrant family may have suffered from multiple moves from bed-and-breakfast or refugee hostels to cramped council flats and facilities for cooking traditional meals may be poor. Familiar vegetables may or may not be available. Some local markets have excellent food stalls but elsewhere vegetables and spices for cooking may be unavailable or very expensive. Egg custard is an example of a much-used unsuitable weaning food. Many children are raised on crisps, Coca-Cola and Rice Krispies. In homes with no dining table, it is difficult for the family to sit together and mealtimes become irregular and disturbed.

Here again, I have found health visitors and health advocates and the community dieticians invaluable. There is currently a wealth of knowledge about suitable foods for all kinds of diets and this can and should be disseminated very successfully. There is no doubt, however, in my experience, that the more sympathetic and successful advisers tend to come from ethnic minority backgrounds themselves.

Haemoglobinopathies

Thalassaemia, sickle cell disease, and Hbc disease are more common in Afro-Caribbean and Asian minority groups. In some health authorities, for example Brent, the proportion of the population from such minorities is high enough to warrant neonatal population screening for haemoglobinopathy and this is done using a spot of blood, like the Guthrie test.

The Haemoglobinopathies can be classified into two subgroups:

- where there is an alteration in the amino acid structure of the polypeptide chains of the globin fraction of haemoglobin, commonly called the abnormal haemoglobins. The best known example is haemoglobin S found in sickle-cell anaemia. Some 'abnormal' haemoglobins function as normal variants.
- where the amino acid sequence is normal but polypeptide chain production is impaired or absent for a variety of reasons: these are the thalassaemias.

Abnormal haemoglobins are caused by amino acid substitutions in the polypeptide chains. These in turn reflect mutations in the structural genes controlling the production of these chains. There are several hundred known haemoglobin variants, some functionally normal, most not. Originally they were designated by letters of the alphabet, such as S, C or E. Now this does not suffice and for some years new variants have been given names, often of the towns or districts in which they were discovered. Sickle-cell haemoglobin or haemoglobin S is the most important in Afro-Caribbean groups but haemoglobin C, D and E are also significant in Asia and the Mediterranean area, particularly when inherited along with haemoglobin S or with beta thalassaemia.

Haemoglobin C disease

This is a benign haemoglobinopathy found in Afro-Caribbean and Asian populations. In its homozygous form, it is not associated with much morbidity. It may cause megaloblastic anaemia in pregnancy and considerable splenomegaly in adult life. No specific treatment is required other than folic acid supplements in pregnancy.

The thalassaemias

Thalassaemia is an inherited impairment of haemoglobin products in which there is partial or complete failure to synthesize a specific type of globin chain. The exact nature of the defect varies and it is probable that a number of different faults occur along the pathway that translates genetic information into a polypeptide chain. The gene itself may be deleted –

and usually is in thalassaemia. When the abnormality is heterozygous, synthesis of haemoglobin is only mildly affected and little disability occurs. Synethesis is grossly impaired when the patient is homozygous and there is an imbalance in polypeptide chain production. The chains produced in excess precipitate in the cell, forming Heinz bodies.

Beta-thalassaemia

Failure to synthesize beta-chains (B-thalassaemia) is the most common type of beta-thalassaemia and is seen most frequently in the Mediterranean area. Heterozygotes have thalassaemia minor, a condition in which there is usually mild anaemia and little or no clinical disability. Homozygotes (thalassaemia major) are either unable to synthesize haemoglobin A or, at best, produce very little and after the first four months of life develop a profound hypochromic anaemia.

Clinical features of B thalassaemia minor

The anaemia is crippling and the probability of survival for more than a few years without transfusion is low. Bone marrow hyperplasia early in life may produce head bossing and prominent malar eminences. Skull radiography shows a 'hair on end' appearance and general widening of the medullary spaces which may interfere with development of the paranasal sinuses. Development and growth are retarded and folate deficiency may occur. Splenomegaly is an early and prominent feature. Hepatomegaly is slower to develop but may become massive, especially if splenectomy is undertaken. Transfusion therapy inevitably gives rise to haemosiderosis. Cardiac enlargement is common and cardiac failure, in which haemosiderosis may play a part, is a frequent terminal event.

B-thalassaemia minor is often detected only when iron therapy for a mild hypochromic anaemia fails. Symptoms are absent or minimal. Intermediate grades of clinical severity occur.

Prevention

It is possible to identify a fetus with homozygous B-thalassaemia by obtaining chorionic villus material for DNA analysis sufficiently early in pregnancy to allow termination of pregnancy. This examination is appropriate if both parents are known to be carriers (B-thalassaemia minor) and will accept a termination.

A community-based genetic counselling service for haemoglobinopathies and other conditions prevalent among ethnic minorities has been set up in Brent and at the Institute of Child Health in London and has had some success for many years.

G6PD deficiency

This is inherited as an X-linked disorder with a high frequency among Asians of Chinese origin and African blacks among whom there are electrophoretic enzymes. The enzymes are A-type (A-) in deficient African blacks. In Caucasians only the normal B-type enzyme is found and the deficient type is also B (B-). In West and East Africa about 20% of males (homozygotes) and about 4% of females (homozygous for the abnormal gene) are affected and the enzyme activity is about 15% of normal heterozygous females worldwide.

The deficiency in Caucasian and Oriental populations is more severe, enzyme activity being less than 1% of normal. Favism (haemolytic anaemia from the ingestion of the broad bean, *Vicia faba*) is due to deficiency of G6PD of the severe variety (B-). Some cases of haemolytic disease of the newborn are caused by this deficiency. Other rare types of G6PD, biochemically different from the above, may be associated with congenital nonspherocytic haemolytic disease and occur sporadically in all races.

Many drugs in common clinical use, such as some antimalarials and sulphonamides, are capable of precipitating haemolysis in individuals with G6PD deficiency. Infections may also potentiate the haemolysis in individuals with G6PD deficiency, and may also potentiate the haemolytic action of drugs such as aspirin, chloramphenicol and chloroquine.

Clinical features

Persons with G6PD deficiency normally enjoy good health but are liable to haemolysis if certain drugs or foods are ingested. However, the haemolytic effect is dose related and will not be clinically detectable if the amount does not exceed a critical level. It is often possible to employ doses that are not toxic. The anaemia, when it occurs, may be rapid in onset, becoming obvious between two and 10 days after exposure to the precipitating agent, and may be sufficiently severe to cause haemoglobinuria as well as the other classical signs of haemolysis. In the relatively mild type of deficiency prevalent in blacks, only older cells that have lost enzyme activity are involved so that the haemolysis is to some extent self-limiting even when the offending agent is continued.

Young red cells have some G6PD activity and remain viable until their enzyme complement decays. The enzyme deficiency is much more severe in the B-variety and destruction tends to be greater. Anuria is an infrequent but serious complication.

Investigation

The diagnosis can be confirmed by estimating the G6PD activity of the red cell but this may not be entirely accurate if there is a considerable reticulocytosis. A number of screening tests are also available. The characteristics of intravascular haemolysis are usually present: haemoglobinaemia, methaemalbuminaemia, haemoglobinuria, ahaptoglobinaemia and later haemosiderinuria.

Management

This is by removal of the toxic agent. Recovery is usually rapid but if the anaemia is severe, transfusion of red cells with a normal enzyme comple-ment may be required. Thereafter the patient should be advised to avoid drugs that may precipitate the disorder. Splenectomy is valueless.

Congenital conditions and child development – the importance of health surveillance programme

Mothers who have recently arrived in Britain may not have participated in a neonatal screening programme for haemoglobinopathy, hypothyroidism or phenylketonuria such as those that exist in this country. Some years ago I came across a family that had recently arrived in the country from the Persian Gulf. The 6-year-old daughter presented with moderate learning difficulties. Some months after their arrival, another child was born in the UK and phenylketonuria was diagnosed with the Guthrie test. The older child was tested and found to have phenylketonuria which had remained untreated from birth and was the cause of her learning difficulty. I have come across other children who have had undiagnosed cataracts and untreated congenitally dislocated hips.

In this country the routine child health surveillance (or child health promotion programme as it is now called) aims to pick up common major conditions that affect health and development in early childhood. We take this for granted but in newly-arrived immigrants or children of refugee families and asylum seekers, the paediatrician has to start from scratch and assume no prior screening. Cardiac conditions may present for the first time at the age of 10 for example. It is particularly important to do a thorough physical examination and take a detailed history from the school-age child who underperforms.

One problem here has been in explaining the child health surveillance programme to all new arrivals and making sure that they use it. Many par-ents have difficulty with the concept of taking an apparently well child to a doctor or health visitor. Other groups, perhaps from authoritarian regimes, will be wary of health professionals and will fail to attend because, in some regimes, a doctor is the tool of a totalitarian state.

Other problems arise with the screening programme for diseases such as Down's syndrome or HIV, where mothers can choose to opt for a more detailed screening – for example serological testing for HIV or amniocentesis for Down's syndrome. Here colleagues have often found that it is the male partners who take all the decisions, and the females may or may not agree even for something like amniocentesis or abortion for abnormality.

Counsellors need to be sympathetic towards the view of some anti-abortion religious communities.

Play

Commonly I have found that isolated young mothers do not know how to play with their children. Houses may suffer from a dearth of toys, or toys may be treated as decorative ornaments. Access to public libraries for children's books will be a new concept. Mothers, perhaps without a car, may lack access to safe open spaces for the children to play ball games. As a result, developmental delay due to lack of stimulation may occur. Advice needs to be given, not just to the parents, but also to the members of the family who may be involved in care giving. I have to say that in my experience, although this does happen, often in minority groups from Asia, the safety net and support of the extended family, particularly from grandparents, can offset the other cultural disadvantages and Asian children can be very high achievers as a result.

Learning difficulties

Educational performance is often taken to be due to difficulties experienced with English as a foreign language. I am often asked whether English should be the only language spoken in the home setting. My response is to enquire which language the parents speak between themselves. This is the language that should be spoken in the home setting. If grandparents, as is common with immigrant groups, speak a different language in preference, then it is perfectly advisable to recommend that the grandparents speak their own language at home and to the children. The reason for these recommendations is that the development of language occurs in the Broca's area of the brain and is independent of the particular language spoken, but does depend on the quality of the language spoken. Children's language comprehension is in advance of expression and they learn most by listening to adults. Children learn the depth and breadth of language by listening to adults conveying the whole gamut of feelings and emotions in speech and, unless they are exposed to this, their language development will be retarded. The received wisdom is that children who learn a mother tongue will be able to learn a second language easily, whereas children who do not even learn one language well will find it hard to pick up a second one. I can still remember the intense look of pleasure on a Bengali-speaking grandfather's face when I told him it was all right and indeed preferable to speak his mother tongue to his grandson and that he did not have to speak broken, unfamiliar English.

Difficulties due to English as a second language contribute to learning difficulties at school but the pediatrician's duty is to exclude other contributing illnesses. Cataracts or vision problems may occur. I have seen undiagnosed sensorineural hearing losses. Severe untreated mastoiditis may cause conductive hearing losses, cerebral palsy and congenital cardiac disease and epilepsy may also not be diagnosed unless specifically looked for.

School nurses in the UK are the lynchpin of the school health service, just as the health visitors are responsible for co-ordinating the core child health surveillance programme for the under-five's. The pediatrician works closely with the primary health care team to detect physical causes of delayed development, ill health or poor school performance. In Camden and Islington, we put together multi-agency guidelines for good practice in identifying and dealing with health issues in refugee children, many of these being applicable to new immigrant children.

Accidents

Children from ethnic minority families, and particularly boys, are more accident prone than those from Caucasian groups.

Data from the National Household Survey, a cohort study of all children born in the UK in one week in April, which began in 1959, shows that boys from ethnic minorities are more accident prone at all ages. The reasons are likely to be related to differences in social class, large family size, overcrowding, urban lifestyles and poor housing but there is also a lesson to be learned in accident prevention, for it may be that families from ethnic minority groups are less likely to have a 'DIY' culture and so less likely to fit stair gates, locks on windows, smoke alarms and the like. The message here is that health promotion advice should be targeted to ethnic minority groups and this is best done by community staff such as health visitors.

Local health promotion departments and voluntary agencies, such as 'Home Start', can be very helpful in providing advice, written leaflets and translations, and often equipment. Another useful contact is the 'Child Accident Prevention Trust'.

Vaccination

One question that often arises concerns vaccination. Many countries in the world have excellent WHO-based immunization programmes, and refugees or newly arrived immigrants will have a record indicating their vaccination status. Diphtheria, tetanus, pertussis and polio vaccinations are universally given and if a good record or history of repeated injections in infancy is obtained, then it is safe to assume the child has had a full primary course of vaccines. However, those coming from migrant or war zones may not be immunized.

Tuberculosis (TB)

Children from Asian ethnic minorities are at high risk of contact with TB and much of this is imported, although by no means all of it. As a result, a neonatal bacile Calmette-Guérin (BCG) programme has been adopted in some London boroughs. New arrivals may be screened by the port authority, by their general practitioner or by the school nurse, who use skin testing with tuberculin purified protein derivative (ppd). Children with a scar who test more than Grade 3 heaf positive or children without a scar who test Grade 2 heaf positive should be referred to a specialist chest clinic for diagnostic tests to exclude TB, and those in direct contact with the disease, and cases where TB is confirmed, will need treatment.

Asthma

There is a well-described increase in the prevalence of asthma in children from Asian ethnic minorities. This may be atopic or it could be related to parental smoking or housing in urban environments; it is not yet known. The asthma often resolves with visits to rural areas in the home country but children visiting the cities in the home country are well advised to take their medication with them.

Migrant workers

A rather interesting effect has been described by researchers into the effect of pesticides on families of immigrant farm workers. As they were not indigenous, these workers were not subject to the same safety standards and safeguards as other workers. The drift and run-off of agricultural pesticide pollutes the air, soil and water, supposedly resulting in chronic outcomes such as adverse reproductive outcomes, delayed neuropathy, neurobehavioural effects, and even cancer.

Lead poisoning

Related to this is the problem of lead poisoning, which is more common in children from ethnic minorities, presumably due to residence in socially deprived areas with poor housing, likely to have lead-containing paintwork. The increase in lead poisoning, however, is also said to be related to a lack of preventive counselling. The symptoms of lead poisoning are similar to other symptoms of emotional and behavioural disorder – hyperactivity, poor concentration and difficulty in learning. High serum lead levels are diagnostic, as are the rarely seen 'lead lines' of lead deposition in bones revealed by radiology, and basophilic stippling of red cells on blood films.

Surma

This is a lead powder usually imported from India used as an eyeliner in infants and Asian women. Through contact with the fingers when being applied, or when a child sucks his thumb, it can be ingested causing varying degrees of lead toxicity. The doctor should advise replacing the *surma* with *Kajal* which is made of ash collected from a *diva*, an Indian lamp commonly sold at Diwali time. *Kajal* is sold commercially and is safe and inexpensive and is a satisfactory substitute.

Moving

Other problems of ethnic minority groups are those resulting directly from multiple-moves from temporary accommodation, often to a different borough, until permanent housing is finally found. Moving is a family stressor that has a significant effect on the child, particularly, as is often the case, when it is associated with school moves as well. Anxiety, poor concentration, poor peer relationships and isolation contribute to learning difficulties and mental health problems.

The other effect of moving is that transfer of health information and access to the core child health surveillance programme decreases with increasing mobility. Professor Taylor in Camden and Islington Community Trust has shown that immunization data are 95% complete for children who are stable in one area but only 60% complete for children who move in or out. Clearly, immigrant children, more likely to be from ethnic minorities, are more at risk of having an incomplete immunization programme or child health surveillance programme, even when they have been in the country for some time, unless they are in stable accommodation.

Conclusion

I have attempted to describe some of the health issues which face Asian children today as I have come across them in my clinical practice. There are two concluding points. The first is that the best health workers are motivated parents from the ethnic minority groups themselves. The other is that most children of Asian parents who immigrate start with a huge environmental and ethnic advantage which is that their parents are likely to be flexible, adaptable and have initiative, drive and intelligence or they wouldn't have survived being here!

Bibliography

'Exercise-induced bronchoconstriction by ethnicity and presence of asthmas in British nine year olds', Jones, CO; Qureshi, S; Chinn, S. Department of Public Health Medicine., St Thomas' Hospital, London UK. Thorax, 1996 Nov. 51 (11): 1134-6

'The biology of intelligence?'; MacKintosh-NJ. British Journal of Psychology, 1986 Feb; 77 (Pt 1): 1-18

'National Study of Health and Growth: social and biological factors associated with height of children from ethnic groups living in England.'; Rona, RJ; Chinn, S. Annual Human Biology, 1986 Sept-Oct; 13 (5): 453-71

'Vegetarianism and growth in Urdu, Gujarati and Punjabi children in Britain.' Rona, RJ; Chinn, S; Duggal, S; Driver, AP. Department of Community Medicine, United Medical School of Guy's Hospital, London. Journal of Epidemiology and Community Health. 1987 Sept; 41(3):233-6

'Iron deficiency in ethnic minorities: associations with dietary fibre and phytate.' D'Souza, SW; Lakhani, P; Waters, HM; Boardman, KM; Cinkotai, KI. Early Human Development. 1987 Mar; 15(2):103-11

'AIDS in minority populations in the United States.' Hopkins, DR. Centres for Disease Control, Atlanta, GA 30333. Public Health Report 1987 Nov-Dec; 102(6): 677-81

'The intelligence of six year olds in Hong Kong.' Chan, J; Lynn, R. Journal of Biosocial Science. 1989 Oct; 21(4): 461-4

'Extrapulmonary tuberculosis in the United States.' Rieder, HL; Snider, DE Jr; Cauthen, GM. Division of Tuberculosis Control, Centers for Disease Control, Atlanta, GA30333. American Review of Respiratory Disease, 1990 Feb; 141 (2): 347-51

'Ethnic minorities, migration and risk of undernutrition in children'; Pelto, GH. Department of Nutritional Sciences, University of Connecticut, Storrs. Acta -Paediatrics Scand. Supplement. 1991; 374: 51-7

'Prevention and control of tuberculosis in US communities with at-risk minority populations. Recommendations of the Advisory Council for the Elimination of Tuberculosis.' MMWR Morb. Mortal Weekly Report., 1992 Apr 17; 41 (RR-5): 1.11

'Standards for pediatric immunisation practices. Recommended by the National Vaccine Advisory Committee.' MMWR Morb. Mortal Weekly Report. 1993 Apr 23: 42 (RR-5) 1 -10

'Cystic fibrosis in children from ethnic minorities in the West Midlands.' Spencer, DA; Vankataraman, M; Higgins, S; Stevenson, K; Weller, PH. Cystic Fibrosis Unit, Birmingham Children's Hospital, UK. Respiratory Medicine. 1994 Oct; 88(9): 671-5

'The changing face of tuberculosis'. Huebner, RE; Castro, KG. Division of Tuberculosis Elimination, Centres for Disease Control and Prevention, Atlanta, GA 30333. Annual Review of Medicine 1995; 46: 47-55

'Parents' views of health surveillance.' Sutton, JC; Jagger, C; Smith, LK. Arch. Dis. Child. 1995 Jul; 73(1): 57-61

Chapter 9
Educational issues

DEV SHARMA

The education of children of Asian origin has been a matter of continuing concern for parents and professionals since large-scale immigration into the United Kingdom started following the Second World War. Understandably designed for the majority society, the British education system was hardly in a position to meet the manifold needs of this group of children. Early approaches perceived their particular needs predominantly in terms of poor linguistic competence in English. It was hoped that if they could be equipped with sufficient skills in English they would be able to function adequately within the school system. Despite the availability of research evidence and experiences of several other countries with large minority populations (Banks, 1986; Moodley, 1986), the British education system at the time showed little awareness of any other issues that may have a possible bearing on the educational development of these children. The following three decades or so witnessed what at times became a lively debate under various headings such as the education of ethnic minority children, multicultural education, anti-racist education and the education of bilingual and bicultural children.

This chapter examines how Asian children have fared in the British education system. What particular problems and predicaments have they encountered and what problems do they continue to encounter? How have these children adjusted to the British education system and how, in turn, has the system accommodated to their particular needs and the wishes of their parents and families? The chapter begins with a brief overview of general developments in the area of the education of ethnic minority children in Britain, without which any account of the education of Asian children would be incomplete.

Education of ethnic minority children in Britain: a brief overview

It is beyond the scope of this chapter to provide a full review of the large body of literature that has accumulated on this subject. Nor it is necessary to do so. Only a brief account of the developments in general thinking and theoretical perspectives on the subject of multicultural education is necessary to put the education of Asian children and young people in context.

Lynch (1986) provides a comprehensive, authoritative and provocative account of the development of multicultural education in Britain, including similar developments in the United States, Canada, Australia and some European countries. He uses the phrase *multicultural education* as a generic term to cover various aspects of the education of ethnic minority children, in contrast with some other authors on this subject who have used different terminology. It is useful to consider his analysis of the development of multicultural education in Britain in some detail.

According to Lynch (1986: 40), there are 'five clearly identifiable chronological and conceptual phases' in the development of the education of ethnic minority children in Britain. He calls the first period, lasting until the beginning of the 1960s, the *laissez faire* phase, which, in his view, was marked by ignorance and neglect. The system took little cognizance of any particular problems posed by the presence of an increasing number of children arriving with families from the new Commonwealth countries. It was hoped that they would be absorbed in the system without any allowance being made to accommodate their particular needs. Initiatives to consider their particular educational needs, both at national or local level, were conspicuous by their absence during this period.

The report, *English for Immigrants,* published by the Ministry of Education in 1963, was the first initiative by the central government that ushered the education of ethnic minority children into the next phase, called the 'immigrant and ESL phase', which lasted until approximately the mid-1970s. Several other reports on this subject were published by central government sources during this period (*The Education of Immigrants*, HMSO, 1971; Department of Education and Science, 1972; Schools Council, 1973). This phase was marked by a growing realization of the particular educational needs of ethnic minority pupils. However, the needs of minority pupils were largely seen in terms of improving their English language proficiency. Section 11 of the Local Government Act 1966 made extra resources available for teaching the English language to immigrant children. This phase also saw the publication of government Circular 7/65, which introduced a policy of dispersal of non-English speaking children in schools so that no school should have more than 30% of such children on its roll. This measure proved controversial, however, and was soon withdrawn. Towards the end of this phase, a grudging but dawning recognition of needs other than mere help with English language became noticeable, particularly in areas with a large concentration of ethnic minority children.

The third phase, lasting from mid-1970s to the early 1980s, has been described as the 'deficit phase'. During this period, as a result of a steady stream of reports on the educational performance of ethnic minority pupils (Little, 1975; Mackintosh and Mascie-Taylor, 1985) and the deep concerns expressed by parents, the underachievement of minority pupils became a matter of notable public and professional concern. The poor performance of ethnic minority pupils was explained in terms of the consequences of social, cultural and economic disadvantages suffered by the minority communities.

The 1980s witnessed a mounting debate on the education of ethnic minority children and ushered in the genuine beginnings of the next phase, the multicultural education phase. Several major reports were published (Department of Education and Science, 1981e; *Multicultural Education*, Schools Council, 1982). Many national and regional conferences were held. Many research studies were carried out; papers and books published. Scores of local education authorities published policy statements on multicultural education. Major subject areas took cognizance of minority cultural values. Teacher-training programmes began to include multicultural ideas in their curriculum content. Despite these developments, the whole area of the education of ethnic minority children was marked by a strong ambivalence, scepticism and lack of clear policy at the national level.

As multicultural ideas gained ground, they started attracting criticism from the proponents of multicultural education as well as detractors. The more enthusiastic supporters of multicultural education described the measures so far as merely palliative and even condemned them as a strategy of social control. Its critics, mainly in the establishment, on the other hand condemned it as dangerously subversive and undermining of traditional British values and standards. For a while the proponents of anti-racist education, as Lynch described this final phase, held sway and pushed for more radical measures such as challenging teachers' own latent racism and argued that multicultural education should be a means towards prejudice reduction in society. As such, although they criticized the 'establishment' for using multicultural education as a means of social control, they showed little hesitation in advocating its use for what can only be described as an instrument of social engineering.

During the past decade there have been momentous changes in the education system in Britain and the issue of the education of ethnic minority children has been overtaken by these events. Extra resources made available under Section 11, meagre though they already were, have been further curtailed. The hopes raised by the publication of Swann Report (*Education for All*) in 1985 have come to nothing. The education system, creaking under the weight of unprecedented and incessant

changes starting with the 1988 Education Reform Act, hardly appears in a
position to accommodate radical ideas such as anti-racist education. The
rumblings over multicultural education, faint though they are, nevertheless continue.

A brief consideration of Tomlinson's (1983) book, *Ethnic Minorities in
British Schools*, which provides an excellent review of literature in this field
between the years 1960–82, would add an important and necessary dimension to the developments in multicultural education described above. This is
the period during which the debate on the issue of the education of ethnic
minority children was at its hottest. The publication of the Swann Report in
1985 was a culmination of the developments that took place during this
period, though sadly the Report had little real impact on the educational
scene in Britain.

Tomlinson (1983) draws interesting parallels between developments in
the education of ethnic minority children and working-class children in
general. One of the central concerns about the education of working-class
children in Britain during the twentieth century has been, and still is,
their low levels of achievement (Halsey, 1972). Likewise, one of the major
concerns about the education of ethnic minority children is their low level
of achievement. The relatively poor educational performance of ethnic
minority children was put down to factors external to school. Factors such
as cultural differences, migration processes, family background and economic disadvantage were considered to explain relatively poor school
achievements (Oakley, 1968; Pollack, 1972). The poor educational
achievements of working-class children were similarly explained in terms
of economic disadvantage and home factors such as restricted language
codes (Bernstein, 1973). In both cases, as Jencks (1972) has argued, there
was pessimism over the extent to which school could make much difference. The movement for comprehensive schooling reached its peak
around the same time as the education of ethnic minority children
became a national issue, which added a further dimension to the educational debate in quest of what Halsey (1972) described as the 'strategy for
educational roads to equality'.

It is in the light of these general developments in the education of ethnic minority children that the issue of the education of Asian children can
be best considered.

Language issues

Tomlinson (1984: 114) states that 'language issues in the education of ethnic minority children are by no means as simple as they first appear'. They
are deeply and inextricably intertwined with the history and politics of the
majority society and the settled minority communities. Language is not
merely a mode of communication. It is as, as Hernandez-Chavez (1988: 45)
argues, 'the symbolic expression of community, encoding a group's values,

its folkways and its history'. The Bullock Report (Bullock, 1975) underlined the crucial importance of language as the 'kingpin' around which education revolves. Sadly, despite recognizing the enormous importance of language in education, the British education system dismally failed to implement this principle in the education of Asian children. The language policy in the education of Asian children never really progressed beyond a diet of English as second language teaching and grudgingly ritualistic respect for the child's home language.

Teaching of English as a second language

The early approach to the education of Asian children in Britain, as indicated earlier in the chapter, was completely oblivious to the deeper cultural and sociological significance of the children's home language to their social, emotional and intellectual development. The focus was entirely on English. The home-language skills of even those pupils arriving in schools with well-developed oral and literacy skills were ignored. They were considered as more of a hindrance than an advantage. This approach fitted in with the assimilationist educational and social perspectives of the period, which regarded 'the process of education for an immigrant in this country . . . as a process of adapting not only his way of life, his habits and actions but his whole personality' (Schools Council, 1967: 5). In order to achieve this goal, teaching the English language was considered as 'the key to cultural and social assimilation and co-operation' (Schools Council, 1967: 4). This approach also conformed to the view that held language difference to be an inherent deficit in children whose home language happened to be other than English.

One of the first national initiatives in the education of Asian children was, therefore, understandably in the teaching of English. The Ministry of Education (1963) published an advisory pamphlet, *English for the Children of Immigrants,* which set out advice on staffing, organization and teaching of English including preparation and the use of materials. The majority of local education authorities with a significant proportion of Asian children used Section 11 funding to employ extra staff for this purpose, but there was a shortage of appropriately trained teachers in this subject. There was also confusion about methods and purposes for the teaching of English to this particular group of pupils. The pedagogical approaches to the teaching of English to children growing up in a predominantly English language environment outside of their home had not been fully thought through and it took some time before the discipline of teaching English as a Second Language (ESL or E2L) became established. The advice offered by the Ministry of Education was tentative and feebly pointed to the need for research in this area. During the early period, most such teaching took place in English language centres where children were withdrawn either on a long-term basis or attended for a part of the week. However, the provision was piecemeal and patchy and there was considerable variation from one authority to another.

By the 1970s, thinking on the education of Asian children widened to include other issues such as the role of the mother tongue and multicultural curriculum and the 'steam had gone out of the debate on the teaching of English as a second language' (Derrick, 1977: 11). However, the protestations against the over-emphasis on the teaching of English to the exclusion of other, wider issues were ideological, and the necessity to provide specialist English teaching to children who have poor language skills because their home language is other than English continues to be recognized as an important need to this day. Most local education authorities with a significant number of such children provide for the teaching of English as a second language. By and large, however, this provision is limited to the initial stage at the primary level. Despite the concerns expressed by professionals, the Department of Education and Science (1972) and the Bullock Report (Bullock, 1975) over the relatively poor, and in many cases non-existent, ESL help for older pupils, the situation in this area has neither improved nor are there any signs of it doing so in the foreseeable future. Tomlinson (1984: 7) notes that 'even the one policy that most LEAs and schools agreed was needed to assist minority pupils educationally was still underdeveloped'. The provision of extra support in teaching English-language skills to Asian pupils who start school with insufficient skills has been and will continue be an important curriculum objective. The teaching of ESL has played, and will continue to play, a vital and unquestioned role.

Role of the mother tongue

One of the most complex aspects of the language issues affecting the education of Asian children is the role of the mother tongue. *Racial Disadvantage*, a report by the Home Affairs Committee (1981: 14) stated that 'of all the various issues which arise concerning the education of ethnic minority children . . . few are at present generating more argument than that of mother tongue teaching'. A few years earlier, the Bullock Report (Bullock, 1975) emphasized the importance of addressing the language issues of children whose home language was other than English in the broader perspective of language for life. It argued forcefully that children should not be expected to 'cast off the language and culture of home at the school threshold'. Similar developments were taking place worldwide as the maintenance of the mother tongue came to be regarded as essential to the retention of minority cultures as a result of the influence of multicultural ideas that had gained ground (Bhatnagar, 1981; Megarry, 1981). The European Council Directive of 1977 gave further impetus to this idea by requesting the member states to take appropriate measures to promote the teaching of mother tongues, although the intention of this directive as it applied to Asian children in Britain was disputed by the Department of Education and Science (1981a).

The Linguistic Minorities Project (Saifullah-Khan, 1983) regarded the presence of children speaking languages other than English as a resource to be exploited, and argued that these languages be accorded the same status as other modern languages. This view was also echoed by the National Union of Teachers (1982). This argument had a rather cool reception. The Swann Committee, in 1986, advanced arguments for the teaching of mother tongue at the secondary level, but 'peremptorily dismisses the case for teaching them in primary schools' (Parekh, 1988).

Research into the educational implications of including mother-tongue teaching into the curriculum has been minimal in Britain, whereas other countries have made better advances in this area. Brown (1979) suggested that the effect of children's home language not being recognized and accepted by the schools results in them being disadvantaged. Ure (1981) concluded that bilingual teaching is academically useful. Skutnabb-Kangas and Cummins (1988) who have carried out research in Canada and Sweden respectively forcefully argue in support of bilingual education. Cummins (1976; 1979a; 1979b; 1980; 1981) has made a forceful plea for the child's first language to be accorded an active and positive role in the school curriculum. On the basis of his own research and many other papers cited by him (Baker and De Kanter, 1981; Katsaiti, 1983; Malherbe, 1978), he argues that bilingual education and teaching that accords an active, positive and direct role to the child's first language provides wide-ranging benefits for these children, including an enhanced level of cognitive functioning.

Some local education authorities have taken steps to provide for the teaching of mother tongue in secondary schools. Some other LEAs have made some sort of mother tongue support available at the early stages of education in the form of bilingual assistants as a transitional measure. These measures are half-hearted to say the least and reflect a distinct lack of clarity and commitment to the role of mother tongue in the education of Asian children. The majority of Asian parents wish their children to learn their home language (Wilding, 1981) but find the situation quite unsatisfactory. The various reports referred to above sound hollow and rather pious pronouncements. The nettle of the educational implications of the mother tongue in the education of this group of children has not really been grasped, which leaves teachers and parents in a state of uncertainty and perhaps even confusion.

Curriculum issues

In the debate on the education of Asian and other ethnic minority children, curriculum issues are subsumed under the label of 'multicultural education'. The multicultural debate began with the recognition of the need for curriculum reform, the mainstream curriculum being regarded as inadequate to meet the needs of a modern multicultural and multiracial Britain. There were concerns about the negative presentation of minority peoples in the curriculum, particularly in history. Even until the 1970s, it was not uncommon to find books such as *Little Black Sambo* in school libraries, which were deeply racist and downright offensive. One of the main objects of the curriculum reform movement was to eliminate such Eurocentric stereotypes of former colonial countries 'as despised places inhabited by savages' (Williams, 1979: 126).

Lawton (1975: 75) argues that school curriculum is 'essentially a selection from the culture of a society'. The school curriculum of the period, however, was exclusively Eurocentric which made little allowance for minority cultural values, history and way of life. Since then there have been obvious changes in the 'ethos' of schools, with visible signs of recognition of Asian and other minority languages and cultures. Most schools with a fair number of Asian children display 'welcome' signs in community languages. Celebration of community festivals such as Diwali and Eid and some Sikh festivals has become a common feature of many schools. There are more Asian faces to be seen in staff rooms. Occasionally, community language books may also be seen. Beyond this, as far as curriculum content is concerned, no real dent has yet been made and the changes are no more than cosmetic and tokenistic. Asian children find little in the curriculum to which they can relate culturally. A pupil of Asian parentage in the mid-1980s recounts her experience thus: 'I used to write down all this stuff about kings and queens and all the European history because I wanted to get through. There was nothing about Asian or black history. It is as if we did not exist' (Mac an Ghaill, 1989: p. 282).

As mentioned earlier, the multicultural movement which aimed to bring school curriculum in line with the needs of a multicultural society was put on the defensive by its critics and this took the wind out of its initiatives. One of the major weaknesses of the concept of multicultural education was a lack of theoretical underpinning in the sense of there being no 'articulated body of theoretically valid knowledge' (Lynch, 1981: 8). Bullivant (1981: 8) also laments the 'immense confusion that exists about what multiculturalism and multicultural education means . . . in general a good deal of the curriculum is in a mess'. Such vagueness, which has marked the concept of multicultural education and the lack of consensus over its aims and objectives, has undermined its thrust. As such it has not fulfilled the hopes it had raised to bring about the much-needed changes in the curriculum to accommodate the needs of Asian pupils.

The introduction of the National Curriculum, and a plethora of other changes in the education system mentioned earlier, has put schools and indeed the whole education system under tremendous strain during the past few years. Financial resources have also been restricted. Under the circumstances, the whole system has become inward looking and unable to spare the energy and resources required to develop new initiatives. There is little mention of multicultural issues in the National Curriculum other than a few pious sentiments here and there. Klein (1988: 3) describes National Curriculum as 'monocultural . . . narrow, elitist and nationalistic'. The Commission for Racial Equality also expressed its extreme disappointment over the disregard of multicultural issues in the national curriculum.

Attainments

The relatively poor educational performance of ethnic minority children has been a source of parental and professional concern since the 1960s. To begin with, the focus of concern concentrated on children of West Indian origin but, as evidence of underachievement of Asian children accumulated, this group of pupils began to arouse similar concerns about their education.

Early studies showed Indian and Pakistani pupils consistently under-performing compared with British white pupils in a range of basic skills (Saint, 1963; ILEA, 1967; Dosanjh, 1969; Sharma, 1971). The National Child Development Study of 1969 quoted by Mackintosh et al. (1988) also found Asian pupils significantly lagging behind their white peers in basic literacy and numeracy skills.

After this period of initial underperformance, Asian pupils started making gains and by the late 1970s had nearly caught up with the majority pupils. According to the research into the GCE examination performance for the years between 1978 and 1982 reported by the Swann committee (1985), Asian pupils did as well as white pupils. Driver and Ballard (1979) found some groups of Asian pupils achieving higher grades in CSE and GCE examinations than white pupils. Craft and Craft (1983) in their study of secondary schools in an outer London borough found Asian pupils the most motivated group to stay on into further and higher education. The Department of Education and Science (1981) also noted that Asian pupils achieved slightly better examination results than other pupils, including white children. An analysis of the public examination performance of pupils in inner London during the late 1980s (ILEA, 1990) showed some groups of Asian pupils outperforming their white peers. The relatively poor educational performance of some other groups of Asian children continues to be a cause for concern for parents as well as teachers. Children of Bangladeshi origin in the London Borough of Tower Hamlets is one such group whose GCSE and A-level attainments in school examinations have consistently lagged behind both their white and other Asian peers.

Asian children and young people, particularly Indian pupils, have continued to make advances in educational achievement. Jon Salmon, in his review of the Inspectorate report published in the Sunday Times (1 September, 1996) described Indian pupils as outclassing all other groups .

According to this report, 'Indians are the most highly qualified students in British schools and colleges' achieving results consistently in excess of their white counterparts.

Some researchers argue that the claims about Asian children's achievements may not be entirely justified. Mackintosh, Mascie-Taylor and West (1988) provide an analysis of the child development study of 1980 in which they found the performance of Indian and Pakistani pupils significantly below that of white children. In their own study, carried out in three LEAs, they found that Asian children of 7, 9, and 11 years 'lag well behind . . . White children' (p. 91) in vocabulary, non-verbal reasoning, reading and mathematics. Tanna (1990) also argued that many studies that show Asian children doing as well as, or even better than, white children were conceptually flawed and used questionable and unsound procedures.

Despite this scepticism, there is strong evidence that Asian children and young people have made advances in academic achievement despite the heavy odds stacked against them. Many of them start school with poor English language skills. They do not appear to be getting a fair deal in schools. According to a report by the Commission for Racial Equality (1992), *Set to Fail,* which studied the setting and banding practice of a secondary school, Asian pupils were experiencing discrimination in a number of areas of school life. They were more likely to be placed in sets below their general ability. They were less likely to receive special needs support. There was inadequate support for the teaching of English as a second language. In general, the organization and the setting system worked to the significant disadvantage of Asian pupils.

Attitudes and expectations of teachers

Teachers play a crucial role in the educational process. In the case of ethnic minority children, this role is even more vital because, as Tomlinson (1983: 73) argues, 'a society in which the majority is largely hostile to minorities, teachers have a key role to play in educating the majority towards knowledge, understanding and accepting of the minorities'. It is also only through understanding and respecting minority cultural values that they are able effectively to facilitate the process of learning and provide motivation for minority pupils.

Research in America shows that white teachers have lower expectations of black pupils and that it can negatively influence their educational performance (Rubovits and Maehr, 1973). Rist's (1970) study, carried out in one of the American inner-city ghettoes showed that even black teachers had lower expectations of black pupils and suggested a link between low teacher expectations and attainments. These findings are consistent with other studies that have suggested that teachers have lower expectations of

working class children. Studies in Britain by Pidgeon (1970) and Rogers (1981) point to a link between low teacher expectations and poor educational performance.

The Rampton Committee (1981) reported that it found many teachers whose views and perceptions of West Indian pupils were patronizing, stereotypical and negative. Earlier, Coard (1971) argued that negative teacher attitudes were responsible for the grossly disproportionate admission of West Indian children into the schools for educationally subnormal children. Green (1982) showed that teachers' attitudes influence not only expectations but actual classroom practice. They found that West Indian pupils, particularly boys, were given the least positive attention compared with other children in class. Asian girls also received less teacher attention and time, but Asian boys were perceived rather positively by teachers. Mac an Ghaill (1989) found that teachers were inclined to view Asian pupils as being of high ability, more motivated and well behaved.

Studies thus indicate that, whereas West Indian pupils receive least positive attention and are more likely to receive negative attention in school, the situation of Asian pupils is different. As the Asian community, like the West Indian community, is over-represented in working classes, it would be logical to assume on the basis of some of the studies mentioned above, that Asian children are also more liable to be affected by low teacher expectations. It appears, however, that through their own commitment and that of their parents, Asian children and young people have done very well educationally and have won the regard of teachers. Gillborn (1990: 100), in his study of a city high school states that 'in direct contrast to the Afro-Caribbean case . . . Asians were well-disciplined, hardworking students who came from stable families where educational success was highly valued'.

Parental aspirations

The influence of home has traditionally been regarded as of critical importance in children's education. Family factors such as socio-economic status, and parents' education and aspirations have been found to have a significant bearing on educational achievement. The first generation Asian immigrants to Britain, nurtured in the particular social and economic circumstances of their countries of origin, regard education as the key to social and occupational mobility (Tomlinson, 1984). Many studies show that Asian parents have relatively higher educational and occupational aspirations for their children. Dosanjh (1969), in his study carried out in Derby and Nottingham, found Asian parents to be more ambitious about their children's educational and occupational attainments. Gupta (1977) in his study of Pakistani and English school leavers concluded that Asian parents exert positive influence over their children in their educational

performance because of their high aspirations and greater personal interest in their education. Many teachers have come to regard Asian parents' aspirations about their children to be so high as to be unrealistic. Tomlinson (1984) stated that it is common to find teachers who complain about Asian parents' unrealistic aspirations about their children.

Asian parents are also anxious about many other aspects of school life and how it may influence their children. They are particularly anxious, indeed zealous, to maintain their cultural and religious values. There are strong anxieties, particularly among Muslim parents, about the religious curriculum, which may be inconsistent with their faith. There are similar concerns about some other areas of school life such as swimming for girls, dress, and appropriate school meals. Most schools and education authorities are far more willing to take on board the parental concerns in these areas than in the past.

Views and experiences of children and young people

Gillborn (1990: 85), in his analysis of life in a comprehensive school, states that 'very little research has examined the ways in which Asian pupils have experienced and responded to schooling in this country'. His own study concludes that Asian pupils experience schools differently from Afro-Caribbean and white children. They are subject to stereotyping, although not all of this is negative. Bhatti (1995), in her ethnographic account of Asian children, also notes the teacher stereotyping of Asian children and the discomfort and disapproval expressed by them. She quotes a Bangladeshi girl who said: 'your teachers treat you as though you will get married and have a dozen children' (p. 73). She also concludes that Asian boys and girls also experience school differently.

One of the most deplorable and worrying aspects of school life for Asian pupils is the extent of racist abuse, including physical attacks suffered by them. Gillborn (1990: 75) in his study cited above observed that 'Asian pupils were frequently attacked by their White peers'. The Commission for Racial Equality (1988) in its Survey of Racial Harassment in Schools and Colleges (*Learning in Terror*) highlighted the seriousness of the racist abuse and bullying occurring in schools. In 1985, the Swann Report also drew attention to this problem and Asian pupils' perception that teachers did not take the situation really seriously. The Report cites the following observation by a pupil of Pakistani origin:

> I attended a middle school where approximately 90 per cent of the pupils were white . . . The Asians were constantly in fear of being attacked by several gangs of white boys. As we ran towards the staff room a teacher would come out and disperse the white gang, throw us back into the playground and then walk back as if nothing had happened. The teachers had no idea of what we were experiencing. (p. 34)

Inadequate pre-school provision

The quality, type and level of pre-school provision generally available in Britain have been matters of continuing debate and discussion for the past three decades (Select Committee on Race Relations and Immigration, 1973; Home Affairs Committee, 1981; Rampton Committee, 1981). The particular needs of pre-school provision for ethnic minority children were underlined by the Select Committee on Race Relations and Immigration in 1973 when it drew attention to its concern that 'a contributory factor in the underachievement of minority group children in our education system is the inadequacy of pre-school provision' (Select Committee on Race Relations and Immigration, 1973, vol.3: 438).

A report by the Commission for Racial Equality (1996) also reiterates the need to improve pre-school provision for ethnic minority children. It lists a number of reasons in support of its arguments to augment pre-school services for minority children. Firstly, minority groups have a greater share of children of pre-school age in proportional terms and as such have a greater need. Secondly, socio-economic factors such as higher unemployment, low pay, poor housing and unsocial working hours place children from minority groups in greater need.

Language is a major issue in pre-school provision for Asian children (Tomlinson, 1984). The vast majority of Asian families mainly speak a language other than English at home and, as such, many children arrive at school with poor English language skills although they may be quite fluent in their home language. This makes transition to school difficult and presents obvious dilemmas for teachers. The case for the use of child's home language at this stage, at least to ease the transition to school life for these children, is strong. Not to do so is to fly in the face of received pedagogical wisdom. London Borough of Redbridge (1984) undertook a small project to 'teach non-English speaking children in their home language' for part of the day when they first started school. It was found that, apart from the obvious benefit of children feeling 'at home' in a familiar language environment, there were other benefits such as children being more able to establish friendships with other children, an important goal of social development at this stage.

Adolescent difficulties and educational consequences

Asian adolescents, especially girls, face particular difficulties and dilemmas as a result of cultural expectations and pressures. Anwar (1976) described Asian adolescents and young people as 'caught between two cultures, whose world is neither the "old" nor "new" but both'. Several other authors have discussed the predicament of Asian adolescents in terms of cultural conflict.

Watson (1977) views cultural conflict as one of the major issues facing this generation and its parents, which, in his view, has a major effect on their personal and family lives. Taylor (1976) described the second generation British Asians as the 'halfway generation'. Such cultural ambivalence on the part of Asian adolescents and fears on the part of their parents that their children are straying away from their cultural values often leads to conflict situations within their homes. This is likely to make them more vulnerable to stress. Sharma and Jones (1997) in their study of stress in Asian adolescents found that they feel significantly more constrained within their fam-ilies – girls far more so than boys. They perceive their families as interfering more in their daily lives. They concluded that this state of affairs leads to' more 'hassles' between parents and young people. They also found that British Asian girls perceive themselves as less valued by, and less emotionally close to, their parents.

A number of other studies show a worrying picture of the situation of Asian girls and young women. According to a study by Merril and Owens (1986), Asian females aged 15–19 years are significantly more likely to attempt self-harm compared with white British females. Soni Raleigh and Balarajan (1992), in their study of the national data on suicide and attempted suicide, found that young women of Indian origin in the 15–24 year age group were three times more at risk of suicide compared with the national sample. Kingsbury (1994) found higher rates of depression and hopelessness in Asian adolescents and concluded that social and parental relationships showed a picture of isolation in the Asian adolescents. Handy et al. (1991), in their study of adolescent self-poisoning, concluded that 'cultural conflicts (with parents) were of paramount importance in precipitating self-harm amongst Asian adolescents and parental expectations were also influential' (p. 161).

No systematic studies of the educational consequences of this aspect of Asian adolescents' situation appear to have been carried out. Its effects on their education, particularly that of girls, are obvious. They are at a critical stage of their education when most of them are studying for examinations. As such, the extra stresses or strains mentioned above are undoubtedly likely to affect their educational performance adversely. Girls around this age are frequently sent back to countries of origin for an arranged marriage or a long stay, although it does not appear to be as common as it used to be.

Home–school relations

Good home–school relations have in recent years come to be recognized as of obvious and vital importance to children's education. The Plowden report (1967), which stressed the need to improve home–school contact, led to a tremendous upsurge of interest in this area.

Home–school relations have historically been marked by tension. This tension is potentially more marked between ethnic minority parents and schools because of the mutual lack of knowledge and understanding about each other. Bhatti (1995: 67) states that 'for parents who did not go to school in Britain, the education system is shrouded in mystery'. Schools and teachers on the other hand, 'with little information or preparation, have struggled to accommodate ethnic minority children in a system designed for a white majority, and to understand views of minority parents' (Tomlinson, 1984: 117). In the case of Asian parents, communication difficulties because of language further add to the problem of establishing effective home–school contact. Some local education authorities such as Sheffield and Bradford have tried to ameliorate this problem by employing bilingual ethnic minority teachers to provide more effective home–school links. The attempts have been half-hearted and have been further thwarted by lack of resources.

There is scarcity of published research on the subject of contacts between Asian parents and schools. It is widely believed that links between Asian homes and schools are relatively weaker. Townsend and Brittan (1972: 82) note with serious concern that 'home–school relations appear to be one of the most unsatisfactory areas of life in multiracial schools'. Bhatti (1995) found Asian parents 'apprehensive, awkward and inhibited' in relating to schools. She quotes (p. 68) several parents who thus expressed their feelings, difficulties and experiences in relating to school:

> Because I haven't been to school here I feel awkward, Baji [sister] . . .and stupid. The teachers are so clever, so sure of themselves aren't they? You just feel silly. [Pakistani father, translated from Punjabi.]

> I went to my son's school once. They [teachers] were very polite when I got there but I will not go there again. It smelt strange [embarrassed laughter] and I felt afraid. I should have taken my sister . . . You see the children stare at you and you don't belong. You are in a strange place. [a Pakistani mother]

There is an obvious need to be more responsive to the particular sensitivities and experiences of ethnic minority parents in order to establish more effective and positive relations between Asian parents and schools. As Tomlinson points out, 'relationships between homes and schools are not a minor issue, they are crucial to the success of a multicultural society' (p. 123).

Conclusion

The education of Asian children and young people, like that of other minority group children in Britain has raised some complex pedagogical, social and political issues. The education system, during the past four decades, has struggled to find ways and means to meet the particular needs of Asian children. The radical ideas espoused by the proponents of multicultural and anti-racist education never really caught on and the system has plodded along in a patchy and piecemeal manner. The history of the education of Asian children in Britain has been largely a saga of failed promises and unfulfilled hopes. In recent years, the concerns about their education have been further overshadowed by other events in the educational world. It is a testimony to the determination of Asian parents to obtain the best education for their children that despite the heavy odds stacked against them and lack of sufficient support from the system, most groups of Asian children and young people have done quite well educationally.

References

Anwar M (1976) Between Two Cultures: A Study of the Relationships between Generations in the Asian Community in Britain. London: Commission for Racial Equality.

Baker KA, De Kanter AA (1981) Effectiveness of Bilingual Education: A Review of the Literature. Washington DC: Office of Planning and Budget, US Department of Education.

Banks JA (1986) Race, Ethnicity and Schooling. In JA Banks and J Lynch (eds) Multicultural Education in Western Societies. London: Holt, Rinehart & Winston.

Bernstein B (1973) Class, Codes and Control. London: Routledge & Kegan Paul.

Bhatnagar J (1981) Educating Immigrants. London: Croom Helm.

Bhatti G (1995) A journey into the unknown: an ethnographic study of Asian children. In M Griffiths and B Troyna (eds) Antiracism, Culture and Social Justice in Education. Chester: Trentham Books.

Brown D (1979) Mother-Tongue to English: The Young Child in Multicultural School. Cambridge: Cambridge University Press.

Bullivant M (1981) Pluralist Dilemma in Education: Six Case Studies. Sydney: Allen & Unwin.

Bullock A (1975) Language for Life, Report of the Committee of Inquiry into the Teaching of Reading and other Uses of English. London: HMSO.

Coard B (1971) How the West Indian Child is made ESN in the British Education System. London: New Beacon Books.

Commission for Racial Equality (1988) Learning in Terror: A Survey of Racial Harassment in Schools and Colleges. London: CRE.

Commission for Racial Equality (1992) Set to Fail, Setting and Banding in Secondary Schools. London: CRE.

Commission for Racial Equality (1996) From Cradle to School. London: CRE.

Craft, M, Craft A (1983) The participation of ethnic minority pupils in further and higher education. Educational Research 25(1): 10–19.

Cummins J (1976) The influence of bilingualism on cognitive growth: a synthesis of research findings and explanatory hypotheses. Working Papers on Bilingualism 9: 1–43.

Cummins J (1979a) Linguistic interdependence and the educational development of bilingual children. Review of Educational Research 49: 222–51.

Cummins J (1979b) Cognitive/academic language proficiency, linguistic interdependence, the optimum age question and some other matters. Working Papers in Bilingual Education 19: 121–9.

Cummins J (1980) The construct of language proficiency in bilingual education. In JE Alatis (ed.) Georgetown University Round Table on Language and Linguistics. Washington DC: Georgetown University Press.

Cummins J (1981) Bilingualism and Minority Language Children. Toronto: The Ontario Institute for Studies in Education.

Department of Education and Science (1971) The Education of Immigrants. Education Survey 13. London: HMSO.

Department of Education and Science (1972) The Continuing Needs of Immigrants. London: HMSO.

Department of Education and Science (1981a) Directive of the Council of the European Community on the Education of Children of Migrant Workers. Circular 5/81. London: HMSO.

Department of Education and Science (1981b) West Indian Children in our schools, A Report of the Committee of Inquiry into the Education of Children from Ethnic Minority Groups (Rampton Report). London: HMSO.

Department of Education and Science (1981c) The Education of Children from Ethnic Minority Groups. Consultative Document. London: Department of Education and Science.

Department of Education and Science (1985) Committee of Inquiry into the Education of Children from Ethnic Minority Groups: Education for All. London: HMSO.

Derrick J (1977) Language Needs of Minority Group Children. Slough: NFER.

Dosanjh JS (1969) Punjabi Immigrant Children. Their Social and Educational Problems in Adjustment. Education Paper 10. University of Nottingham.

Driver G, Ballard R (1979) Comparing Performance in Multiracial Schools at 16 Plus. New Community 7: 2.

Ghuman PAS (1981) Educational Attitudes of Bengali Families in Cardiff. Journal of Multicultural and Multilingual Education 2: 2.

Gillborn D (1990) Race, Ethnicity and Education. London: Unwin Hyman.

Grannis JC (1992) Students? Stress, distress and achievement in an urban school. Journal of Early Adolescence 8: 391–403.

Green PA (1982) Teachers? Influence on the Self-Concept of Pupils of Different Ethnic Groups. Unpublished PhD thesis. University of Durham.

Gupta YP (1977) Educational and Vocational Aspirations of Asian Immigrants and English School-Leavers. British Journal of Sociology 28(2): 185–98.

Halsey AH (1972) Educational Priority, Problems and Policies. London: HMSO.

Handy S, Chitiramohan RN, Ballard CG, Silveira WR (1991) Ethnic Differences in Adolescent Self-poisoning: A comparison of Asian and Caucasian groups. Journal of Adolescence 14: 157–62.

Hernandez-Chavez E (1988) Language policy and language rights in the United States. In T Skutnabb-Kangas and J Cummins (eds) Minority Education. Clevedon: Multilingual Matters.

Home Affairs Committee (1981) Racial Disadvantage. London: HMSO.

ILEA (1967) The Education of Immigrant Pupils in Primary Schools: Report of a Working Party of Inspectorate and Schools Psychological Service (959). London: ILEA.

Inner London Education Authority (1990) Ethnic Background and Examination Results 1987. London: ILEA, Research and Statistics Branch.

Jencks C (1972) Inequality. New York: Allen Lane.

Katsaiti L. (1983) Interlingual Transfer of a Cognitive Skill in Bilinguals. Unpublished Master's Thesis, University of Toronto.

Kingsbury S (1994) The psychological and social characteristics of Asian adolescent overdose. Journal of Adolescence 14: 131–5.

Klein G (1988) Editorial: the nature of the beast. Multicultural Teaching, 6(2): 3.

Lawton D (1975) Class, Culture and the Curriculum. London: RKP.

Little A (1975) Performances of children from ethnic minority backgrounds in primary schools. Oxford Review of Education 1(2): 117–35.

London Borough of Redbridge (1984) Language Development Project. An Unpublished Report.

Lynch J (1986) Multicultural Education: Principles and Practice. London: Routledge & Kegan Paul.

Mac an Ghaill M (1989) Coming of Age in the 1980s England: reconceptualising black students? Schooling experience. British Journal of Sociology of Education 10(3): 273–86.

Mackintosh NJ, Mascie-Taylor CGN, West AM (1988) West Indian and Asian Children's Educational Attainments. In GK Verma and P Pumphrey (eds) Educational Attainments: Issues and Outcomes in Multicultural Education. London: The Falmer Press.

Malherbe EG (1978) Bilingual education in the republic of South Africa. In B Spolsky, RL Cooper (eds) Case Studies in Bilingual Education. Rowley MA: Newbury House.

Megarry J (ed.) (1981) The Education of Minorities. The World Yearbook of Education. London: Kogan Page.

Merril J, Owens, J (1986) Ethnic differences in self-poisoning: A comparison of Asian and White Caucasian groups. British Journal of Psychiatry 148: 708–12.

Ministry of Education (1963) English for Children of Immigrants. London: HMSO.

Moodley KA (1986) Canadian Multicultural Education: Promises and Practice. In JA Banks, J Lynch (eds) Multicultural Education in Western Societies. London: Holt, Rinehart & Winston.

National Union of Teachers (1982) Mother Tongue Teaching. London: NUT.

Oakley R (1968) New Backgrounds. London: Oxford University Press.

Parekh B (1988) The Swann Report and Ethnic Minority Attainments. In G Verma, P Pumphrey (eds) Educational Attainments: Issues and Outcomes in Multicultural Education. London: The Falmer Press.

Pidgeon D (1970) Expectations and pupil performance. Slough: NFER.

Pollack M (1972) Today's Three Year Olds. London: Heinemann.

(Plowden Report) Committee of Enquiry into the Education of Primary Age Children (1967) Children and their Primary Schools. London: HMSO.

(Rampton Committee) Committee of Enquiry into the Education of Children from Ethnic Minority Groups (1981) West Indian Children in Our Schools. London: HSMO.

Rubovits PC, Maehr M (1973) Pygmalion black and white. Journal of Personality and Social Psychology 25: 2.

Rist R (1970) Student social class and teacher expectations, The self-fulfilling prophecy in education. Harvard Educational Review 40: 3.

Rogers CR (1981) A Social Psychology of Schooling. London: RKP.

Saifullah-Khan V (1983) Linguistic Minorities Project. London: University of London Institute Of Education.

Saint CK (1963) Scholastic and Sociological Adjustment of Punjabi-Speaking Children in Smethwick. Unpublished MEd thesis, University of Birmingham.

Salmon J (1996) Indian pupils outclass all other pupils. Sunday Times, 1 September 1996.

Schools Council (1967) English for the Children of Immigrants: Working paper No 13. London: HMSO.

Schools Council (1973) Multiracial Education: Needs and Innovations. Working Paper 50. London: Schools Council.

Schools Council (1982) Multicultural Education. London: Schools Council.

Select Committee on Race Relations and Immigration (1973) Education. London: HMSO.

Skutnabb-Kangas T, Cummins J (1988) (eds) Minority Education. Clevedon: Multilingual Matters.

Sharma R (1971) The Measured Intelligence of Children from the Indian Sub-Continent. Unpublished PhD thesis, University of London.

Sharma D, Jones D (1997) Cultural and family influences as sources of stress in adolescence. Paper presented at the British Psychological Society conference at Edinburgh.

(Swann Report) Committee of Enquiry into the Education of Children from Ethnic Minority Groups (1985) Education For All. London: HMSO.

Soni Raleigh V, Balarajan R (1992) Suicide and self-burning among Indians and West Indians in England and Wales. British Journal of Psychiatry 161: 365–8.

Tanna K (1990) Excellence, equality and education reform: the South Asian achievement levels. New Community 16(3): 349–68.

Taylor JH (1976) The Halfway Generation. London: NFER.

Tomlinson S (1983) Ethnic Minorities in British Schools. London: Heinemann.

Tomlinson S (1984) Home and School in Multicultural Britain. London: Batsford.

Townsend HER, Brittan E (1972) Organisation in Multi-racial Schools. Slough: NFER.

Ure J (1980) Bilingualism and achievement in schools. Journal of Multicultural and Multilingual Education 1: 253–60.

Watson JL (ed.) (1977) Between Two Cultures: Migrants and Minorities in Britain. Oxford: Basil Blackwell.

Wilding J (1981) Ethnic Minority Languages in the Classroom: A Survey of Asian Parents in Leicester. Leicester: Council for Community Relations.

Williams J (1979) Perspectives on the multicultural curriculum. The Social Sciences Teacher 8(4): 126–33.

Chapter 10
Similarities and differences: working respectfully with the Bangladeshi community

HAROON-UR RASHID AND SHILA RASHID

Introduction

The Bangladeshis in Britain have their roots in a country that gained its independence and identity by breaking the manacles of oppression in a war that also caused devastating and immeasurable national and personal losses. Experiencing adversity, surviving losses and building anew are familiar tasks for many Bangladeshis, being subject to the often debilitating and destabilizing repercussions of natural disasters such as floods and famine. In Britain, too, some Bangladeshis have had to manage adverse experiences such as racial abuse and violence, discrimination in many spheres of their life, as well as poverty, unemployment and social marginalization. Tenacity and resilience, although important concepts in mental health, are qualities rarely applied to the Bangladeshi communities in Britain, especially by the indigenous population.

Instead, certain images are portrayed of Bangladeshis that are negative and stereotypical, if not inaccurate and derogatory. Examples of such commonly held ideas are the notion that all Bangladeshis have arranged marriages, and that these marriages are usually oppressive to women; women are passive and submissive to their husbands; men are over-controlling; young people, especially girls, are in cultural conflict with their parents because they want freedom like their Western peers, and so forth. Although some of these statements can equally be applied to other cultural groups, they have become associated with South Asian communities to such an extent that they have acquired the status of 'facts'.

Through various systems of transmission, these 'facts' have become part of the knowledge base of people, influencing their personal and profes-

sional dealings with members of that community. On occasions, the outcome of such an encounter is a pathologizing of the culture; often, the reason behind this lies not in the presence but an absence of adequate and
appropriate information about the 'norms' of a group. For instance, a white
child-and-adolescent psychiatrist, on a home visit, observed an 8-year-old
Bangladeshi girl being fed by her mother and concluded in her assessment
that the child showed a developmental delay in being unable to feed herself. Later on, a Bangladeshi colleague was able to change her views by
informing her that it was a common child-rearing practice for Bangladeshi
mothers to feed their children, even if the children had acquired the skills
to feed themselves.

In this chapter it is argued that such professional maps that narrow and
belittle the narratives and lived experiences of certain cultural groups are
both detrimental and counterproductive when engaging them as clients.
In order to establish a meaningful and respectful premiss for dialogue and
collaboration it is suggested that professionals need to take account of
both the familial influences on an individual and the other multiple contexts in which families are embedded, such as race, gender, culture, religion, socio-economic and political positioning. A parallel task for
professionals is to be aware of, and critically evaluate, how their own
familial, racial, socio-economic and cultural experiences affect and organize their work with clients from different cultural groups (McNamee and
Gergen, 1992). In the absence of such knowledge and practice, attempts
to intervene effectively may, at best, be incongruent and, at worst, may be
experienced as a form of subjugation, if not oppression.

By focusing specifically on Bangladeshi children and their families in
Tower Hamlets, this chapter attempts to highlight some of the dilemmas
and difficulties for both professionals and clients, in addressing issues pertaining to mental health.

Using some clinical vignettes, and illustrations of present deficien-
cies, suggestions are offered for ways to create more culturally accessible, congruent and meaningful services. Our aim is not to be
prescriptive. Rather the intention is to raise questions about current
thinking and practice and highlight the importance of working flexibly
and respectfully with cultural differences.

Facts and figures: a profile of the Bangladeshi community

According to the 1991 census, the total Bangladeshi population in the UK
was 162 835, of whom 71 016 are resident in Inner London (see Chapter
1). The highest concentration is in the borough of Tower Hamlets, where
Bangladeshis constitute about 22.94% of the local population.

The migration of Bangladeshis to Britain dates back to the time of the
East India Company, in the eighteenth and nineteenth centuries, when as

seamen they landed in the docklands of the East End. Another wave of immigrants arrived in the 1950s and 1960s looking for social, economic and educational betterment, and these individuals were later joined by their spouses and families throughout the 1970s and 1980s. The present Bangladeshi community in Tower Hamlets is a rich mixture of first, second and third generations, sometimes all living in one household.

The majority of Bangladeshis in Tower Hamlets originate from the district of Sylhet, and speak a dialect of the Bengali language, called Sylheti. They are Muslims, following the Islamic religion.

The average household size is 5.3 persons, compared with 2.5 persons for the general population. There is a high degree of overcrowding and poor living conditions. Nearly a fifth of the households live at the highest density given by the census of over 1.5 persons per room. Almost 24% of households lacked central heating compared with the national average of 19% (Coleman and Salt, 1991). Such poor housing conditions may contribute to the existence of 9% of men aged 16 and over, and 2% of women, who are permanently sick. Housing tenure is 50% below the national average for owner occupation and 50% higher for council and housing association properties.

Family structure

There is a pattern of nuclear and extended families, with relatively little manifestation of Western patterns of co-habitation.

The majority of the population is in the 0–19 age group. The British-born Bangladeshis show an even younger second generation, the largest proportion of which is aged between 0 and 4 (Eade, Vampleu and Peach, 1996).

Socio-economic profile

Unemployment rates are very high among the Bangladeshi population. Over one-third of the economically active women (35%) and one-third of men are unemployed. The majority of those who work are pushed, through lack of qualifications and lack of ability to speak English, towards manual jobs, such as working in restaurants and the rag trade. Almost 63% of Bangladeshi men aged 16 and over are in manual employment (classes III, IV and V) compared with 41% for the total population. Only 16% of men are in the professional and managerial classes (I and II), which is less than half of the national average of 36% (Coleman and Salt, 1991).

The socio-economic position of women is difficult to analyse given their low participation in the national workforce, except that they seem to be polarized in their distribution in both professional and skilled manual work. Educationally, girls seem to be doing better than boys up to A levels, which is similar to the general population. However, overall,

Bangladeshis seem to be significantly underachieving educationally, in comparison with other ethnic groups.

Social adversity

Many studies document the direct relationship between social adversity and mental health. That migration itself has a deleterious effect on the mental health of the immigrant population is also well documented in several studies. For instance, a study of Bangladeshi residents in Inner London housing estates compared with their native-born neighbours showed that the Bangladeshis were found to be experiencing more serious life events and chronic difficulties, and reported more symptoms of psychological disturbance than their indigenous neighbours. These higher rates of distress appeared to be accounted for by the higher levels of adversity to which they were exposed (MacCarthy and Craissati, 1989).

In general, the combined effects of poverty, poor housing, over-crowding, high unemployment rates, racism and racist attacks (some of which have led to the death of family members), poor access to healthcare and other services, large and extended families to care for, discrimination, stigmatization and social isolation, make the Bangladeshi community in Tower Hamlets more vulnerable to life stresses and mental health difficulties than the white indigenous population. Given the very young age structure of the community and the social adversities and life events they may encounter, the mental health of children and adolescents is of particular concern. It becomes even more worrying in light of the fact that, despite the significant proportion of potential users, counselling the Bangladeshi community currently underutilizes psychological and psychiatric services. Young adults aged between 16 and 19 years also appear to be experiencing difficulties, but do not seem to be receiving appropriate attention due to a gap in existing services aimed at this specific age group.

Ethnicity, culture and mental health

Ethnicity and culture are important determinants of people's internal and external realities and experiences, and are therefore integral, if not central, in any discussion pertaining to mental health. These influences 'pattern our thinking, feeling and behaviour in both obvious and subtle ways . . . cultural norms and values prescribe the "rules" by which families operate, including how family members identify, define and attempt to solve their problems and how they seek help' (McGoldrick, Pearce and Giordana, 1982). In relation to mental health, such 'cultural filters' will shape individual perceptions about normality/abnormality when defining situations/events as problematic and in need of outside assistance, and will influence expectations about the kind of help needed, and the relationship with the helper (Lau, 1998). The models used by mental health professionals, and the institutions in which they train and deliver services are themselves shaped by cultural notions of what constitutes and improves illness and good health (Kareem and Littlewood, 1992).

Fernando (1995) elucidates how that process may operate:

> Anyone trained in Western schools of thought will naturally see ideals of self-sufficiency, personal autonomy, efficiency and self-esteem as the correct basis for discussions about mental health. In other words, the ideals of mental health, implicit in the thinking that underlines training would naturally adhere to the values which are derived from Western culture . . . Racism affects our perceptions of culture and these assumptions are incorporated into the training of professionals.

Dominant stereotypes in popular culture undoubtedly filter through into the personal and professional consciousness of practitioners and affect their perceptions and dealings of certain ethnic groups, as illustrated by the following example.

> An Asian (non-Bengali) therapist was seeing a Bengali family, where there were some concerns about their 12-year-old daughter showing developmental delay. The therapist's assessment was that the mother was very passive and father seemed to be talking for everyone. Her view was that although father's dominance may have arisen due to the mother's limited ability to speak English, she speculated that his style of 'taking over' may be culturally determined. To engage the mother more, a Bengali-speaking colleague was brought in to do a joint session. In these conversations, what emerged were shared parental fears and sadness about the possible long-term consequences of the learning disability for their daughter, one manifestation of which was extreme social withdrawal. In the absence of an interpreter/cultural consultant it may have been 'easier' for the non-Bengali therapist to stay with the theme of father's dominance rather than the one of shared parental sadness and concern, which generated a different way of engaging the parents.

Some practitioners have attempted to remedy this issue of conducting therapy without adequate knowledge of the clients' presenting culture by providing descriptions of the beliefs and practices of different ethnic groups (for example, McGoldrick and Carter, 1980; McGoldrick et al., 1982). These 'manuals', although useful in introducing the idea of cultural differences, may themselves run the risk of perpetuating, rather than removing, stereotypes, with their suggestion that all families from a particular ethnic group act in certain ways all of the time. Cultures are not static but subject to different influences over time: families, too, change and evolve over the life-cycle, and professionals need to be aware that diversity and difference exist in cultural ascriptions both within and across families of an ethnic group. Moreover, although cultures will differ in many respects, they may share similarities too. For instance, worrying about their children's future is a universal theme for most parents in most cultures but the degree and manner in which the concern is manifested may differ according to cultural values about the roles and responsibilities of parenting.

For those practitioners who have some knowledge about the cultural practices and beliefs of their clients, the challenge is how to use these constructively without the knowledge becoming a 'straitjacket' that stifles movement in the therapeutic relationship. Learning from the client(s), maintaining curiosity, seeking consultations from colleagues may help to avoid the pitfalls of stereotyping (Casement, 1985). However, the other risk is to be 'too' organized by culture: 'Ascribing all that one sees to cultural or ethnic factors, may lead one to overlook important personal difficulties experienced by one or more members of the family' (Burnham and Harris, 1996). Sometimes, this practice of attending to culture may arise from a perceived pressure by professionals to be 'politically correct' rather than based on a judgement of therapeutic need, and may be experienced as potentially disingenuous by both the professional and the client(s).

Evolving families

The Bangladeshis in Britain are not a homogenous community, and the presentation of individual and family life may vary in terms of the degree to which they uphold certain cultural and religious practices and beliefs. The profile is changing, with a rapidly growing second and third generation whose values and aspirations are, in some respects, different from their first generation parents and grandparents. These differences are shaped by gender, educational, occupational, cultural, regional, political and religious developments that have taken place locally, nationally and globally. This is reflected in the numerous self-descriptions of ethnic identity – often not represented in ethnic monitoring forms – such as British Asian, British Bangladeshi, Bangladeshi, Black British, Sylheti and Bengali.

Just like any other cultural group, the Bangladeshi community experiences a dual force – to maintain the *status quo*, but also to respond in more adaptive ways to changes in the external environment. Perhaps due to their physical proximity – living, working and socializing with and alongside each other – the Bangladeshi community in Tower Hamlets has preserved many aspects of its cultural and religious identity and traditions. Another reason may be that upholding one's traditions is a counter-response to racism and racist experiences of a devaluing of Bangladeshi culture and the Muslim religion. Indeed, one may come across second- and third-generation people who are proud of their identity as Bangladeshis and Muslims. For instance, some young women will choose to wear *hijab*, or headscarf, to mark their commitment to observing religious practices. Parallel to such individuals, there are also others who adhere more loosely to cultural and religious norms – for example, those choosing mixed marriages. Thus, the cultural mosaic of the Bangladeshis must be viewed within this context of stability, evolution and change.

Explanatory models about mental health and psychological difficulties

As there is a diversity of different family forms, so there is a range of beliefs about the origins of mental illness and psychological difficulties and accompanying ideas as to its treatment. These ideas have evolved from folk culture, religious beliefs, wider social developments (such as urbanization) and have been shaped by the level of education, information and exposure to other ways of thinking in relation to mental illness. Thus, in one family, there may be a range of views about the causes and treatment of mental illness, with the first-generation members influenced by ideas in Bangladesh, and second and third generations who may have similar ideas to their parents and additional ones arising from the socio-cultural influences in Britain.

Some of these ideas are as follows:

- Mental illness and/or psychological difficulties are transmitted through blood ties – they are genetically inherited. The expression used is *roktber modbey* which is literally translated as 'in the blood'. This can include schizophrenia, aggression, delinquency, any forms of social deviancy or behaviour that are seen as family traits, passed from generation to another.
- One's destiny or fate (*vaggo, kopal*) leads one to having such difficulties.
- Difficulties may be stress related; arising from adverse/traumatic life events.
- There is a belief that bad spirits (*vhut*) can affect people's psychological and physical state, and even take them over.
- There is a belief that supernatural bodies (*jinns*) can possess someone's body and cause him or her to think or act in socially unacceptable ways – for example, as severely withdrawn, aggressive, violent to others or themselves; hallucinations, or speaking in an unrecognizable voice.
- Something in the air (*batash*) can affect a person who is exposed to it, causing unusual physical and mental symptoms, such as aches and pains in the body, anxiety, or distress.
- There is an idea that mental illness or social and psychological adversity can be 'wished upon' a person by the power of another's expression of envy or jealousy towards them. This can act like a curse (*ovishap*) which can be given verbally, or implied through the 'evil eye' (*chok laga*).
- Similarly, there is an idea that certain people practise a form of witchcraft or sorcery in order to harm others, causing serious physical and mental illness, even death.
- There is an idea that people who commit certain sins against God,

contravening religious practices/teachings, will be punished by the visitation of physical and psychological ailments, in an act of divine retribution.

As some of these ideas about causes of mental illness/psychological difficulties are based on a premiss that there is an imbalance or deficit in the religious/spiritual life of the person, the treatment is often about restoring this inbalance. Help is sought from 'specialists' in religious teaching or spiritual healing. These consist of the following:

- *Moulovi* (religious leader). Many people will consult their local *moulovi* in the mosque when affected by such illness. He will normally provide a *tabiz* or amulet, which consists of Quranic verses written on a small piece of paper and folded into a small metallic container to wear on certain parts of the body, such as the upper arm, neck or the waist.
- *Pir/fakir* (a saint or spiritual leader). Some people will visit a *pir* or *fakir,* as they are believed to possess special spiritual power to heal illnesses. They will normally recite a verse from the Holy Quran and blow it over the affected part of the body or a glass of water to be drunk by the affected person. *Pirs* can also provide *tabiz.*
- Folk magician or exorcist. These practitioners are supposed to have special powers to exorcize clients affected by black magic or possessed by evil spirits, such as *vhut* or *jinns.* They perform various healing rituals mostly in public or in the client's home.
- *Kabiraj* (herbalist). This is generally a practitioner in Ayurvedic or traditional herbal medicine and will administer various concoctions according to the complaint.

Messages from research

Some Bangladeshis, when presented with a member of the family behaving in an unpredictable or inexplicable manner will often seek out the help of religious specialists. Others may seek help of experienced or more senior members of the extended family or community. Some, however, will seek out, or be referred to mainstream services. In comparison to the general population there is an underrepresentation of Bangladeshis in the utilization of mainstream counselling, psychological and psychiatric services. A paucity of specific research pertaining to the community make it difficult to describe quantitatively or qualitatively its use and experience of such services, and its outcome. Such audit and research is clearly needed in establishing clarity as to the relevance and appropriateness of these services in addressing the diverse mental health needs of the Bangladeshi community.

However, research that is available about the experience of ethnic groups in general perhaps offer some tentative clues. For instance, a study in north-west London, of GP consultation for mental health and psychological difficulties revealed equivalent rates of non-psychotic psychiatric morbidity in both the Asian and white samples and no differences in the way their symptoms were presented. Certainly, our collective personal experiences of working as a general practitioner in primary care and family therapist in a child and adolescent mental health service, respectively have found that Bangladeshis approach, or are referred to, services with the same range of difficulties as their indigenous counterparts.

Another study, in trying to understand the factors contributing to the underutilization of mental health services by Asian immigrants found that Indo-Chinese clients took longer to receive psychiatric treatment for their first episode, and tended to receive initial help from family members or traditional healers. The implication is that for this client group the route into mainstream services also occurred at a much later stage from the initial presentation of difficulties, often after they have made use of their own familial and community support systems (Kavanagh and Lam, 1996).

One may speculate about the factors, on the side of both the professional and the client(s) influencing the underutilization of services among the Bangladeshi community. Research shows that professionals are less likely to refer ethnic minorities for psychotherapy and/or counselling, and more likely to prescribe medication such as anti-depressants (Fernando, 1995). Professionals may also have difficulties in identifying or eliciting information about mental health difficulties. For instance, primary care physicians often mention somatization as a frequently encountered problem during consultation. They report increasing numbers of Bangladeshi patients complaining of very diffuse and vague physical symptoms such as headaches, dizziness, lethargy, palpitations, diffuse aches and pains all over the body, burning sensations, sweating, and urinary problems. Cecil G Helman (1994) describes somatization as 'the cultural patterning of psychological disorders, into a "language of distress" of mainly physical symptoms and signs'. The north-west London study previously quoted also found that the Asians were more likely to state that they were consulting the GP for a physical problem than their white counterparts, and that GPs were more likely to identify psychiatric morbidity in white than in Asian patients. The findings suggest the possibility of an interaction between the ways in which some patients experience and communicate psychological distress, their ethnic origin and their GPs' modes of responding (Kavanagh et al., 1996). To avoid misdiagnosis in such situations, primary care workers may need to go beyond the surface 'presentation' of physical symptoms to elicit information about underlying psychological difficulties. Professionals may also find it useful to elicit the client's construction, or explanatory model, of their difficulties.

Clients may themselves feel constrained by certain influences in approaching services. For instance, there may be a worry about expos-

ing private issues to the public scrutiny of others and facing the stigmatization connected with mental illness. In common with the indigenous
population, Bangladeshis also find it difficult to accept mental illness as
a possible diagnosis, even if the effects of illness are distressing to the
individual and their family. Similarly, in common with white parents,
Bangladeshi parents are also concerned when their children present
with psychological or psychiatric difficulties, as they feel this may reflect
badly on their parenting abilities. For Bangladeshi parents there may be
an additional worry about how they will be judged by other
Bangladeshi families, as well as the white community, so there sometimes may be a pressure to keep things hidden. This issue becomes
much more complicated with female children as it directly affects their
chance of getting married. In some instances, therefore, rather than
seek treatment and risk being 'found out' by friends and relatives here,
some Bangladeshi parents may take their daughters back to their country and get them married quickly. This can also be seen as a solution to
difficulties with daughters who are seen to be behaving in socially unacceptable ways – for example, becoming involved in emotional/sexual
relationships with the opposite sex – in an attempt to save 'face' or rescue one's honour, or *izzat*. It may be helpful, therefore, to have conversations with Bangladeshi clients about the socio-emotional 'costs', or
consequences, of seeking help for mental health issues. There is also
research to suggest that the low uptake of services may be due to a lack
of knowledge of, and/or faith in, these services. For instance, a report
published by Minara Karim in 1995 entitled, *Access to Mental Health
Services for the Bangladeshi community in Tower Hamlets – A User's
Perspective*, identified the following criticisms of existing services:

- lack of involvement in care;
- lack of information about the range of services available, processes,
  procedures and entitlements;
- lack of consultation with their consultant;
- lack of interpreting and advocacy services.

Karim's report also mentioned the users' suggestions for an improved service, which included provision of information about their care/treatment
and access to alternative therapy. Indeed, over the years, Tower Hamlets,
and other boroughs, have commissioned and collated several documents
relating to the use of mental health provisions by ethnic minorities,
including Bangladeshis. These reports have made recommendations
about ways to re-address issues of inequality, inaccessibility and inappropriateness of services, but have produced little in the way of structural
changes to services.

The existence of these reports suggests that some form of consultation
has occurred. However, the fact that these reports continue to gather dust
on the shelves of decision-making institutions, rather than to become live,

workable realities, indicates that there is a blockage in institutions at the level of action and implementation.

Fernando (1995) suggests that institutional racism may be one such blockage and a powerful factor in maintaining the *status quo,* both in relation to the conceptualization and delivery of services.

This can result in institutions adopting a 'colour-blind' approach of seeing all people as individuals irrespective of their ethnicity. This may seem, on the surface, a considered if not benign view, but on closer scrutiny is at risk of assuming that everyone is the same, thereby negating any differences and indeed the impact of these differences on individual psyche and development.

In a study comparing return rates and outcomes with ethnicity in specific mental health programmes in Los Angeles it was found that ethnic clients who attended such programmes had a higher return rate and stayed in the treatment longer than those using mainstream services. These findings seem to support the notion that ethnicity-specific programmes may help to increase the use of mental health services among these groups (Takeuchi, Sue and Yeh, 1995).

It may be interesting to compare mainstream services with specialized services for ethnic minorities in Britain (such as Nafsiyat, Shanti, Kalb, the Asian Counselling Project in Marlborough Family Services) to see if there are any qualitative differences in use and experience of these provisions by the Bangladeshi community. At present no such evaluation research exists.

Specific issues in the mental health of the Bangladeshi community

Although the Bangladeshi community show a similar range of psychological distress to their white counterparts, there are also certain specific issues that some members of the Bangladeshi community may present.

Transgenerational differences

Professionals often encounter the issue of transgenerational differences when working with Bangladeshi families, whether these differences are presented by the family or identified by the professional working with or referring the family.

Anecdotal evidence suggests that some white professionals see such presentations purely in terms of 'culture conflict', a clash between the traditional beliefs of parents and the more contemporary Western-influenced values of the young person in the family. A progression of such thinking may often be a pathologization, and hence a distancing from/rejection of the parental belief systems/concerns, perceived as the alien other, and a closer alliance with the young person, seen as being similar to, if not the same as, the white professional. It is interesting to contrast this with work that is carried out with white families presenting similar issues of trans-generational differences/conflict. Here, although the professional may still feel an inward sympathy towards the position of the young person, the outward intervention is likely to focus on developing a more positive relationship between the parent(s) and young person, through which negotiation of the differences between them could then begin to be explored.

In such cases, the thinking and practice of the professional is perhaps more influenced by the culture rather than the clinical presentation of the family, in a way that seems to impede rather than enhance the therapeutic relationship.

Depression

As a general practitioner one sees a significant number of men and women suffering from depression, which in the main probably remains mostly undiagnosed and untreated. Many feel discouraged and inhibited from seeking mainstream services due to concern about social stigmatization and professionals themselves trivializing their symptoms as mere somatization.

In Tower Hamlets, bilingual advocates and counsellors – mostly based in GP surgeries and outpatient clinics – are able to support some clients, but do not access the large numbers who need the service. This is partly due to a lack of resources and partly due to a lack of community consultation and participation in setting up these services.

Self-harming

There is increasing concern about the levels of suicide and attempted suicide among Asian young women, including Bangladeshi women. Various factors such as social isolation, racism, intracultural and familial conflicts, marital difficulties, loss of the usual kinship and community support structures that would have been available in their country of origin, coupled with adverse situations here such as unemployment, overcrowding and homelessness, all act as precipitating and perpetuating factors. Here again, as a practitioner, one would need to hold a much broader view of the presenting difficulties, rather than simply attributing them to culture.

Changes in family forms

Due to a lack of available research, it is difficult to quantify these changes. However, both in GP practice and child and adolescent mental health services, there is a presentation of family forms other than the traditional nuclear and extended family systems. So, for instance, there are racially mixed marriages, post-divorce families and stepfamilies. Clearly, more research needs to be conducted on the particular experiences of Bangladeshi families undergoing these transitions.

Drug addiction

There is recent evidence, in the form of presentation at GP surgeries, suggesting increasing use and abuse of drugs amongst the young people in the Bangladeshi community. This is not unexpected given the high level of deprivation, poverty, unemployment, and lack of general youth and community support services. Projects such as the Asian Drug Advisory Service are trying to address this problem, which has just come to the surface, but its resources are limited. Local health and social services departments have yet to formulate and implement clear strategies for tackling this issue. Conducting research on the incidence and psychosocial impact of the problem and establishing a comprehensive multi-disciplinary and bilingual team aimed at helping young people and their families would clearly be a step in the right direction.

Respecting cultural differences: snap-shots from primary care

The following clinical vignettes given by Dr H Rashid (HR) illustrate how primary care professionals can facilitate the assessment, diagnosis, management and outcomes of their clients.

Case 1

HR received an urgent request for a home visit from the family of a young Bangladeshi woman who were concerned that she was not eating at all and losing weight. On visiting her at home, the patient was found to be very withdrawn. It was difficult to take a detailed history as she was not forthcoming. However, information emerged indicating that, for the past year, she had been having difficulties eating, she was losing weight, was unhappy with her college, and was mainly staying at home. The father and other members of the family were quite concerned at the state of her health and seemed to be quite supportive, especially her sister-in-law. However, the structure of the family seemed authoritarian with the father being very protective and also in some ways restrictive with regard to the movements and personal development of the patient.

HR decided to offer her an appointment at the surgery to explore matters further. When she came to the surgery she was still not very forthcoming and did not provide any detailed history. However she did show an interest in seeing a local psychiatrist at the local hospital and a Bengali counsellor who worked with the psychiatric team. She agreed to attend the surgery to check her weight and discuss her progress with HR.

It also seemed appropriate that the family, especially the sister-in-law, should be involved in the management plan. She seemed to be very supportive and co-operative during the sessions. A referral was made to the Bangladeshi Mental Health team in the Social Services Department, which specialized in dealing with Bangladeshi clients. A few joint assessments were made by the Bangladeshi social worker and the psychiatrist, which elicited more detailed history, including the patient's family problems, which were quite complicated with issues of personal relationships, interference by the family and the patient's desire to have some freedom and space in her life. However, the involvement of the family members, especially the sister-in-law, helped to reassure the other members of the family that the professionals who were involved in the treatment of the patient were sensitive to the cultural and social standing of the patient's family. This helped in gaining the confidence of the patient and her family in the therapeutic management of the patient. The patient was put on regular anti-depressants and was also referred to the local gastroenterology department to manage her complaints of dyspepsia and heartburn. Within a year the patient started to put on weight, was eating much more regularly, seemed happy, and was planning to start her studies and making efforts to organize her life positively. The family was also quite happy that the patient had started to put on weight, interact with other members of the family and make positive decisions about going back to college. HR did not see the patient for another six months, when she came on her own to say she had now moved on to separate accommodation with the help of the local Social Services Department, and started college. She is maintaining a relationship with her family and there has been no reoccurrence of the eating disorder.

This illustrates that, while working with Bangladeshi female clients, it is very important for professionals to understand the various interactions within the family and outside the social parameters, so that an intervention strategy involves the confidence of the family members, includes the patient's near relatives and does not offend the cultural and social sensitivities of the family.

Case 2

HR was seeing a Bangladeshi family with six children where the mother was complaining about marital problems including emotional abuse by her husband. On going through the history, it seemed that for the past few years she had involvement from the local social services and her previous GP without making much headway in resolving her marital difficulties. The children, especially, seemed to be affected, showing signs of hyperactivity, and the mother indicated that her two adolescent children were also showing signs of disturbance at school. They were reluctant to come to the surgery and she was finding it difficult to cope. HR put her in touch with the appropriate local services to help her in resolving her marital problems and their effects on the children.

After a few consultations it seemed that the situation was getting worse. The children were showing increasing signs of disturbed behaviour. A case conference was called and attended by HR, a social worker, and the psychologist involved in their care. During the case conference, HR was quite surprised by the attitude of the psychologist. The psychologist did not appear to be very objective in dealing with the family and seemed to be taking sides in this conflict, which seemed unhelpful to both the patient and the interest of the children. HR discussed the attitude of the psychologist with the manager of the service, and how it may adversely affect the outcome of the joint intervention to help the patient and the children through this situation.

It is interesting to note that some professionals can identify too much with their clients and bring their own personal values and judgement in dealing with clients from minority ethnic groups, including Bangladeshi families. A greater understanding of their religious, cultural and social values would go a long way in making interventions more meaningful to the everyday lives of the clients. Such an approach would help to foster a sense of partnership with the client, which would make interventions more easily acceptable and probably achieve a better rate of success.

Case 3

HR was urgently called to the local psychiatric hospital to assess and section a young Bangladeshi man under the Mental Health Act. When visiting the hospital ward, the patient appeared to be quite agitated but was happy to be interviewed by a fellow Bangladeshi professional. HR spoke to him in Bengali and it transpired that he was admitted having assaulted his parents at home. He said he was living with his parents but was very angry with them as they were not helping him to bring his wife and children from Bangladesh. He had been married for the past five years and repeated attempts to bring his family to London had failed due to the refusal of the Immigration Department to allow the family entry into the United Kingdom. He appeared to be religious and expressed various religious beliefs including the statement that the Prophet met Allah by crossing seven skies and that one of the religious figures, Imam Mehdi, would be coming to the world to help Muslims.

This was considered by some professionals as expressing deluded ideas, including thought broadcasting. However, someone with knowledge of the religious content of his statements would not necessarily come to this conclusion. These ideas are coherent religious beliefs and normally would be acceptable by members of the Muslim community.

A good knowledge of the religious and cultural values of clients and their families is important in making the correct assessment and diagnosis of psychosis or other mental health problems as there is a danger of overdiagnosing or underdiagnosing mentally ill patients where sectioning may not be appropriate.

There are also serious medico-legal issues involved in dealing with clients from such ethno-cultural backgrounds. HR offered his opinion to the team treating the patient that the patient was not exhibiting signs of paranoid delusion or hallucination although he may be suffering from chronic mental illness. He was discharged later into the community, and put on anti-psychotic medication, with regular monitoring by the community psychiatric nurse who, fortunately, was also Bengali speaking. He gradually improved enough to stay at home with his parents.

The consultant psychiatrist wrote a letter to the Immigration Department at the British High Commission in support of his application for his wife and children to join him in the UK. HR also wrote a letter supporting his application as the separation between him and his family appeared to be one of the main causes of his frequent admissions and sectioning, and a barrier to his long-term recovery.

This illustrates that an immigration policy that is not fair and equal, especially for mentally ill patients, who suffer double discrimination, in that they are mentally ill and come from an ethnic minority group, is detrimental to the long-term health of these patient groups.

Professionals need to be sympathetic and understanding of the predicament and help as much as possible in this matter.

The Moitri project

The Moitri project is an innovative project in cross-cultural medicine that was founded in 1995 to support educational exchange and development of training in family medicine between general practice in East London and the Dhaka Community Hospital Trust in Bangladesh. *Moitri* means *friendship* in Bengali and seeks to establish an ongoing mutually beneficial programme sharing knowledge and skills between primary care professionals in both countries, which will ultimately benefit the patients.

In Tower Hamlets the project will enable general practitioners and other primary healthcare professionals to have first hand knowledge of the culture and tradition of healthcare in Bangladesh, thereby making them more effective in delivering appropriate healthcare to their Bangladeshi patients. The project is based at the Department of General Practice and Primary Care, St Bartholomew's and the Royal London School of Medicine and Dentistry at Queen Mary's and Westfield College, and is supported by the International Committee of the RCGP and the local health authority.

Some closing thoughts

In the field of mental health, it is generally accepted that mental well-being is mediated by the external social realities in which the individual is 'embodied' and 'embedded' (Flaskas and Perlesz, 1996), such as race, gender, culture and family circumstances. It seems imperative, therefore, to pay due consideration to these influences if practitioners are to avoid negating certain significant systems framing people's experiences and the meaning they ascribe to them.

For some white, and to a lesser extent Asian, professionals, certain Asian families and individuals present particular challenges in being able to think and work creatively and meaningfully. The tendency is to establish a relationship between the professional and client(s) based either on familiarity and sameness ('they are people, just like us') or difference ('they come from another planet').

We should like to suggest Bangladeshi families and individuals are in some respects the same as, and in other ways different from, both European families and other Bangladeshi families. Perhaps this is an obvious fact but sometimes it is useful to state the obvious. If practitioners were to adopt this position they would espouse a view that Bangladeshi families, like families from other non-Bangladeshi backgrounds, share certain universal human qualities and circumstances, and other unique features arising from their own cultural, historical, socio-economic and familial contexts. This would then involve a process of engaging with the individual's or family's narratives about their significant meaning systems, in defining their understanding both of self and of relationships with others.

The extent to which practitioners attend to such issues is perhaps partly influenced by individual style of relating and thinking, but largely also a product of the training received and the culture of the training institutions. Personal experience and informal discussions with colleagues who are health professionals suggest that cultural issues are not given adequate attention in courses or training, even though in principle there is a commitment to incorporating these issues in relation to theory and practice. What little literature is available on trainee feedback on training courses seem to confirm our anecdotal evidence (Hildebrand, 1998).

Perhaps one change that might make a difference in the way mental health professionals engage with Bangladeshi clients is to scrutinize critically and modify existing theoretical paradigms and practices underpinning the teaching of disciplines such as medicine, psychiatry, clinical psychology, family therapy, and psychotherapy. To date, these institutions are largely biased towards Western constructions of individual and family development, good health and ill health, normality and abnormality, ways to engage with helping systems, and so forth. Within these structures, there is very little information about, or exposure to, the experiences of other cultural groups.

Incorporating such information in training about other culturally determined systems of meanings, constructions of reality and wider experiences of people would help to broaden the professional's repertoire of thinking and practice. As Mason (1989) states:

> For change to happen we need to become less certain of the position we hold. When we become less certain of the position we hold we are more likely to become receptive to other possibilities, other meanings we might put to events. If we can become more open to the possible influence of other perspectives we open up space for other views to be stated and heard.

In working with individuals from different cultures it seems important to be 'open' to alternative descriptions and explanations in order to validate, respect, and celebrate differences within and across human lives.

References

Burnham J, Harris Q (1996) Emerging Ethnicity: A Tale of Three Cultures. In Dwivedi KN, Varma VP (eds) Meeting the Needs of Ethnic Minority Children: A Handbook for Professionals. London: Jessica Kingsley.

Casement P (1985). On Learning from the Patient. London: Routledge.

Coleman D, Salt J (eds) Ethnicity in the 1991 Census Vol. 1, London: OPCS.

Eade J, Vampleu T, Peach C (1996) The Bangladeshis: the encapsulated community. In Peach C (ed.) Ethnicity in the 1991 Census. Vol 2, London: OPCS.

Fernando S (1995) Social realities and mental health. In Fernando S (ed.) Mental Health in a Multi-ethnic Society. A Multi-Disciplinary Handbook. London: Routledge.

Flaskas C, Perlesz A (1996) The Therapeutic Relationship in Systemic Therapy. London: Karnac Books.

Helman CG (1994) Culture, Health and Illness. Oxford: Butterworth-Heinemann.

Hildebrand J (1998) Bridging the Gap: A Training Module in Personal and Professional Development. London: Karnac Books.

Kareem J, Littlewood R (eds) (1992) Intercultural Therapy: Themes, Interpretations and Practice. Oxford: Blackwell.

Karim M (1995) Access to Mental Health Services for the Bangladeshi Community in Tower Hamlets – a User's Perspective. London: Karim.

Kavanagh DJ, Lam AP (1996) Help seeking by immigrant Indo-Chinese psychiatric patients in Sydney, Australia. Psychiatric Services 47(9) : 993–5.

Lau A (1998) Family Therapy and Ethnic Minorities. In Street E, Dryden W (eds) Family Therapy in Britain. Buckingham: Open University Press.

MacCarthy B, Craissati J (1989) Ethnic differences in response to adversity. A community sample of Bangladeshis and their indigeneous neighbours. Social Psychiatry and Psychiatric Epidemiology 24(4): 196–201.

Mason Barry (1989) Handing Over. London: Karnac.

McGoldrick M, Carter EA (eds) (1980) The Family Life Cycle: A Framework for Family Therapy. New York: Gardner Press.

McGoldrick M, Pearce JK, Giordana J (1982) Ethnicity and Family Therapy. New York. Guilford.

McNamee S, Gergen KJ (eds) (1992) Therapy as Social Construction. London: Sage.

Takeuchi DT, Sue S, Yeh M (1995) Return rates and outcomes from ethnicity-specific mental health programs in Los Angeles. American Journal of Public Health 85(5): 638–43.

Tamura T, Lau A (1992). Connectedness versus separateness: applicability of family therapy to Japanese families. Family Process 31(4): 319–40.

Webb-Johnson A (1991) A Cry for Change: An Asian Perspective on Developing Quality Mental Health Care. London: Confederation of Indian Organisations.

Wilson M, MacCarthy B (1994) GP consultation as a factor in the low rate of mental health service used by Asians. Psychological Medicine 24(1): 11, 3–9.

Chapter 11
Psychological Problems in Asian children

QUEENIE HARRIS

Introduction

It is difficult to make general statements about the mental health of British Asians because of the great variation between groups and the cultural diversity that exists. Epidemiological research to show the presence of mental problems and the need for services to cater for them in the Asian population, along with ethnic monitoring, continues to be problematic. As Bird (1996: 43) acknowledged, 'a widely accepted methodology for epidemiological surveys of mental disorders of children and adolescents that can be used systematically with different cultural groups and applied in different cultural settings is yet to be developed'.

This situation is likely to continue as long as current methods of research, rooted as they are in Western world-views and forms of communication, are pursued. Their use in assessing people of different cultures with different world-views and using different explanatory models is the subject of ongoing debate. As Barnett Pearce (1989: xvii) points out: 'persons who live in various cultures and historical epochs do not "merely" communicate differently, but experience different ways of being human because they communicate differently'. The controversy lies in the degree to which consideration is given to the influence of cultural variation in the data collected, and social issues in the interpretation of the results of surveys. This presents a major dilemma in epidemiological research and continues to exercise the minds of epidemiologists, most of whom agree on the importance of developing culturally sensitive research methods. While service provision continues to be dependent on epidemiological research, comments on the strengths and weaknesses of existing services are difficult to make for the reasons stated above.

This chapter is concerned with the broad picture of mental health in Asian children, and is set in the context of the shortcomings of research done in this area. It begins with a brief literature review of research on psychiatric morbidity in Asian children in their countries of origin, and in this country, which will highlight difficulties in this area of research. Against this background, possible factors that militate against the development of psychological problems, and those that make for greater vulnerability among Asian children, are explored through some personal reflections, reference to literature and case studies. Some useful theoretical concepts that facilitate ways of working with Asian children and their families are also outlined.

Brief literature review

Psychological problems in Asian children from studies carried out in India.

The presence of significant morbidity from child psychiatric disorders is reflected in studies carried out in India (Verghese and Beig, 1974; Lal and Sethi, 1977; Gupta, Dutta and Dutta, 1978). The disorders identified, included emotional and behaviour problems, developmental delays, psychosis, learning difficulties, and epilepsy with associated behaviour disturbance. Several of these studies of the rates of emotional and behavioural psychiatric disorder of children living in the Asian subcontinent seem to suggest that rates of disturbance are similar to those seen in the West and are higher in urban areas compared with rural areas. This pattern is similar to that demonstrated in the West.

However, the populations used in the studies carried out in India on behaviour problems in children vary widely, and are often not clearly defined, making interpretation and comparison with British studies difficult (Newth, 1986). Furthermore, these studies have mostly been carried out by Western-trained/influenced mental health workers, who have applied Western-based research criteria and instruments validated for use in Western psychiatry rather than for these culturally different and diverse groups. While not discounting the merit of such studies, one wonders how the 'entities' arrived at might have been constructed if more 'locally evolved' explanatory and culturally sensitive models were employed.

Psychological problems in Asian children and young people from UK studies

Studies like those of Stern et al. (1990) and Jawed (1991) confirm the view that children in the Asian population are underrepresented in referrals to mental health clinics. Whether the low referral rate or low rate of uptake of services could be related to a low rate of disorder, cultural issues that inhibit the seeking of outside help, somatization of emotional distress, different meanings given for disturbed behaviour, or the perceived inappropriateness of services delivered, is not yet clear. Newth and Corbett's study of behaviour problems in 3-year-old Asian children concluded that 'Asian parents of pre-school children are less likely to see difficult behaviour as a problem that can be dealt with although they may be just as distressed by it' (Newth and Corbett, 1993: 349). The common experience of professionals working in child mental health clinics, for Asian children to be referred at a later stage in their childhood, was validated in an audit of referrals from the Asian community in two similar districts in the West Midlands. This audit also showed that in one of these districts there was no difference in the numbers of boys and girls referred, but male children tended to be referred at a younger age. The types of disorders presented, and the differences between the sexes, were similar in both populations studied. Emotional disorder and overdoses were more common as a presenting problem in girls (A Solomon and P Forster, personal communication).

Ken Fogelmann's (1983) national development study indicated a large difference between first and second generation Asian children, with second generation Asians appearing much closer to the indigenous population. The problems presented by those seen in mental health clinics do seem to reflect this.

Changing pattern of mental health in Asian children and young adults.

Numerous earlier studies suggested that less mental illness is found among most groups of British Asians than might be expected (Cochrane and Stopes Roe, 1977). Some have speculated, from a comparative study of two groups of schoolchildren, that the lower rate of behavioural problems in the Asian group of children might be due to possible, but not yet established, differences in family life (Kallarackal and Herbert, 1976).

This perception of a lower rate of symptomatic behaviour appears to be changing, especially in the young female population. Self-harm behaviour and bulimia are two problem areas identified, where there appears to be an increase higher than the general rate for white women of corresponding age (Wright, Trethowan and Owens, 1981; Merrill, 1986; Mumford, Whitehouse and Platts, 1991). The young married Asian women represented in the former studies usually overdosed in the context of marital difficulties whereas, for the young unmarried girls, intergenerational tensions related to cultural expectations and adaptation to a Western way of life were common reasons given (Merrill, 1986). In addition, Asian females in the age group 15 to 24 showed levels of completed suicide 80% higher than the general rate for white women of a corresponding age (Soni-Raleigh, Bulman and Balarajan, 1990). The increased prevalence of eating disorders among Asian adolescent girls was thought by the researchers to reflect hidden cultural conflict and distress, arising in a context of traditional family life and of growing up in Britain (Mumford et al., 1991).

Discussion of some protective factors

'Protective factors refer to influences that modify, ameliorate, or alter a person's response to some environmental hazard that predisposes to a maladaptive outcome . . . the concept is not at all synonymous with a positive or beneficial experience.' 'Protective influences operate indirectly through their effects on interpersonal interactions' (Rutter, 1985: 600, 606).

This is clearly a complex issue and what follows is not intended to provide answers. It is a collection of thoughts that perhaps address certain facets of this large area.

American studies on migrants seem to suggest that a preservation of some of the cultural traditions, rituals and ceremonies, have a protective function. The significance of this association as a possible protective factor in Asian families in this country is yet to be studied, although the idea is a persuasive one and worth exploring further.

The maintenance of cultural ties

In one study of Mexican American migrants, a pervasive sense of cultural heritage among migrants was positively related to indicators of mental health (Warheit, Vega, Auth and Minhardt, 1985). Many Asian families maintain connections in two or more locations over extended periods of time. These are effected, for example, through commuting between countries and long-distance telephone calls. The connections maintained between different geographical locations and meaning systems leads to a 'trans-context lifestyle' (Turner, 1991), which refers to a lifestyle that spans both contexts. Such a lifestyle incorporates cultural changes occurring in the countries of origin, which enable the calibration of rules governing the cultural practices and beliefs of settled communities outside these countries. Asian radio and television programmes in the UK, and Indian films and videos, provide the means for those not able physically to visit the countries of origin to keep abreast of the evolving cultural and societal changes occurring there. Modern Asian comedy television programmes in the UK, written by Asian scriptwriters and using Asian actors, provide sources for reviewing and reflecting on values and styles of living in the Asian community both in the UK and in India, Pakistan and Bangladesh. Not all Asians may view this as a positive experience. Television talk shows and programmes for young British Asians foster their emerging identity in the Asian community in the UK. All these influences have the potential to promote, through a strong cultural identity, the self-efficacy and self-esteem that enable positive responses to problem-solving.

Implications for the Asian Community in UK – personal reflections

The development of 'family-like' ties, usually forged by first-generation Asian families, is commonly found, and is the personal experience of the author who is embedded in such a network. Common interests and backgrounds provide a mutually supportive social milieu, in which old stories are retold, social customs and practices are adhered to or modified, and new stories and beliefs are created. A context is created in which evolving ethnic identities can emerge. Such processes can be said generally to reflect adaptation in a new and hostile environment, and are therefore shared by other migrant ethnic groups. A strong sense of cultural heritage and striking differences in appearance and lifestyle that the Asian group presents perhaps makes these apparent cohesive processes more pronounced. The influence of these processes on emerging lifestyles is particularly noticeable in the area of arranged marriages and in the further education of girls and young women.

The 'modern' arranged marriage

Arranged marriages are effected differently now, although the processes still differ widely, both in the countries of origin and in the UK. Prospective partners of a marriage are given greater choice in many groups in the Asian community, some being effected in novel ways. For example, a largely middle-class Gujerati community in London has organized regular social events, when young people of marriageable age attend with their families, in a forum approved of and supported by the whole local Gujerati community. The impetus for this has come from recognition by parents of the need to understand the emerging differences in values and outlook on life in their children brought up in a different environment from themselves. From talking to the young people at one such event, I learned that they approved and understood the purpose of these meetings. They welcomed the opportunity to socialize freely, and to have a say in their choice of partner, at the same time as feeling no obligation to do so. They reported that they did not feel forced into marriages they did not want.

Such attempts to build bridges between generations enables families to evolve in a way that supports the maintenance of family ties, and the young people's connection with their community and cultural heritage. The supportive network in which such marriages are embedded promotes the likelihood of a potentially stable background environment for the children of these marriages. It is not suggested, however, that this process alone guarantees the emotional well-being of children or of stable marriages. More marriages appear to be arranged between young men and women born and brought up in the UK or with a Western background. This is in contrast to the earlier and common practice of husbands or wives being found in India, Pakistan or Bangladesh, and joining their respective partners in the UK. Many Asian parents, influential community and religious leaders, increasingly recognize the potential difficulties inherent in the latter form of arranged marriage – for the couple and for the children of the marriage.

Education

The further education of girls with an accompanying deferment of marriage to a later-than-usual age, is increasingly encountered in many families. More educated Asian women are thus able to hold jobs in various walks of life, although the task is still hard, both by virtue of them being women and of being Asian. Education has afforded Asian women a sense of empowerment and a degree of 'independence', which enables them to challenge, for example, lifestyles of enslavement in abusive relationships. The implications of this changed dynamic in relationships between couples merits further study.

Strengths and weaknesses in patterns of close family and community ties

The role of the extended Asian family in the exacerbation of, or protection from, child psychological disorder has not been studied enough in Britain. It is important to remember that there can be both strengths and weaknesses in a pattern of close family and community connections. For example, an Indian teenager presented with depression in a context of domestic violence. Her mother had, through the courts, effected the eviction of the teenager's father from the family home and ultimately divorced him. Mother and daughter came under considerable pressure from the immediate family and community network against taking such action and were urged to consider reconciliation with the father. They felt unsupported by the family and the community, whose advice, based on considerations of 'honour' and 'shame' on the family and the larger community, superseded considerations of the mother's and daughter's experience of humiliation, personal injuries and danger.

In another example, a young UK-born Indian woman exercised her choice of husband in an arranged marriage but, within months, difficulties ensued in the marriage of such proportions that it was doomed to fail. Her beliefs led her to try to stay in the marriage because of the shame she thought she would bring on her family if she left. She was also fearful of the likely consequences on her sisters' chances of marriage if she left. She became depressed, and contemplated taking her life as the situation became intolerable. She found the courage to tell her family of her suffering and returned to her family. She remained sad and depressed, however, as she perceived her widowed mother's sadness, which she felt resulted from her mother's sense of failure to effect a good marriage for her daughter. When she became aware that members in her close community were sympathetic to her and supportive of her, she felt enormous relief and was able to continue with her career and life again. Here, support in the family and the immediate community network was of a positive nature, and sustained not only the young girl concerned but also her family, especially her unmarried sisters.

In India, living with the extended family is common, and the woman who has to live with her husband's family has to 'reconstruct' her identity and status associated with this position (Ramanujam, 1975). There are potentially new tensions to be overcome, for example within the female kinship network, and with the mother-in-law in particular. The tensions that are sometimes generated in the couple's relationship as a result of this can have an impact on the woman's mental health, the marriage and the upbringing of the children, who can potentially present with behaviour problems. On the other hand, there are positive elements in such a structure of living, such as an environment that can potentially be supportive to a young mother in caring for her young child, thereby enabling a less stressful environment for the child to grow up in. A similar structure of joint family living is common in the Asian community in the UK. The effect of changing patterns in raising children, such as mixing with different cultures, can make such a 'reconstruction' of roles a more difficult process. Further exploration and study of this is needed.

Discussion of some vulnerability factors

All children and adolescents face many stressors in their lives. They can therefore be vulnerable at different stages of their development. The manifestation of this vulnerability is usually the result of an interaction between a number of factors at the social, intellectual and biological levels. Violence, marital conflicts, mental illness in parents, sexual and physical abuse, neglect, low social status, overcrowding or large family size, paternal criminality, and other harmful influences are risk factors for all children (Rutter, 1978, 1979, 1985) regardless of their cultural background. In some families, family responsibilities seem to contribute to an increased vulnerability in the eldest son (Al-Issa, 1989).

The effects of racial abuse, and other social injustices surrounding the life of an Asian family, as with other minority groups, make for added vulnerabilities in Asian children that are not shared by their white counterparts (Littlewood and Lipsedge, 1989). The experience of negative images of their ethnic background, and conflict between values at school and those of the family, can sometimes promote a sense of inferiority and disadvantage in these children as individuals or as a group.

A growing incidence of marital breakdown and, with it, the increasing presence of single-parent families, usually mothers on their own, could be expected to have an effect on child-rearing practices. The vulnerability of children in one-parent families would depend on, among other socio-economic factors, whether or not their mothers have the support of their family or community. Such factors could be deemed as having influence generally, but in communities that exist in perceived or actual 'hostile' cultural environments, and whose values for family life are based on interdependence, the importance of intra-community cohesion may become more important.

Other conflicts and sources of stress can exist between different ethnic groups and within any one group. Conflicts based on cultural values, beliefs, and practices, between the values of the emergent culture of second and subsequent generation Asian children and those of first generation Asian families and communities, are a common source of tension and stress for Asian children and adolescents. As the children grow up in a milieu that includes mixed schools, the social and religious constraints on relationships between boys and girls from different groups are sometimes weakened and boundaries transgressed. Conflicts that can arise from romantic alliances formed between members of two different groups can sometimes have far-reaching and adverse consequences, usually for the girl involved. The consequences of being found out in these circumstances can sometimes include death, usually of the girl, in order to preserve the honour of the family. The girls who decide to leave their families in these situations, usually face being ostracized by their family. They often live in fear of being found, and spend their lives in fear and 'on the run' for many years. They experience a sense of alienation and rejection from their family and extended community network, and feel an acute sense of loss of the close relationships they had in the family. They often remain in an estranged relationship with their families for many years, although some manage to meet secretly with some members of the family. The fear, isolation and lack of support felt by them often takes its toll on their mental well-being. Some of these young girls who have been brought up in sheltered environments are particularly at risk when they are separated from their families. The plight of some of these girls has been the subject of many television documentaries.

Discussion of service provision

The concept of ethnic identity and ethnic monitoring in the National Health Service is controversial (Hodes, Creamer and Woolley, 1998) and complicates epidemiological research. It is suggested that ethnicity is a complex variable 'whose everyday use, often as a euphemism for race may be difficult to alter since a replacement variable is hard to find' (Singh, 1997: 307). The interpretation of current ethnic monitoring in the NHS, which overlooks certain ethnic groups large enough to deserve special attention at a local level because of the limitations of categorization, results in a lack of provision of adequate/appropriate services for these communities (Aspinall, 1995).

Such difficulties as exist are not surprising if one takes the view that ethnicity and culture are constantly emerging. 'Given that ethnicity is constituted through a variety of meanings and contexts, any one way to describe it will have some limitations' (Hodes et al., 1998: 20). It is desirable for conversations about ethnicity, which may take place at different times in the course of therapy, to be useful in therapy, rather than having only a research or monitoring function.

As mentioned elsewhere, 'ethnicity is proposed, as referring to a client's "definition of self" in relation to their race and culture at a particular point in time. As such it cannot be defined by another and can only be created in a conversation between therapist and client/s' (Burnham and Harris, 1997: 131). That ethnicity has an enduring and powerful influence determining family patterns and belief systems, although it may be modified in successive generations of a community, is increasingly recognized. This view is supported by recent research that suggests that adolescents take some aspects of their cultural identity from their parents but are also active participants in constructing new identities (Tizard and Phoenix, 1993; Ballard, 1994; Baumann, 1995; Hodes et al., 1998).

Aspects of service delivery and the importance of creating a context for therapy

General considerations in service delivery developed so far in the health and social services, such as the employment of interpreters, health education initiatives, matching ethnic groups in fostering and adoption decisions, and equal opportunities policies, are important in achieving respectful and useful services for Asian families.

Specific considerations for therapists working with Asian families

Monica McGoldrick stresses the need for an understanding of the frame of reference of the person seeking help as well as that of the helper, without which problems, whether physical or mental, can neither be diagnosed nor treated (McGoldrick, Pearce, Giordano, 1982: 6). Each will derive/bestow meaning about the problem and consultation according to his or her differing sets of beliefs. The consultation can be regarded as a negotiation between two or more belief systems which, to be successful, needs to take into account clients'/patients' explanations for their problems/symptoms (Messent, 1992).

This has relevance for paediatricians dealing with Asian families presenting with acutely ill children, or managing chronic illness in them. For example, take the case of a child on the ward with a physical illness who is not responding to treatment in the expected way, or is having to be admitted frequently to the ward with recurring problems of a similar nature, such as diabetic control-related problems, frequent epileptic seizures or recurrent abdominal pain. As with children in general, factors in the child, school, in the family, in the interplay between the family and staff on the ward and between the staff all need to be examined in gaining an understanding of the factors that are sustaining or maintaining the problem.

In the case of the Asian family, however, particular attention needs to be paid to finding out what explanations the families have for the problem and their ideas about medication. One needs to be open to hearing explanations for the symptoms that might sometimes sound alien, as will be seen in the case example below. Explanations of the nature of the illness, and the treatment regime given to the child and the family, need to be given in the light of information gained through such conversations. This may need to take into account the value placed on injections, or the significance attached to timing and dietary considerations associated with taking drugs (Bavington and Majid, 1986).

Attitudes to, and expectations of, therapy.

The concept of therapy as it is thought of in Western cultures also needs to be reappraised. Therapists who assume they can stand outside of that which they observe are vulnerable to the pitfalls of negatively judging family members for not measuring up to normative standards subscribed to by the therapist, blaming the culture for contributing to the problem, and directing the family to conform to the therapist's ethnocentric standards.
It is important for a therapist working with Asian families to remember the following (see also Harris, 1995):

- The idea that most Asian families prefer to have problems dealt with within the family or close network should not lead the therapist to think that family meetings would be the best format for discussion of problems. To invite the whole family to a first meeting poses problems.
- In most Asian families there is an inhibition about seeking help. Family conflicts, mental illness and so forth are considered embarrassments not to be disclosed to outsiders. The stress caused by the problem may be severe enough for an individual to overcome inhibitions about seeking help from an outsider, but not severe enough for other members of the family.
- Family meetings with expectations for free exchange of ideas between members in the presence of an outsider, especially asking children to talk in front of and about their parents, transgresses intergenerational and cultural rules about such communication.
- Respecting hierarchical rules means being prepared to work separately. with the various subsystems of the family Depending on the receptivity of the family and the degree of trust established between the worker

and the family, brief joint meetings with the parents and the referred child, or with a couple, to discuss agreed issues can eventually be negotiated.

● It is important to keep an open mind. One may need to be open to the possibility that some families are not supportive at all, contrary to one's expectations of Asian family life.

● Where there is conflict between family and individual interests, it is important for the therapist not to side automatically with the individual – a pitfall for Western therapists.

● Formal information-gathering in early sessions, as required for a psychiatric interview, is generally experienced as intrusive by Asian parents.

● Expectations at the point of contact with professionals are often for advice and concrete ways of solving problems, and not for insight therapy. In this respect, expectations are perhaps like those of some white families, but they are articulated more often by Asian families.

● There may be an expectation for the therapist to take an active role in helping to resolve the problem, to play the role of adviser, act as a resource person, or sometimes to work in conjunction with faith healers, Imams and other religious community leaders.

A case example.

The referral to a child psychiatrist of an 11-year-old Pakistani boy, RK, by a paediatrician, concerned his repeated admissions for continuing episodes of apparent loss of consciousness. Extensive investigation showed no physical basis for his 'attacks'. He had just started secondary school and shortly afterwards had an accident in PE, from which he made a satisfactory recovery, he developed episodes when he would go very limp, apparently unconscious, and then come around but not in a normal state. He was discharged from the ward as he was better while there and was referred to the child psychiatrist for outpatient follow-up.

Response to referral

The senior registrar, (a white Australian) who saw him on the ward worked sessionally in the child psychiatry department and was able to continue to be involved with him and his family with supervision from the child psychiatrist. Problems at school were identified while he was on the ward, which included bullying. Her initial interventions involved meeting with important members of the family as identified by them, and included an important uncle.

Commentary

This illustrates the willingness of a non-Asian professional actively to enquire about and accept different family structures, such as an important uncle. Readers may wish to consider what kind of questions they would ask, and with what tone, to create a context in which families could feel confident that their ways of doing things would not be judged as pathological or wrong because they were different from the ways in which professionals organized their own lives or had been taught to regard as 'normal'.

RK was not able to cope with the rough elements in school and the bullying he experienced there, and his symptoms were thought to be a manifestation of anxiety in school. The social worker and the therapist did home visits and liaised with the head of his school, which included advice about the management of the attacks in school. A short period of improvement followed, for approximately six months, with RK being escorted to school by an uncle and returning home for lunch. The staff in school were supported by the reassuring visits made by the senior registrar in response to the few anxious calls they made. RK's attacks gradually returned, however, increasing in severity and frequency both at home and at school. A meeting with his mother at this time found her unable to cope with him, as she reported the family's distress over RK's attempts to jump out of a window during an attack, and to get a knife out of a drawer in the kitchen. A plan to seek admission to a child psychiatric ward was provisionally made, and put to the mother in a subsequent meeting that included an important uncle. This was accepted, as was the fact that there might be a delay in effecting this. However, when a home visit by the in-patient staff took place, the family asked them if his admission could be delayed for a short while.

A scheduled appointment with the therapist came up in the meanwhile, which was supervised. The mother and the children attended the meeting together with an uncle.

Important aspects of this interview

The therapist's attempts to connect with the uncle, who was new to her, revealed her knowledge of the family and extent of her involvement in the family network. The interview began by finding out the names of the various members present, and the therapist had an early indication of the need to address other members of the family via the uncle, by the various interjections he made in this process.

Therapist: I am very glad you could come. Now I have not met you before have I? Which uncle are you? The one that takes RK to school or . . .?

Uncle: Yes that's right.

Therapist: I see you are the one that drives RK to school. I have met another uncle who comes sometimes and there is another uncle who lives in Derby isn't there?

Uncle: Yes that's right.

Therapist: And it's your daughter who has been ill? How is she?
Uncle: Well, she's on dialysis, you know . . . the bags.

The therapist proceeded to enquire respectfully about their understanding and explanations for the continuing symptoms that RK presented and, more particularly, to enquire about their change of mind about admission. The 'uncle' assumed the role of the spokesperson in the interview, even when questions were put to RK's mother. This was noted by the therapist but not commented upon or confronted.

Commentary

The therapist here was gaining an idea of the hierarchical and gender rules observed in this Muslim family. A therapist working with a non-Asian family would have dealt with this differently. They would have used various techniques gained from their training to facilitate views being expressed by every family member. Observers of such a situation with similar views as the therapist might have attached negative connotations to the process. Comments like 'he is too dominant' or 'the mother's views need to be heard' would have been made and attempts to 'give RK's mother a voice' would have been advised. If the therapist had applied this way of working, engagement with the family would have been jeopardized. The stance that the therapist took was of a respectful acceptance and curiosity, which produced information that was fascinating.

The family's explanation and beliefs

The uncle put forward the view that the explanation all the family had come to was that RK was possessed by a spirit. They recalled he had urinated by the side of the road, under the shade of a tree (a place that is usually inhabited by spirits) while accompanying another uncle on his milk round. The uncle explained that the act of urinating facilitated the entry of the spirit into him through the stream of urine.

He said

> At that place there was evil spirits living there. So when he finished passing water and came back home, his body felt heavier – he felt something heavy in his body and then he started having pains in his stomach – just on top of his appendix operation. Somebody said instead of going to the doctor take him to the priest, our priest you know, who knows about evil things, can catch them in their hands sometimes, when they are reading the Koran or something like that. So we went to the priest and he agreed to treat him.

It had been two-and-a-half months since they had seen the priest, who had given them a sword to carry with them wherever they went with RK. They were instructed to point the sword at his chest whenever he had an 'attack'. They had to seek permission of the priest before they went to anybody's house, because 'that thing does not give you permission to go to somebody's house'. The therapist referred to the troubling behaviour shown by RK, to which the Uncle replied that this had occurred only once. He went on to say that following an attack, RK had said that he could see evil ladies.

Uncle: First when he started to be sick that thing was speaking from his body and she was telling us why she was giving him trouble. 'It was because he passed water on me. They were eating their dinner up there and he started passing water on me.' When he was unconscious it was speaking from his body.

The therapist proceeded to enquire whether all the members of the family shared this belief and if it was one that would be shared by most in the culture, to which the uncle replied that all the family and all Muslims believed this. He explained that such things happened to children of friends he knew, that it usually took about six months for the spirits to come out, and after that the children are perfectly all right. He added 'it is almost four months and he is much better than before.'

He said that the priest has 100% success in these cases in Pakistan, adding that in other hot countries there were more spirits. He explained that in the absence of good toilet facilities, people in his village used the great outdoors for these functions! They 'did not urinate or defecate in the "shadows" because the spirits are always resting there, so if anyone passes water on them they catch the things' .

Therapist: And do you catch the same sort of thing as RK?
Uncle: Exactly the same thing. That is why we understand what has happened. The people in our country tell us there is nothing to worry about – he should be all right.

Commentary

The therapist, in elaborating the questions in an accepting and respectful way, about the nature of the spirits, the manner of inhabitation, and the shared beliefs in the family and community, was gaining valuable information about the family's explanations and beliefs that would influence the therapy on offer.

The family discussed the plans for admission with the priest, who said he had no objection but requested a delay, during which time no medication was to be given.

In the course of the interview, RK began to have one of his 'attacks' , which was dealt with calmly by the uncle and his mother. His uncle explained that they had forgotten to tell the Imam before leaving the house, as instructed by him, and had forgotten to bring the 'dagger/knife' with them. They were sure that had they done this they would have been to able to bring his symptoms under control.

They were invited by the therapist to phone the Imam from the interview room. While they struggled to recall his number, they asked RK while he was having an attack, if he knew the telephone number of the Imam, and he was able to give it to them! While they were waiting to get through to the Imam, the therapist asked what the family would do if the Imam was unsuccessful in getting the spirit out. They confidently replied, that they would go to Pakistan to a senior Imam with greater powers who would be able to get the spirit out.

Commentary

This case demonstrates the importance of enquiring about, and treating with respect, the family's explanations for the problem at different times in the course of contact with them. Their earlier anxieties would have been based on an idea that he had something wrong in his brain. When the investigations did not substantiate this, and they noticed his improvement while on the ward, they co-operated with the strenuous efforts that were made to help RK get to school and stay there as they saw his continuing education as important. The school's co-operation in helping RK was viewed positively by the family. When his turns at school started to reappear the family sought reassurance that there was no physical basis for this, which was given to them.

There followed a consultation process within the family and community network, which led to an explanation that would have been unknown to us had we not enquired again about their explanations for the continued symptoms.

In the light of what emerged, it can be appreciated that medication, if administered without this knowledge, would probably not have been taken. Admission, if taken up before the Imam had begun his 'treatment', would have placed the family in a dilemma. Admission would perhaps not have been a good idea as any treatment regime would have run contrary to the family's beliefs. The respectful curiosity shown by the therapist in order to find out about their ideas, and the invitation to contact the Imam, would have been seen by the family as respect for and acceptance of their ideas. In agreeing to the delay in admission, the Imam would have seen us as allies in helping RK and the family, avoiding triangulation of the therapeutic unit with the Imam and family network.

RK's symptomatic behaviour was associated with school stresses and was a form of school avoidance. Being the eldest child in the family would have probably made it difficult for him to voice his concerns to his family. As the lack of a physical basis for his symptoms had come to be accepted by his family, the new meaning given to his continuing symptoms, which were supported by strong beliefs that he could be cured, offered him a way out. The disappearance of his symptoms could be paced by him, helped by the other interventions in place.

This case demonstrates that customs, religious beliefs, or attitudes, all affect the meaning that the family may give to symptoms, which are not always readily offered unless enquired about.

It is therefore important to enquire about their understanding of the referral, what they think about the meeting with the specialist, whether they are in agreement with the referral, and about their expectations of the visit. While these may be important questions to ask all families, the value of their use with Asian families is the access it provides to the particular beliefs and explanatory models that the family subscribes to and their implications for the therapeutic approach on offer. A therapist working with Asian families needs to resist the temptation of certainty through a process of respectful co-ordination, when the coherence (logic) of the professional(s) differs from the coherence (logic) of the family. Questions relating to the beliefs and practices of ethnic groups may assume different levels of importance, compared with other clients, within a particular therapy or therapeutic setting. Professionals require particular resources and practices that allow them to co-create ethnically sensitive practices with the families and individuals with whom they are working. Some useful theoretical concepts that can help therapists develop their practice follow.

Theoretical concepts

The theoretical concepts that underpin a systemic approach, provide a means for considering the problems presented by children from Asian backgrounds at different stages of development (see Harris, 1994). Some of the ideas that have been most useful will be highlighted here, and readers are referred to the source material for their further exploration.

The significant system

The idea of the 'significant system' (Boscolo, Cecchin, Hoffman and Penn, 1987) or the 'meaningful system' – that configuration of relationships and beliefs in which the family's problems and issues make sense (Imber Coppersmith, 1985) was an influential and important development in the Milan-based practice of systemic therapy. This concept invites therapists to avoid labelling individuals, families or cultures as dysfunctional and to consider the meaning of symptomatic behaviour in various relational contexts, including that created between the family and the therapist/therapeutic team.

Therapeutic co-construction of meaning

1. Observed and observing systems

Sometimes a therapist works with families in ways that aim, directly and indirectly, to change the family. Such an 'observed system' position adopted by some researchers has generated much useful information (see McGoldrick, Pearce and Giordano, 1982; McGoldrick and Rohrbbaugh, 1987; Boyd-Franklin, 1989; McGoldrick, Almeida, Moore-Hines, Rosen, Garcia-Preto and Lee, 1991; Lau, 1984, 1986, 1988).

This approach gave way to an increasing recognition that the observations made by professionals/teams included what they contributed to the dialogue between those professionals and the client/s (the 'observing system'). This derived from the theoretical ideas subscribed to, professional and personal experience, and their own cultural patterns and beliefs. Scientists in the biophysical sciences instigated such a view in the 1980s, challenging the idea that one could acquire objective knowledge about the world and about others independently of one's own constructions.

Other important influences came from the ideas of social constructionists who proposed that realities are constructed socially between people by communication over time. The conversations between the therapist and the individual and/or family members take place in the context of the multiple levels of meaning that are significant to the participants of the therapeutic conversation. Mendez, Coddou and Maturana (1988) proposed the term 'multiverse' to emphasize that there are many equally valid ways of perceiving the world, although one might add that they may not all be equally desirable. Meanings emerge in the therapeutic conversation between the therapist and family members. Cecchin (1987) suggests that the therapist, when curious, questions her own premises as well as those of the family she is interviewing. This fits with Bateson's ideas about multiple levels of context in interpersonal systems that give meaning to behaviours or symptoms as well as current interactions.

Multiple levels of meaning.

A theoretical framework that is particularly useful for work with families is the co-ordinated management of meaning (CMM) approach developed by Cronen and Pearce (1980) with many further developments. (Most recently see Pearce, 1994, and Cronen and Lang, 1994). Specifically in relation to culture see Hannah, 1994. The different levels of meaning (Cronen and Pearce, 1980) enable one to examine in greater detail the context that gives meaning to the problem under study. This framework elegantly elaborates Bateson's idea (1973) that there is 'no meaning without context'. Cronen and Pearce propose a hypothetical hierarchy of levels of context in which the meaning of any level can be understood by reference to a higher level. They stress a flexibility in its application such that any level of context can be privileged in discerning the meaning of a given episode.

The contexts that give meaning can be arranged as follows (in ascending order): content (of a statement), the speech act (the utterance as a whole); episode (the particular social encounter); interpersonal relationship (the definition of the relationship between the people creating the episode); life story (stories people have about themselves); family narratives (family mottos and ways of behaving in the world); social mores (laws, regulations and social prescription for the citizens of a particular society) and cultural patterns (the beliefs, values and practices that distinguish a culture as unique, different from other cultures).

In the example of RK, given above, the act of urinating at the side of the road was given meaning in the context of the life story ('in our country urinating in the shadows is avoided as spirits reside there'). The episode of his 'attacks' gained new meaning in the context of family narratives and cultural beliefs ('after discussion with the family someone said to take him to the priest, as he had become possessed by a spirit – he would be cured, if not by this priest then by a more senior and powerful one'). The respectful curiosity of the therapist keen to understand the family's explanations brought forth these meanings by the questions she asked and by her acceptance of the explanations.

Therapeutic curiosity

Adopting a position of 'therapeutic curiosity' (Cecchin, 1987) about a person/family's world view, offers greater opportunities for understanding beliefs that give meaning to behaviours. The beliefs that are shared by many Eastern cultures contextualize the different meanings given to symptomatic behaviours, patterns of extended family networks, kinship and hierarchies, in ways that are different to those held in Western cultures.

Ethnicity as a context

It is important to consider contexts such as ethnicity, gender, age, race and so forth in all meetings with individuals/families. They are contexts that are privileged at different times in the course of therapy or social interaction. The questions are 'how is ethnicity to be privileged when the difference between therapist and the family is not so obvious?' and 'what aspects of an interview prompt the therapist to privilege ethnocultural factors as a context for understanding?' Is it only when a physical difference is obvious between the therapist and one or more members of a family? Some of the cues for making ethnicity a context for exploration may include: something the family members say or do; something the therapist feels or thinks; something a team member experiences or observes.

When there is no physical difference that might give a cue to ethnic differences then it may be less likely that ethnicity becomes an important context for the conversation because it may be assumed that the family and therapist share ideas and beliefs, and curiosity is likely to be diminished. If one is working with a team, they may be helpful in sustaining the therapist's curiosity. It is necessary in these circumstances to adopt a 'discipline of curiosity' (Cecchin, 1992). Questions related to ethnicity need to be sensitively and carefully explored with the family in these situations. The posture of curiosity about beliefs and cultural practices can be experienced as intrusive, interrogative and make the therapist appear 'distant'. Family members may also think: 'she should know – why is she asking?' Questions may be viewed as the therapist dissociating herself from the culture, being 'anglicized', pretending not to be the person she is, and so on, all of which potentially risk processes that alienate rather than promote engagement with families. My colleague John Burnham and I have developed an approach that makes explicit the reasons for asking questions about ethnicity in such a context. The conversation opens with a statement such as 'I would like to ask some questions about how your life is. It may be that because we look the same and roughly share the same cultural background, that we would think the same. But I would like to be sure that we are talking about your ideas and beliefs rather than me assume that we think the same. So when I ask you some questions, it may seem "as if I know nothing" about the things we are discussing. Of course I do have ideas and views but I would like to be sure that we are talking about how you see things.' Many people have expressed an appreciation of this and have become more willing to answer questions about things that they may have assumed the therapist, as a member of the same community, would understand already.

Therapists with such an orientation are invited to examine how their own prejudices, values, passions and theories are situated within their own ethnicity and culture. The worker is freed from the idea of fitting everyone into the same set of beliefs and practices and therefore is less likely to impose the values and practices of the dominant (majority) culture upon persons from a minority culture. The worker is more inclined to elicit different views and perceptions of the problem. Enquiring about the client's cultural background, beliefs and practices needs to be carefully and thoughtfully done. It is important to avoid the temptation, inherent in gaining more knowledge of a culture, of creating a 'grand narrative' about cultures that can lead to a static view of them (Burnham and Harris, 1997).

In conclusion, it seems evident that current research methods need further refinement. While the newer multiaxial classification acknowledges the relationship between diagnosis, personality, physical health and preceding life stresses, it still lacks an acceptance of cultural variation within societies and across societies.(Acharyya, 1992). A further complexity in research is presented with the subtle differences of experience in British-born second and third generations. The influence of these differences and responses to them have been alluded to here, although they have yet to be studied. Although the difficulties in epidemiological studies continue to exist, making statements about service provision difficult, ways of developing ethnically sensitive practices, such have been described, need to continue.

Note

1. Acknowledgement: My grateful thanks to my friend and colleague Mr. John Burnham, for his encouragement and helpful comments towards the completion of this chapter. Our professional relationship has spanned more than 20 years, and some of the ideas and practices described reflect co-evolved developments during this time.

References

Acharyya S (1992) The doctor's dilemma: the practice of cultural psychiatry in multi-cultural Britain. In Kareem J, Littlewood R (eds) Intercultural Therapy: Themes, Interpretations and Practice. Oxford: Blackwell Scientific Publications.

Al-Issa I (1989) Psychiatry in Algeria. Psychiatric Bulletin of the Royal College of Psychiatry 13: 240–5.

Aspinall PJ (1995) Department of Health's requirement for mandatory collection of data on ethnic group of inpatients. British Medical Journal 311: 1006–9.

Ballard R (1994) Desh Pradesh. The South Asian Presence in Britain. London: Hurst.

Barnett Pearce W (1989) Communication and the Human Condition. Carbondale and Edwardsville: Southern Illinois University Press.

Bateson G (1973) Steps to an Ecology of Mind. London: Paladin, Granada Publishing.

Baumann G (1995) Managing a polyethnic milieu; kinship and interaction in a London suburb. Journal of the Royal Anthropological Institute (NS) 1: 1725–41.

Bavington J, Majid A (1986) Psychiatric Services for Ethnic Minority Groups. As cited (page 106) in Bavington J (1992) 'The Bradford Experience'. In J Kareem and R Littlewood (eds) Intercultural Therapy; Themes, Interpretations and Practice. Blackwell Scientific Publications .

Bird HR (1996) Epidemiology of childhood disorders in a cross cultural context. Journal of Child Psychology and Psychiatry 37(1): 35–49.

Boscolo L, Cecchin G, Hoffman L, Penn P (1987) Milan Systemic Family Therapy: Conversations in Theory and Practice. New York: Basic Books.

Boyd-Franklin N (1989) Black Families in Therapy: A multisystems Approach. New York: Guilford Press.

Burnham J, Harris Q (1997) Emerging ethnicity: a tale of three cultures. In K.Dwivedi and VP Varma (eds) (1997) Meeting the Needs of Ethnic Minority Children. London and Bristol PA: Jessica Kingsley.

Cecchin G (1987) Hypothesising, circularity, neutrality revisited: an invitation to curiosity. Family Process 26: 405–13.

Cecchin G (1992) Constructing therapeutic possibilities. In McNamee S, Gergen KJ (eds) (1992) Therapy as Social Construction. London: Sage Publications.

Cochrane R, Stopes Roe M (1977) Psychological and social adjustment of Asian immigrants to England and Wales. Social Psychiatry 12: 25–35.

Cronen V, Lang WP (1994) Language and action: Wittgenstein and Dewey in the practice of therapy and consultation. Human Systems 5(1–2): 5–43.

Cronen VE, Pearce WB (1980) Toward an explanation of how the Milan method works; an invitation to a systemic epistemology and the evolution of family systems.' In Campbell D, Draper R (eds) Applications of Systemic Therapy: The Milan Approach. London: Grune & Stratton.

Fogelmann K (ed.) (1983) Growing up in Great Britain. Papers from the National Child Development Study. London: Macmillan.

Gupta PR, Dutta AK, Dutta P (1978) Growth and development. A cross sectional study of pre-school children. Indian Journal of Paediatrics 45: 189–95.

Hannah C (1994) The context of culture in systemic therapy: An application of CMM. Human Systems 5(1–2): 69–81.

Harris Q (1995) A systemic approach to working with families from ethnic minority backgrounds. In CONTEXT: 20, 31–36.

Hodes M, Creamer J, Woolley J (1998) Cultural meanings of ethnic categories. Psychiatric Bulletin 22: 20–4.

Imber Coppersmith E (1985) Families and Multiple Helpers, A Systemic Perspective. In D Campbell and R Draper (eds) Applications of Systemic Therapy: The Milan Approach. London: Grune and Stratton.

Jawed SH (1991) A Survey of Psychiatrically Ill Asian Children. Br J Psych 158: 268–70.

Kallarackal AM, Herbert M (1976) The happiness of Indian immigrant children. New Society 4: 22–4.

Lal N, Sethi BB (1977) Estimate of mental ill health in children of an urban community. Indian Journal of Paediatrics 44: 55–64.

Lau A (1984) Transcultural issues in family therapy. Journal of Family Therapy 6(2): 91–112.

Lau A (1986) Family therapy across cultures. In John Cox (ed.) Transcultural Psychiatry. London: Croom Helm.

Lau A (1988) Family therapy and ethnic minorities. In Street E, Dryden W (eds) Family Therapy in Britain. Buckingham: Open University Press.

Littlewood R, Lipsedge M (1989). Aliens and Alienists: Ethnic Minorities and Psychiatry. 2 revised edn. London: Unwin Hyman. (Originally published 1982.)

McGoldrick M, Almeida R, Moore-Hines P, Rosen E, Garcia-Preto N, Lee E (1991) Mourning in Different Cultures. In Walsh F, McGoldrick M (eds) (1991) Living Beyond Loss. London, New York: Norton Publications.

McGoldrick M, Pearce JK, Giordano J (1982) Ethnicity and Family Therapy. New York: The Guilford Press.

McGoldrick M, Rohrbbaugh M (1987) Researching ethnic family stereotypes. Family Process 26: 89–99.

Mendez C, Coddou F, Maturana H (1988) The bringing forth of pathology. Irish Journal of Psychology. Special Edition 9: 1.

Merrill J (1986) Ethnic differences in self poisoning: a comparison of Asian and White groups. British Journal of Psychiatry 148: 708–12.

Messent P (1992) Working with Bangladeshi families in the East End of London. Journal of Family Therapy 14: 287–304.

Mumford DB, Whitehouse AM, Platts M (1991) Sociocultural correlates of eating disorders among Asian schoolgirls in Bradford. British Journal of Psychiatry 158: 222–8.

Newth S (1986) Emotional and behavioural disorder in the children of Asian immigrants. A topic for discussion. Newsletter of the Association of Child Psychology and Psychiatry 8(4): 10–14.

Newth SJ, Corbett J (1993) Behaviour and emotional problems in three-year-old children of Asian parentage. J Child Psychol Psychiat 34(3): 333–52.

Pearce WB (1994) Interpersonal Communication. London: HarperCollins.

Ramanujam BK (1975) Psychiatric problems of children seen in an urban centre of Western Indian. American Journal of Orthopsychiatry 45(3): 490–6.

Rutter M (1978) Family, area and school influences in the genesis of conduct disorders. In LA Hersov, M Berger, D Schaffer (eds) Aggression and Anti-Social Behaviour in Childhood and adolescence. Oxford: Pergamon Press, pp 95–113.

Rutter M (1979) Protective factors in children's responses to stress and disadvantage. In Kent MW, Rolf JE (eds) Primary Prevention in Psychopathology: Social Competence in Children. Vol.3. Hanover NE: University Press of New England, pp 49–74.

Rutter M (1985) Resilience in the face of adversity: protective factors and resistance to psychiatric disorder. British Journal of Psychiatry, 147: 598–611.

Singh SP (1997) Ethnicity in psychiatric epidemiology: need for precision. British Journal of Psychiatry 171: 305–8.

Soni-Raleigh V, Bulman L, Balarajan R (1990) Suicides among immigrants from the Indian subcontinent. Br J Psych 156: 46–50.

Stern G, Cottrell D, Holmes J (1990) Patterns of attendance of child psychiatry outpatients with special reference to Asian families. Br J Psychiatry 156: 384–7.

Tizard B, Phoenix A (1993) Black, White or Mixed Race? London: Routledge.

Turner JE (1991) Migrants and their therapists: a trans-context approach. Fam Proc 30: 407–19.

Verghese A, Beig A (1974) Psychiatric disturbance in children – an epidemiological study. Indian Journal of Medical Research 62: 1538–42.

Warheit GJ, Vega WA, Auth J, Minhardt K (1985) Mexican-American immigration and mental health: a comparative analysis of psychosocial distress an dysfunction. In Vega WA, MR Miranda (eds) Stress and Hispanic Mental Health. Rockville MD: National Institute of Mental Health.

Wright N, Trethowan WN, Owens J (1981) Ethnic differences in self poisoning. Postgraduate Medical Journal 57: 792–3.

Chapter 12
Children and families involved in Children Act proceedings

ANNIE LAU AND ANNA BOND

In recent times there has been an increasing emphasis on local authorities working in partnership with parents:

> Whether professionals offer support services or therapy, remove the child or keep the family together, the benefits of involving the family in decisions about their future emerge clearly in several studies. Partnership with parents is now a feature of legislation and guidance but Thoburn and colleagues [*Paternalism or Partnership? Family Involvement in the Child Protection Process*] found that social workers wanted to work with families because they believed it would make their practice more effective. Wanting partnership is a step in the right direction but achieving it is difficult. Thoburn, 1995.

This partnership requirement applies regardless of whether the arrangement is voluntary or involuntary. What does partnership mean? In the ordinary context, it means a person (or persons) associated with others in a common enterprise where they share risks, and profits. The partnership may not have to be an equal one. There must surely, however, be a shared basis of understanding and a common interest. There must be agreement on how the parties will go about effecting the partnership; what each party intends to put into it; the rules of engagement; and expected objectives and outcomes.

This shared basis of understanding is the foundation for all other aspects of the partnership. For it to exist, the partners need to have some knowledge, each of the other, of a nature sufficient to enable the partners to trust one another to forward the partnership.

> Farmer and Owen (1995) concluded: 'that an understanding between parents and professionals was most likely to occur if there was agreement about whether the child had been abused, who was responsible, who was to blame and whether the child was at future risk'.

They continue by noting that 'disagreement – real or perceived – greatly hindered the ability of social workers to achieve desired outcomes for children.'

For local authority professionals, therefore, it is important to have a positive attitude to partnership. They also need to learn how to go about achieving it in situations that are fraught with difficulties, even though the 'partners' begin with similar cultural bases, belief structures and values. The difficulties are increased where those features do not exist.

With Asian families, how do local authorities achieve that shared basis of understanding? This is an increasingly important question, given the commitment of local authorities to take ethnocultural issues into account in their deliberations. The concept of partnership implies that the local authority worker is sufficiently informed so as to be able to take the views of parents, and of children, into account in making plans for the child. This is difficult enough in the adversarial (though theoretically inquisitional) context in which childcare proceedings occur, but even more difficult when dealing with the unfamiliar context of the Asian family.

We conducted a recent review of Child Protection statistics from four neighbouring boroughs: Redbridge, Waltham Forest, Barking and Dagenham, and Tower Hamlets. Redbridge reported a total of 69 children on the Child Protection Register on 31 December 1997, with 17.4% being Asian, compared to 10% in 1996. This reflected the proportion of Asians in the population census.

Waltham Forest reported 118 over 1997 on its CPR, with 2.5% Asian. Over the previous three years, the Asian proportion had varied from 12.8% in 1995 to 2.5% in 1997. Barking and Dagenham reported 35 Asians on its CPR, a high proportion compared to their population percentage. Tower Hamlets had the highest proportion of Asians on its CPR, with 33.5%, of which 26% were Bangladeshi. In contrast, the official statistics of children and young people on Child Protection Registers in England for the year ending 31 March 1997 (Government Statistical Service, Crown Copyright 1997) had no information related to ethnic minorities.

These figures would at least suggest that Asian children and families on the Child Protection Register are a significant presence today on the UK scene and that it is appropriate that the service implications be taken seriously.

We examine, from a local authority's viewpoint, children and their families from a South Asian background who became involved in care proceedings where efforts to work in partnership were not, or were not entirely, successful, because either the shared basis of understanding had not been achieved or because there was disagreement or, at least, a lack of consensus between the partners for ethnic, cultural and religious reasons. The purpose is to try to determine what can be learned for future practice. The questions are those that the local authority professionals asked themselves when examining, with hindsight, what had happened, in an effort to 'make their practice more effective'.

The discussion takes the following format. Anna Bond presents the cases from a legal perspective, and poses relevant questions. Annie Lau then responds with a commentary. The chapter then concludes with a summary of theoretical principles and offers guidelines for good practice.

Case example 1

Placement

The female child of a family of Indian origin and Hindu religion became the subject of emergency protection and care proceedings following one quite serious assault by her father and what she alleged had been similar treatment on other occasions. At the time emergency protection action was taken the local authority had no foster carers who were an ethnic and religious match for the child, who was therefore placed with very experienced white UK foster carers, with whom she settled well.

The parents denied their daughter's allegations. They contested the first interim care order unsuccessfully and had to accept that their daughter would remain separated from them for at least the immediately foreseeable future.

They had from the outset protested vigorously that the carers with whom their daughter had been placed had no knowledge or understanding of her cultural background; she was unable to speak the Indian language in which they conducted their family conversations and would thus lose her facility in its use; her religious observance was compromised and she was being allowed a freedom of dress and association that they did not see as acceptable.

The Children Act 1989 ('the Act') provides, in s22, that in relation to children looked after by them, a local authority shall, before making any decision with respect to a child whom they are looking after, so far as is reasonably practicable, ascertain the wishes and feelings of, *interalia*, the child and his parents regarding the matter to be decided and, in making any such decision, shall give due consideration, (having regard to age and understanding in the case of the child), to such wishes and feelings as they have been able to ascertain. Due consideration must also be given to the child's religious persuasion, racial origin and cultural and linguistic background (s22(5)(c). Furthermore, s23(9) of the Act (which concerns provision of accommodation and maintenance by local authorities for children whom they are looking after) provides that Part II of Schedule 2 shall have effect for the purposes of making further provision as to children looked after. Part II of Schedule 2 provides for Regulations as to placing of children with local authority foster parents and, in Paragraph 12 (e), for securing that where possible the local authority foster parent with whom a child is to be placed is (i) of the same religious persuasion as the child; or (ii) gives an undertaking that the child will be brought up in that religious persuasion. The legislative position is therefore clear and the local authority made very considerable efforts to try to find foster carers who would be a better match.

There was no one within the child's extended family at the time who, upon assessment, was both acceptable to the local authority and willing to undertake the care of the child. The parents put forward other family members as carers, but the local authority feared that, because of their attitude to the allegations, the child would be unsupported, under pressure and possibly at further risk if placed with them. The child, who was old enough to make her wishes and feelings known, wanted to stay with the white UK foster carers, who were willing to keep her.

Then, foster carers newly approved by the local authority who were an ethnic, cultural and religious match for the child, became available. They were members of the same religious congregation as the parents and informed the local authority that they had some acquaintance with the family, though maintaining that this acquaintance was not close. (Much later on, it became apparent that their relationship with the family and, particularly, the child's parents was, in fact, much closer than either they or the parents had told the authority. That could have resulted, and to an extent perhaps did, in the child being in the situation which had been feared for her with the family members assessed as unsuitable to look after her.)

The local authority, recognizing that the experienced white UK foster carers were not a match for the child, and now having available matching, although inexperienced, foster carers, had to decide how to balance the factors. These included the child's wish to stay with the first foster carers; the child's statement that the new foster carers knew her parents well; the parents' vigorous pressure for her to be moved, and a professional opinion that she was 'not an easy child to parent'. The local authority moved the child to the newly approved and matching foster carers. This was done in recognition of the legislative provisions and also in an attempt to assist in forging a partnership with the parents.

Questions

1. Where a local authority provides accommodation for a child whom they are looking after, the legislative factors noted above apply and the local authority shall 'so far as is reasonably practicable and consistent with his welfare, secure that the accommodation is near his home' (s23(7)(a) of the Act). It will not be unusual that members of a community of the same ethnic group and the same religion and culture living in an area will be acquainted, friendly with, or sympathetic to each other. How is that factor to be checked, assessed and weighed when placing a child?

Comment

This is an interesting case and certainly the local authority concerns being raised are not atypical. In responding to these questions, I felt the first point that needs to be established is the issue of the competency of the local authority assessment from a cultural perspective. It is noted elsewhere that the social worker 'did not have extensive experience with families of that background', and the guardian *ad litem* 'did not pretend to any specialized experience in the background'. Under these circumstances it may have been difficult to determine the exact nature of the stresses the family and the subject were experiencing, and what relative weight needed to be put on them. Were there particular cultural-based reasons why the female subject was particularly at risk? For example did she represent an unwanted female child who brought shame and reproach to a young mother, unsure of her own status in her new family? Was this an adolescent who wanted more Western-style freedoms related to boyfriends and going out?

Why was she the subject of 'serious assault by her father' and what did it mean to the father, the mother and the family, and the community? In cases that I have dealt with, the father might take the view that physical chastisement was necessary, even mandatory, in order to bring the girl into line; the mother might or might not have a contrary view; if other siblings support the father's view, then it would not be uncommon for them actively to support father's chosen methods of discipline – for example, an older brother may also be involved in the physical chastisement. So in assessing the suitability of a carer of the same ethnic group and community, it would be important for the local authority to know what the carer's views were with regard to the behaviours of which the girl's family disapproves, and how they would manage potential situations that arise.

Would the local authority approve of their potential strategies, and be supportive of their views and actions? If an ethnic carer was approved by the girl's family it would be presumed that the carer would support the family's views on, say, drinking, dating, going out. Has the local authority been able to offer support to the carer – for example, would the social worker be able to meet with the carer and the subject to spell out the ground rules?

2. In a situation such as this, where a child is placed for care with members of the same ethnic group, information about the child's situation will have to be provided to the carers. While they will be expected to maintain confidentiality, how is the situation to be managed with the family so that it is positive, rather than negative, for partnership?

Comment

The safety needs of the young person are paramount, and so it is important that the carers are sufficiently informed about the subject and her family so they know what to expect, what the likely difficulties are, and what strategies to employ, in order to keep the young person safe. This needs to be openly and clearly communicated to the family. I believe the carer needs to be fully briefed by the local authority in order to be able to manage the behaviour difficulties that will inevitably arise.

3. In partnership terms, in a situation of this kind, whose are the risks and whose are the profits? Where is the shared basis of understanding? In the partnership with parents, where does the child stand?

Comment

Partnership with the parents will not always imply agreement. It needs to imply, however, clear communication between the local authority and the parents so that each other's position is understood.

There will be the inevitable encounter with parents whose views of child rearing will be over determined by their own histories of harsh parenting and childhood abuse. I have known parents who refuse to budge from a position that 'physical punishment does not really lead to lasting damage', despite the evidence of clear behavioural and emotional sequelae to their childrens' development, with corresponding patterns of control, bullying and physical intimidation being acted out in the playground. I believe that all reasonable attempts need to be made to help parents understand the consequences of inappropriate parenting, but when this fails, the smokescreen of 'cultural values' cannot be held out as reasonable grounds for failure to protect children.

4. When do 'cultural differences' in the treatment of children move beyond what is acceptable and by whose standards should the treatment be judged?'

It is generally acceptable that, on one level, the notion of 'child abuse' can be seen as a cultural construct. A large number of Western child weaning practices would be seen as abusive in other societies; for example, practices that promote separation and individuation in the West at an age that would not be considered appropriate in India and the Far East, including the practice of children sleeping alone or away from their mother's bed; early weaning from the breast; the use of boarding schools. It is important to be aware of the motivations of the family or the community behind a practice that might be considered abusive in the West, for example, leaving younger children in the care of older children. From a practical perspective I would suggest that the following findings would require immediate steps towards a thorough investigation, whether or not the worker was familiar with ethno-cultural issues that may have a bearing on the case:

- the presence of actual physical injury;
- discrepancy between the child's account of events leading to the injury and the explanation offered by parents or caretakers;
- corroborative evidence from another agency with considerable opportunity to observe and report on the child's status, e.g. school, nursery or day centre.

It is also important that the child/children be competently assessed to determine whether the treatment of the children (by the parents) leads to impairment, in the terms of the Children Act.

In exploring the limits of partnership between the local authority and the parents, it would suggest that efforts be directed towards exploring whether there is a basis of common ground that can be established from which differences can then be negotiated. The most vulnerable and suspicious parents often benefit from the presence of an advocate of the same ethnic group, who can help translate local authority concerns into effective language. The advocate will often need to be individually chosen and trusted by the family, and capable of bridging the gap between the family and the local authority.

Contact

There were also issues regarding supervision of contact between child and parents. The parents wished, during contact, to use the Indian language in which they were accustomed to talk to their daughter. The local authority, which feared that pressure would be put on her by the parents but could not find a contact supervisor who spoke their language, wished English to be spoken during contact visits so that they could be adequately supervised.

Question

This situation may be a common one, given limited availability of trained supervisors with appropriate language skills and local authority financial resources for funding them. How is 'partnership' between parents and local authority to be established in these circumstances?

Comment

If the purpose of contact is to maintain the relationship and sense of connectedness between the daughter and the family, and if it were really the case that they normally converse in their own language, then to insist on English being spoken does make for an artificial situation that creates more strain on existing relationships. I am curious as to why an interpreter could not be found. An alternative mode of supervision might be to videotape the contact session for later review by someone who understood the language. With families who are known to be bilingual – fluent both in English and the Indian language – then the local authority is on firmer ground in insisting that English be spoken. Otherwise I feel the situation needs to be highlighted as a service deficiency to be remedied.

Matching of those in the partnership

In this set of care proceedings, with the exception of the second set of foster carers, none of the professionals involved, including the social worker and the guardian *ad litem*, were of the same background as the child and her family.

During the course of the proceedings the social worker who, while an experienced social worker, did not have extensive experience with families of that background, had the task of preparing a comprehensive assessment of the family and of preparing a care plan for the child.

The guardian *ad litem*, with more variety of experience, did not pretend to any specialized experience in the background but had to provide a report to the court, upon which it was likely to place considerable reliance.

It seems likely that this is a common experience for families and local authorities.

Questions

1. If it is accepted that to provide a fully informed assessment one 'needs previous experiences with normally functioning members of that ethnic community, where one can see the cultural assumptions and practices . . . operating within the life of that community' (Lau, 1998) and if that is not present in the assessor(s), might the family reasonably question whether the assessment has properly been made 'in partnership' with them?
2. Can it be said that, without such experience, that the assessment has been done on a shared basis of understanding between parents and the local authority?
3. Is it questionable whether the 'comprehensive' assessment, which is, of course, an assessment to assess the risks to the child as a member of the family, is indeed comprehensive as it will lack full insight into the life of the family?

Comment

I would agree that the 'comprehensive' assessment, conducted under the circumstances described above, is unlikely to have taken on board all relevant ethnocultural factors. The workers may not have been aware of their own cultural prejudices, or of how particular issues, or practices, fitted into the spectrum of normal experiences or expectations of that community. The reader is referred to Chapter 2, which goes through some of the normative developmental tasks in the traditional Asian extended family that are dissimilar to those seen in Western European nuclear families. Without previous informed experience of working with Asian families, one is likely to find it difficult to join or engage with them, to explore sources of strength and competence based in the ethnocultural roots and traditions of the group, or to understand the complexities of the social and family context in which the alleged difficulties in individual or group functioning have given rise to professional concern.

Case example 2

Three children of a family of Pakistani origin and Muslim religion became the subjects of care proceedings because of neglect by their parents, who were drug users. Neither at the outset, nor later, was the local authority able to assign to the case a worker of the same background or who had specialist knowledge of, or experience in, ethnocultural issues.

The children had themselves first sought sanctuary from the parental home with members of the extended family. When the case came to its attention, on initial assessment a placement with those family members, at least for the immediate future, appeared suitable to the local authority in terms of care for the children and their ethnocultural and religious needs (i.e. Muslim) and also served to further its duty to keep children within their families whenever possible. Section 23(2)(a)(ii) of the Act permits the local authority to provide accommodation for any child whom they are looking after by placing the child with a relative and s23(6) provides that any local authority looking after a child shall make arrangements to enable him to live with a relative, friend or other person connected with him unless that would not be reasonably practicable or consistent with his welfare. The placement within the family also met, for the local authority, its duty under s23(7)(a) to secure that the siblings were accommodated together.

It emerged, however, that there were considerable differences of religious observance and its effects between the parents and these members of the extended family, which the local authority social workers had not had the background of knowledge to identify when assessing. The parents (whom the local authority had expected would see the placement as a basis for working in partnership with them) were discontented with it because of the differences. The partnership that the local authority had expected would be forwarded by the placement was in fact inhibited by it, partly due to this factor.

Questions

1. Early establishment of trust between the local authority and parents will often be crucial to the progress of the 'partnership' between them. Can pitfalls of this kind be avoided and, if not, how is trust to be established especially when, as here, the children were adamant they wished to remain with the members of the extended family?

2. During the proceedings it was agreed that the parents (with the children) should undergo a residential assessment to look at their ability to provide care. The local authority, having regard to its financial constraints, proposed to place them in its own resource for this purpose. The parents preferred a different resource for which the local authority would be required to pay. The basis of their argument for this was that

the local authority resource would not provide them with sufficient privacy for the female members of the family to preserve the modesty required of them (because of a bathroom shared between the two families in residence); nor would the shared kitchen at the resource enable them to meet the food preparation requirements of their religious observance. They indicated that the local authority had not realized or, if it had, had not understood and had therefore not properly considered this aspect and had consequently failed to take into account the importance of these factors to them and to their children. The question of which resource should be used was eventually brought before the court and a decision made; however, this was hardly helpful to partnership. Local authorities may have a genuine commitment to work in partnership with parents, but how are they to balance honestly felt and stated parental preferences against their undoubtedly constrained financial resources?

Comment

I would be curious here as to whether the 'differences of religious observance and its effects' were significant differences, if reviewed by an independent individual with Muslim religious authority, or otherwise. How is the local authority to inform itself of whether these differences, or lack of religious observance, would lead to a significant deterioration in the child's religious life? Or whether the issues being raised by the parents were actually irrelevant, and may reflect their sense of shame and discomfort that the children were being removed from their care? If we took, for example, the more familiar Jewish case – say, where, in a family of Orthodox Jews, conflict arose between the parents regarding the strictness of observance of *shabbat,* and the children had become drawn into these issues over a period of many years of chronic marital conflict, and had taken sides with the mother against the father. How is a worker with no understanding of Jewish law or custom to make sense of a situation in which the mother and children will partially observe *shabbat* (i.e. participate in Friday evening dinner, light candles) but fights break out between father and the children around whether or not they are to go out with their friends on Saturday? How much was practice and custom dictated by different family traditions, for example Ashkenazi and Sephardi? How much was the father's rigidity and unwillingness to compromise on religious observance a reflection of his resentment of his own marginalized position in the family, as a result of the closer emotional bonding between mother and children? In many districts there is a well-established Jewish Family Service, linked with Norwood and Ravenswood services, able to advise and comment on Jewish cultural and religious issues. It is less likely, however, for local authorities to have established links with Muslim religious leaders, and I believe it is mandatory for links with various sources of religious authority in the district to be established.

With regard to the question for the facilities for the residential assessment, again, I would feel it would be useful to seek the views of the local Imam. Otherwise the local authority is placing itself at risk of accusations of institutional racism, each time Muslim families are offered the residential facilities designed to meet the needs of non-Muslim families. The reader is referred to the Chapter Five in this book by Ali El-Hadi. On the resources, consideration could be given to whether adjustments could be made at the assessment centre e.g. separate storage facilities for food, to provide for the family's religious dietary requirements.

Case study 3

This family consisted of the child, her mother and the mother's second husband. It demonstrated some features of family relationships and dynamics which have also been seen in other cases.

Mother was born and reared in India. There, she was married to her first husband and the couple came to the UK, where the child was born. Soon after the birth, the first husband died and, some time later, the mother met her second husband through family connections. He had the same ethnic origin and background and both were of the Hindu religion. The mother had no close relatives of her own living in the UK and her first husband's family did not continue to support her after the second marriage had taken place.

It eventually emerged that the mother's relationship with her in-laws was uncomfortable and, by her account, oppressive. Her mother-in-law, particularly, became critical of her appearance, her upbringing of her daughter and her housekeeping. The husband supported his mother who, while she did not live with the family, was nevertheless a frequent and influential presence. The husband did not treat his stepdaughter as his own child and both he, his mother and his family were critical and dismissive of her. The marriage quickly ran into difficulties, with the stepfather adopting an often punitive approach to the child. The situation eventually deteriorated to the point where the mother found it unendurable and attempted suicide for herself with the intention that the child should die with her since at that time she could see no bearable future for either of them.

It was at the point of the attempted suicide that the local authority became involved. In that situation, it was the mother's mental health which was the initial focus but it quickly became apparent this was not really the source of the problem. Attention then concentrated on the family dynamics. It proved difficult to unravel these since the mother appeared fearful of the future effects for herself and the child if she was candid about her marital situation. She was also anxious about taking steps for herself, independently of her husband and his family, in case her problems were exacerbated. The husband was unwilling to discuss his marriage or his family relationships, ascribing blame to his wife for her actions and their effects and what he and his family described as her faults of character and behaviour. Nonetheless, neither husband nor wife wished to end their marriage and the local authority concluded that its work with the family should include trying to support them to face their differences and resolve them sufficiently to create a setting where there would be no repetition of the past and a safe and nurturing situation for the child and any other children they might have.

In the context, it became necessary to ascertain:

1. What, if any, ethno-cultural issues had relevance for this situation?
2. What action might be taken to overcome the wife's fears and the husband's intransigence?
3. What support systems were needed and could be obtained to achieve the aim?

Comment

The ethno-cultural issues here are extremely relevant. The organisation of subsystems in Indian families are different to those considered normal in Western nuclear families. The husband-wife dyad, usually the central emphasised relationship in the West (Tamura and Lau, 1992) contrasts with that in the Indian extended family, where other intergenerational subsystems, such as the mother-son dyad, takes precedence (Kakar, 1990). The unwillingness of the husband to 'discuss his marriage or his family relationships' and to ascribe total blame onto his wife's supposed character faults, needs to be understood in the context of the cultural rules, which broadly spelt out, are as follows: for the marriage to succeed, she has to fit in and be one of us (i.e. the family firm).

It follows then, that for a worker to support the family in staying together, one would have to work within a perspective where those rules were acknowledged. In other words, the worker needs to be aware that in a traditional hierarchical Asian extended family, the new wife needs to first acknowledge the authority of the in-laws, especially her mother-in-law. The questions to be asked then may include: what were the expectations of the new wife on moving into the family? What were the corresponding expectations of the husband and his family? How have they failed each other? For example, did the husband's family feel the new wife failed to show sufficient respect to the in-laws?

One can then slowly move towards exploring such questions as: what could help enhance confidence on both sides and what changes might be necessary?

The issue of whether the stepdaughter belonged in this family is an important one, however, to be tackled directly. The husband and his family must be prepared to 'own' this child, otherwise the wife might sacrifice this child and her welfare in the interests of making a new beginning for herself. In this case, alternative arrangements for the child's care may need to be considered.

Case study 4

The child was accommodated by the local authority at the age of four days, as her mother had learning difficulties. Care proceedings began when she was two months old after the local authority had concluded that the mother (with father) and grandmother (who were the only potential carers within the family) would be unable safely to care for her and had decided that its plan for the child would be for adoption without direct contact.

This plan for adoption had been opposed by each of the parents, by the maternal grandparents and by mother's brother, who was a significant person in the family structure. They argued that no placement other than in the family could match the child's ethnic, cultural and religious background and she would therefore lose all the advantages that knowledge of and contact with that background would give her. The maternal grandmother was British and of the Christian religion. The maternal grandfather was Indian and of the Hindu religion and the father was Malaysian Chinese of the Taoist religion. They argued that it would be better for the child to remain for some considerable unspecified time with her foster carer (who was willing to keep her), until an expected change in the family circumstances occurred, than that she should lose them altogether.

The local authority, whilst it had been, and continued to be, willing as far as possible to work in partnership with the parents, had reached its conclusion from an assessment of those in the family, conducted in the first two months of the child's life. It saw no purpose in delaying the plan for the child but was obliged to pursue this through care proceedings because of the family's opposition. It accepted that a precise match for the child with adopters was unlikely, but nonetheless thought other factors relevant to her welfare were more important, including the consideration that she should not have to wait indefinitely for the expected change in the family's circumstances.

During the course of the care proceedings, further assessments of the abilities of members of the family were made at the request of, first, the mother and, when that resulted in the same conclusions as the local authority's, the grandmother, with the same result. During this period, despite the family's knowledge of its adverse conclusions about them, the local authority had to continue to work with the family, arranging and supervising contact (s34(1) of the Act provides that where a child is in the care (which includes interim care) of a local authority 'the authority shall ... allow the child reasonable contact with parents') and in considering its plans, taking their views, objections and feelings into account.

Questions

1. What does 'partnership' mean in these circumstances?
2. How realistic is the concept of 'partnership' once conclusions of this kind have been reached?

Comments

I would interpret 'partnership' to mean a willingness to listen to the views of the 'partner', and to accommodate these wherever possible. Clearly, when conclusions are reached that suggest a clear divergence of views, such as the conclusion that the extended family is not a suitable accommodation resource, the local authority has to make different plans from those desired by the family. I feel, however, the local authority is still obliged to include provision for how the child growing up will be encouraged to acknowledge the various elements in her mixed racial identity. Is any direct contact with the extended family possible or viable? This would be by far the best way of ensuring that these ethnic links could be kept alive. If, however, there would be good reasons against keeping extended family links alive, then the local authority care plan does need to include exposure of the child to the various elements of her diverse ethnic background.

Case study 5

The care proceedings in this case concerned allegations of sexual abuse. The family was of Indian origin and of the Sikh religion. It consisted of grandfather, his three sons, the wives of the two older sons and their children. The male members of the family conducted a business together in which the adult females assisted. The family lived together in one house and all the children were of primary school age. Initially one of the female children and, very soon afterwards, two others, made allegations of sexual abuse by their grandfather; specifically, digital penetration (for which there was medical evidence in support) and inappropriate touching and requests for sexual attention.

At the very beginning, there was acknowledgement by the children's mothers of the anxieties expressed by the local authority and it was hoped that a relationship of partnership could be forged with the family, which, among other aspects, would have included the removal from the household of the alleged perpetrator so that the children could remain in the family home. Schedule 2, paragraph 5 of the Act ('Provision of accommodation in order to protect child') provides that where it appears to a local authority that a child who is living on particular premises is suffering, or is likely to suffer, ill treatment at the hands of another person who is living on those premises, and that other person proposes to move from those premises, the authority may assist that other person to obtain alternative accommodation. Assistance given may be in cash. Had that partnership proved possible, the care proceedings might have been avoided and the desired outcome of protection for the children achieved with the minimum possible trauma and disruption for them.

In the event, the children's mothers withdrew acknowledgement and co-operation. It was the opinion of the local authority social workers that pressure had been brought to bear upon them. The grandfather was clearly an 'authority figure' in the family. He denied the allegations. His married sons appeared to accept the denial and, therefore, to deny any risk to, or need of protection for, their daughters. It was recognized by the local authority, and by the guardian *ad litem* appointed by the court to safeguard the interests of the children under s41(2) of the Act that there were future as well as present issues for the family concerning sexual purity, marriage prospects and maintenance of family relationships, cohesion, structure and harmony; however, the local authority was still left with the problem of how best to protect the children from the perceived harm while at the same time trying to preserve and support the family for their benefit. The guardian *ad litem* had (Family Proceedings Courts (Children Act 1989) Rules 1991, Rule 11(7)) to file a written report with the court advising on the interests of the children.

Eventually, when it seemed possible that care orders might be necessary in order to protect the children, the grandfather left to live with other members of the family with some assurances by the children's parents that the arrangement was intended to be permanent. As there had been some indication, possibly because of the pressure of the proceedings, that the family might accept assistance and, particularly, therapy, the court was able to make supervision orders and the children were returned to their parents.

It might be questioned, however, whether anything resembling partnership or any basis of shared understanding had been achieved in this case. The outcome appeared, from a local authority viewpoint, to be rather the result of pressure from outside than recognition from within the family, although it was probably the best that could have been achieved for the children in the circumstances. It is possible that the family might, within itself, have had more recognition of the causes for anxiety than it was prepared to make apparent but, even if that was so, the local authority professionals were still left with questions.

Questions

1. If it is important to frame the problem within a context that enables the issues to be accepted by the family, how is the local authority social worker, or a therapist asked to work with the family to overcome resistance to recognition, taking into account the meaning and function of the disturbance for the family, the cultural group and the wider community (see Chapter 2)?

2. When families are asked, within a partnership, to examine and question such basic concepts (for them) as authority structures where younger members of the family do not usually enquire into or criticize the actions of their elders, how are they best supported to do this?

3. If the family recognizes and accepts that there is a problem within it (with particular reference to the issue of sexual abuse), how, if at all, can it be helped to deal with the longer-term effects of what has occurred; for example, with issues of sexual purity, virginity, marriage prospects?

Comment

As this is a family in which there was considerable joint work between the local authority and myself, I will go into the case in some detail, before dealing with the questions.

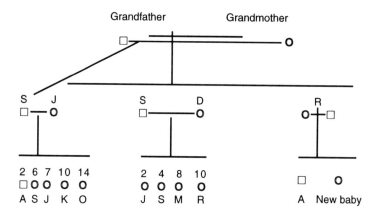

Figure 12.1. Family background

A case conference was held within a few weeks of the eight-year-old girl saying at school that her grandfather had done rude things to her, M, and her female cousins. There were positive findings by the female community paediatrician of hymenal tears and or stretching in three of the female grandchildren, aged six, seven and eight.

The family had closed ranks and said the girls were telling lies. A decision was made that the children were not safe as long as the grandfather was still in residence in the family home. This was the mother of the eight-year-old who had initially disclosed the abuse, and she was now being blamed; for 'inciting her daughter to tell lies'.

At the child protection conference, the police reported that the eight-year-old (M) who initially disclosed at school, told them that the grandfather had been inserting his finger in her vagina for over a year. She had told her mother a few times but her mother had not approached the grandfather. When she again raised it with mother, mother told father but all he said was to 'keep an eye on things'.

The health visitor reported that as the mother's English was poor, she had not responded to a request to give the children 'pre-school English experience'. The two sisters, S, aged six and J, aged seven had little English and were seen as withdrawn in school. By contrast, M, from the other family, who had made the initial disclosures, was more outgoing and articulate.

The GP, who was Asian, felt the two sons, who were primarily resistant to the idea that their father had abused their daughters, needed to have the safety issues of the children emphasized. It was also agreed that a Punjabi-speaking student social worker should also attempt to engage the non-English speaking elements of the family, particularly the grandmother.

The paediatrician was concerned about the girls' mental state and said she would make a child psychiatric referral.

Child psychiatric assessment

I conducted the following series of interview, each of one to one-and-half hours duration.

- Professional network meeting
- Meeting with adult members of the family – two adult sons and their wives
- Meeting with the two adult sons
- Interview with the four girl children with the two mothers
- Discussion with residential unit staff of their group work with the children
- Two meetings with M and her mother.

There was a close working relationship between myself, the local authority Social Worker (white male), social work student (Punjabi speaking female) and key worker from the residential unit (white female). The Asian GP was also closely involved, and facilitated a meeting between local authority staff and the grandmother on the surgery premises. By this time the grandfather was 'in the vicinity', although not living at the family home.

The social worker said that, following the paediatric assessments, there had been concerns that both of the mothers would be stigmatized and blamed in the wider family for allowing the family shame to enter the public arena.

The following family background was elicited from the adults in the family. The grandparents are in their mid-sixties. Grandfather was registered disabled with a history of heart disease. He was not working and stayed at home. He used to be in the army in India, and was described

by his sons as a stubborn man. He came over to the UK 'with nothing'
but was extremely hard working. The sons felt their father had been a
good father, and had worked hard to establish a secure base for their
family, working successively in a factory, then an off-licence, and a
supermarket. The grandfather initially established the family off-licence
business, now run by the two sons.

The two sons, with their wives, are in their early thirties, and have been
married 15 years and 11 years respectively. The older son had five children, ranging in age from 14 to 2. The younger son had four children,
aged 10 to 2. There was a younger sister who was visiting from India.

Over two sessions, which I conducted with the social worker, we established that, by now, the sons and their wives were able to acknowledge
the painful truths, despite the initial denials to the professional community. The older son said he now believed the children, and felt very upset
and disappointed by what his father had done. I felt it had been important
to approach the issue of the grandfather's position and role in the family
through allowing them first to share with me how pivotal he had been in
establishing, through long years of hard work, a secure family base, as
acknowledging their father's responsibility for the abuse of their daughters would entail a psychological letting go of the idealized image they
held of their father. They said their father no longer lived with them. 'If I
see my father I will punish him in my own way', said the elder son.

The social worker and I both felt the sons had now moved to openly
acknowledge the abuse. We brought in the children and, in front of us,
the fathers told the girls they were believed, and they would from now on
be protected. On the basis of this work I felt able to recommend that the
girls could go home.

At the same time we saw the girls with their mothers. We encouraged
the girls openly to go through the painful details with their mothers, to
ensure that there were no secrets, and that the mothers also acknowledged responsibility for protecting them.

A period of group work then followed, in which social work staff conducted five group sessions around the theme of assertiveness and how to
say no (to abuse) using a format described on a tape from the abuse team.
I reviewed some of the videotaped sessions with the workers. The children were able to express themselves openly in play with the sexually
explicit dolls. They also acted out a fantasy in which their grandmother
tried to protect them against a predatory grandfather. In this fantasy,
grandmother left the home with the children. Subsequently, everyone got
back in a family reunion scenario, following an apology from grandfather.

Some work was also done addressing the relationship between the
8-year-old girl who made the initial disclosures and her mother. The mother was more retiring and placid and found her active daughter 'a bit of a
handful'. This girl still had recurrent nightmares that her grandfather
would somehow return, perhaps in disguise; or he possibly still 'has the

key to the house'. I asked her if anyone in the family was still angry or upset, particularly with her. She said 'only my Grandmother, she still cries a lot.' It was generally felt, however, that M had responded enthusiastically to the assertiveness training programme and that she also now felt more confident of protection from her family.

Returning to the questions, therefore:

1. *Working with 'resistance to recognition' of the children's sexual abuse.* In this case, it was extremely important to allow the adults, especially the sons, both space and time to look at what had been important issues for them in their own development. The grandfather had been such an exemplary father that the very idea that he could have committed such a family outrage was unthinkable – therefore these allegations must have been childish pranks, telling lies, or family mischief (incitement by younger daughter-in-law). The carefully conducted separate police interviews of the children, and the paediatric examinations, all offered consistent corroborative evidence that became, in the end, impossible to ignore. In the interviews I invited the sons to share the family narrative that recounts all the struggles and achievements of the family, mainly centred around their father – and then moved them gently on to the present. It was especially difficult for the older son, as he had a great deal to lose in the toppling of a family icon.

2. *Criticism of the actions of their elders.* As suggested by the Asian GP in the case conference, the sons needed to see that the main issue was not, for them, a lack of filial piety implied by being critical of their father, but rather their primary parental task of protecting their daughters from further harm.

3. *Dealing with longer-term effects.* In this particular case, the abuse was one of digital penetration, so in the marriage stakes the girls were still virgins, not having had sexual (genital penetrative) intercourse. Nonetheless, the issue of sexual purity remains a difficult area. One then needs to refocus on the girls' strengths and competencies in learning how to defend and protect themselves with enhanced assertiveness skills.

Bibliography

Almeida R (1996) Hindu, Christian and Muslim families. In McGoldrick M, Giordano J, Pearce JK (1995) Department of Health Child Protection: Messages from Research: Studies in Child Protection. London: HMSO.

Department of Health (1988) Protecting Children: A Guide for Social Workers Undertaking a Comprehensive Assessment. London: HMSO.

Dwivedi KN, Prasad KMR (1999) The Hindu, Jain and Buddhist communities; beliefs and practices. In Lau A (ed.) South Asian Children and Adolescents in Britain. London: Whurr.

Farmer E, Owen M (1995) Child Protection Practice: Private Risks and Public Remedies – Decision Making, Intervention and Outcome in Child Protection

Work. In Department of Health Child Protection: Messages from Research: Studies in Child Protection. London: HMSO.

Lau A (ed.) (1986) Family therapy across cultures. In Cox JL (ed.) Transcultural Psychiatry. London: Croom Helm.

Lau A (1988) Cultural and ethnic perspectives on significant harm; its assessment and treatment. In Adcock M and White R (eds) Significant Harm; its Management and Outcome. London: Significant Publications.

Lau A (1988) Family therapy and ethnic minorities. In Street E, Dryden W (eds) Family Therapy in Britain. London: Open University Press.

Lau A (1990) Psychological problems in adolescents from ethnic minorities. British Journal of Hospital Medicine 44: 201-5.

Lau A (1992) Commentary on Messent and Weiselberg. Journal of Family Therapy 14: 331-6.

Lau A (1995) Gender, power and relationships; ethno-cultural and religious issues. In Burck C and Speed B (eds) Gender, Power and Relationships. London: Routledge.

Tamura T, Lau A (1992) Connectedness versus separateness: applicability of family theory to Japanese families. Family Process 31: 319-40.

Thoburn J, Lewis A, Shemmings D (1995) Paternalism or Partnership? Family Involvement in the Child Protection Process. In Department of Health Child Protection: Messages from Research: Studies in Child Protection. London: HMSO.

Index